ADVANCE PRAISE

Retire on Real Estate

"*Shark Tank* changes lives. *Retire on Real Estate* will change your life too! Dr. K. Kai Anderson is a leader in helping working adults rethink and reclaim their retirement possibilities. This book is brilliant! *Retire on Real Estate* is one of a kind because it connects the dots between retirement planning and real estate. Through clever chicken-and-egg metaphors, *Retire on Real Estate* does an impressive job of explaining the pitfalls of the current retirement system and the nuts and bolts of how to plan for the future using the powerful and surprisingly achievable tool of real estate. Anderson's inspirational, positive, and easy-to-read tone makes *Retire on Real Estate* a must-read for everyone."

> —Kevin Harrington, Original Shark on ABC's *Shark Tank*,
> Inventor of the Infomercial, and Founder of "As Seen on TV"

"*Retire on Real Estate* is a must-read for anyone considering buying residential real estate to rent, whether they are merely curious or totally serious. No get-rich-quick schemes here, Dr. Anderson also provides a step-by-step companion guide to her conservative, disciplined method of building a real estate portfolio and assuring income in retirement."

> —Todd M. Sinai, PhD, Professor of Real Estate and Business Economics and
> Public Policy, University of Pennsylvania, Wharton School of Business

"In *Retire on Real Estate*, Dr. K. Kai Anderson answers one of life's toughest questions facing most new real estate investors: How do I get started? Kai writes not from theory but from her real-life experience as an investor. Learning from someone who has made mistakes, faced challenges, risen above setbacks, and today has a successful track record makes all the difference. Her step-by-step, first-hand knowledge of how to find, manage, and create cash-flowing property can put you in control of your financial future."

> —Kim Kiyosaki, of RichDad.com, and Author of
> *Rich Woman* and *It's Rising Time*

"Dr. Anderson is an inspiration to budding real estate entrepreneurs everywhere. *Retire on Real Estate* presents a simple approach that anyone can use to get started using real estate as a tool for the generation of lasting wealth."

—Ian Parrish, President, Investors United®, America's
oldest school for real estate investing

"*Retire on Real Estate* is one of the best books you can read if you feel like you're behind in saving for your retirement. You'll get a no-guilt proven plan that will let you stop worrying and start taking action."

—Steve Harrison, Original Publicist for Robert Kiyosaki's
bestselling book *Rich Dad Poor Dad*

"All readers, whatever their age, will find much to stimulate their thinking about what they can do to protect their retirement dreams with real estate in this book. Its breadth and scope, the variety of data explored, and the stark nature of the argument will provoke both thought and emotion about their nest egg being at risk. Dr. K. Kai Anderson's book *Retire on Real Estate* helps us plot a plan with the Why and the How to think more clearly about important issues in planning for the future."

—Connie Rankin, Author of *God Gave Us Wings: A Journey to Success:
Theirs, Mine and Yours* and President and CEO, CRES & Associates,
an award-winning commercial real estate firm, Houston, Texas

"Realtors will benefit greatly from this book. Providing *Retire on Real Estate* to clients will be extremely beneficial in helping clients see past their personal residence purchase and incorporate rental properties into their retirement investment portfolios. An exceptional read, *Retire on Real Estate* flows beautifully, laying out and thoroughly examining pros and cons of several retirement investment vehicles. *Retire on Real Estate* presents a comprehensive approach to analyzing successful real estate investment and convincingly argues real estate as the vehicle one can count on to provide ever-increasing cash flow and wealth."

—Michael Anderson, Real Estate Agent (no relation to the author)

"*Retire on Real Estate* has inspired me to buy more real estate than I already own! The guide-like design of *Retire on Real Estate* [and the *R.O.R.E. Blueprint for Success: A Step-by-Step Companion Guide*] makes it easy for me to reference anything I've read if I have future questions. I now have the tools I need to increase my nest egg, and I have a place to turn to for answers. The visual aids and concise explanations made even the most complex subjects easy to understand. If you want to invest in your future, read this book."

—Kalen Bruce, MoneyMiniBlog

"Dr. K. Kai Anderson's seamless analogies and anecdotes speak to readers from all walks of life. Her candor shines through the pages as she shares her expertise and experiences. No matter your level of real estate expertise, Kai can teach you something practical that can get you started in the world of real estate today! As Kai artfully shares her knowledge in real estate, she introspectively examines her decisions, her fears, and her life. Kai not only shares her knowledge in real estate, but she also shares her insights into happiness, retirement, and success. She maintains a work-life-real estate balance, and you can too! *Retire on Real Estate* is a well-rounded financial resource that should be incorporated into every household."

—Justin DeCleene, MBA, author of *Medical Adventures*

"A must-read for anyone interested in investing in real estate, no matter if you're just getting your feet wet or are well versed and an experienced home owner. Retirement financial security is a scary concept, and so is buying property. With all her heart and soul, Kai takes us into her world and the experiences of two of life's scariest decisions. This is a book that will be used as both a reference and a guide."

—Rebecca Walden, Pharmacist, Mom, and Achiever of the Level I Goal

"Dr. Anderson cheers her readers on, while explaining how to reinforce one's retirement with real estate. *Retire on Real Estate* is an eye-opening read, with helpful advice for EVERYONE! It is encouraging and informative without an ounce of condescension. I'm now ready to 'get a chicken'!"

—Louise Suggs, Principal, Louise Suggs Design

RETIRE ON REAL ESTATE

K. KAI ANDERSON

RETIRE ON REAL ESTATE

Building Rental Income for a Safe and Secure Retirement

AMACOM
American Management Association

New York • Atlanta • Brussels • Chicago • Mexico City • San Francisco
Shanghai • Tokyo • Toronto • Washington, DC

Bulk discounts available. For details visit:
www.amacombooks.org/go/specialsales
Or contact special sales:
Phone: 800-250-5308
E-mail: specialsls@amanet.org
View all the AMACOM titles at: www.amacombooks.org
American Management Association: www.amanet.org

This publication is designed to provide accurate and authoritative information in regard to the subject matter covered. It is sold with the understanding that neither the author nor the publisher is engaged in rendering legal, accounting, or other professional service. If legal advice or other expert assistance is required, the services of a competent professional person should be sought.

Library of Congress Cataloging-in-Publication Data

Names: Anderson, K. Kai., author.
Title: Retire on real estate : building rental income for a safe and secure
  retirement / K. Kai Anderson.
Description: New York, NY : AMACOM, [2017] | Includes bibliographical
  references and index. | Description based on print version record and CIP
  data provided by publisher; resource not viewed.
Identifiers: LCCN 2017021214 (print) | LCCN 2017022749 (ebook) | ISBN
  9780814438985 (ebook) | ISBN 9780814438978 (pbk.)
Subjects: LCSH: Retirement--Planning. | Real property. | Finance, Personal.
Classification: LCC HQ1062 (ebook) | LCC HQ1062 .A53 2017 (print) | DDC
  332.024/014--dc23
LC record available at https://lccn.loc.gov/2017021214

About AMA

American Management Association (www.amanet.org) is a world leader in talent development, advancing the skills of individuals to drive business success. Our mission is to support the goals of individuals and organizations through a complete range of products and services, including classroom and virtual seminars, webcasts, webinars, podcasts, conferences, corporate and government solutions, business books, and research. AMA's approach to improving performance combines experiential learning—learning through doing—with opportunities for ongoing professional growth at every step of one's career journey.

Printing number

10 9 8 7 6 5 4 3 2 1

DISCLAIMER

This material is provided for informational purposes only and should not be construed as ERISA, tax, investment, or legal advice. Readers should consult an attorney or accountant for specific applications of the content provided herein to their individual real estate investing and/or retirement planning ventures.

Although care has been taken in preparing this material and presenting it accurately, the author and publisher disclaim any express or implied warranty as to the accuracy of any material contained herein and any liability with respect to it. Similarly, although the author has exhaustively researched all sources to ensure the accuracy and completeness of the information contained in this book, the author and publisher assume no responsibility for errors, inaccuracies, omissions, or any other inconsistency herein. Again, although the author has made every effort to provide accurate Internet addresses at the time of publication, neither the publisher nor the author assumes any responsibility for errors or for changes that occur after publication. Further, the author and publisher have no control over, and do not assume any responsibility for, third-party websites or their content. Any slights against people or organizations are unintentional.

This book is dedicated to YOU, the one holding this book, so that the final third of your life may be just as abundant as it is today . . . or perhaps even more so!

Real estate cannot be lost or stolen, nor can it be carried away. Purchased with common sense, paid for in full, and managed with reasonable care, it is about the safest investment in the world.

FRANKLIN D. ROOSEVELT
32nd President of the United States
(1882–1945)

Contents

CONTENTS

PART THREE

THE CHICKEN: HOW TO PROTECT YOUR RETIREMENT DREAMS WITH REAL ESTATE

Foreword

by Amanda Han, CPA

Are you one of the millions of people who are waking up to the realization that your retirement years may not be as safe and secure as you had once hoped?

More and more people are finding themselves working harder and harder, only to receive less in return for their efforts. With rising prices, higher taxes, and often stagnant pay, the middle-class retirement dream is slowly turning into a nightmare. Even more frightening is the realization that many may have to trade their dreams of retiring at a reasonable age for an undefined number of additional years working.

The good news is that the American dream is still possible for you. That beautiful future is possible regardless of where you are today. As a CPA with more than two decades helping clients achieve financial stability and financial freedom, I find Dr. K. Kai Anderson's book, *Retire on Real Estate*, a must-read for anyone who is looking for a better solution to their financial future, particularly in retirement. Every year, I meet with countless new clients who are either not well prepared for retirement or simply not making smart decisions with their finances.

This book reveals startling statistics that show how the history of saving for retirement has changed over time. It will help you understand why the old methods of saving and investing will no longer help us achieve our dreams and what opportunities exist for today's investors.

Whether you are twenty years old and just starting out, or sixty years old trying to accelerate or even rebuild your wealth, Dr. Anderson's book provides instructions on simple things you can do today to start you on your path toward financial safety, comfort, or even complete self-sufficiency in retirement.

Dr. Anderson skillfully brings together the heart, mind, and financial aspects of our lives, and challenges some of the outdated belief systems that we may have grown up with. This book reveals new ways to look at:

- How you can increase your cash flow without increasing the number of hours you work, using real estate;
- How to take control of your retirement money by taking advantage of lesser-known strategies that Wall Street and your financial planner do not want you to know;
- How to understand the truth behind "debt" and how you can use it to supercharge your wealth; and
- How to rethink your own capabilities and make small changes in your life that have large and lasting results.

As a seasoned real estate investor, Dr. Anderson shares insightful tips on the "Dos and Don'ts" of owning investment property. From analyzing properties and making offers to strategizing on how to trade up into larger properties tax-efficiently, this book provides a solid foundation for new and seasoned investors alike.

Dr. Anderson offers step-by-step guidance on how to use real estate investments to supplement retirement planning, making this book a valuable tool for anyone looking to build additional streams of income without having to continue working indefinitely.

As the title indicates, *Retire on Real Estate* teaches us how to abandon the idea of relying on only one path toward retirement and instead to create multiple streams of income to achieve financial stability. The book masterfully combines the "Why" and the "How" in achieving financial success. If you are looking to take charge of your financial future, especially for your retirement years, this book was written for you.

AMANDA Y. HAN
Certified Public Accountant at Keystone CPA, Inc.,
Real Estate Investor, and Co-Author (with Matthew MacFarland) of
The Book on Tax Strategies for the Savvy Real Estate Investor:
Powerful Techniques Anyone Can Use to Deduct More, Invest Smarter,
and Pay Far Less to the IRS! (Publisher: Bigger Pockets)

Preface

"**A** computer on every desk and in every home." This was the ambitious dream of Bill Gates and Paul Allen when they co-founded Microsoft more than forty years ago.[1] Now, their dream is a reality: Computers (in the form of desktops, laptops, tablets, and smartphones) are indeed on every desk, in virtually every home. And they are in pockets and purses and backpacks. Computers are even strapped to wrists in the form of smartphone watches. They are literally everywhere!

I have a similar dream, though it's not about computers and it's not about smartphones. It's about real estate. *My dream is that every adult will have at least one rental property as a part of his or her long-term retirement plan.* And I mean everyone . . . including you! If you worry that you lack the courage, experience, or even a compelling reason, then keep reading. This book is uniquely designed to show you *why* even just one rental property is a critical component of your long-term financial plan, as well as *how* you can accomplish this goal, strategically. This is why I believe my dream is attainable for virtually anyone, which you will see as you get into the heart of this book.

There are many reasons for my dream. Mostly, I am terrified for the millions of working adults who are living in this post-pension world and hoping to retire one day with financial security. I fear for all of us the potentially devastating impact of relying *solely* on the shaky and highly politicized Social Security system and our inherently risk-laden retirement accounts. More so, if you really stop to think about it, the nest egg model of striving your whole life to build up a pool of savings, then retiring, crossing your fingers and hoping and praying that it won't run out before you die, just doesn't make sense. On top of that, you'll be lucky if there is anything left over to pass on to your loved ones after you're gone.

This is why I've started a movement to inspire working adults everywhere to—Think beyond the nest egg and get a chicken! Not a real chicken, but a metaphorical one: a rental property. Because just as chickens lay eggs day after day, rentals provide income month after month . . . forever. This income never runs dry, and, in fact, is likely to increase gradually with time. Plus, if kept in good repair, rental properties typically appreciate in value over the *long term*, meaning that, instead of passing down the dregs of your 401(k) to your kids when you die, you pass down an often-appreciating, income-producing asset that will be there to help protect *their* economic security for years to come as well.

Here are some of the ways owning even just one rental property can benefit you, once you pay off the mortgage:

1. It will diversify your plan and serve as a backup in the event of a widespread stock-market crash, computer glitch, identity theft, or cyberterrorist attack.
2. It could pay for your kids' college tuition or other large expense, either expected or unexpected.
3. It will supplement whatever modest income you might receive from Social Security once you retire.
4. It will add a sustainable asset to your plan that pays you every month, so that you will not be exclusively reliant on your retirement savings—which, by definition, could run out.
5. It could lower the taxes that you pay on your retirement account withdrawals and Social Security income in retirement.
6. It will give you an asset, which you can sell or refinance, if or when you need a large sum of money.

7. It will give you a transferable, willable, income-producing asset that you can pass down to your loved ones (or favorite charitable organization) upon your death for continued prosperity.

In addition to these long-term benefits, there are many benefits to owning a rental property that you can enjoy right away, even before the mortgage is paid off:

1. The property can reduce your annual income taxes (or increase your refund).
2. It can generate extra income for you and your family, month after month.
3. It can provide a way for you to leverage into more investment property and attain greater levels of financial comfort and self-sufficiency, if that is what you desire.
4. It can foster a profound sense of empowerment and confidence regarding your future financial security.

As I explain in chapter 5, the Ultimate Goal is to own at least one income-producing rental property with no mortgage. To achieve this Ultimate Goal, you must first purchase or otherwise acquire rental property, usually *with* the help of a mortgage. This is where the three Primary Goals come in. The first step is to decide which Primary Goal is best for you. Do you desire just a degree of financial diversification and safety (Level I Goal), greater financial comfort (Level II Goal), or complete financial self-sufficiency (Level III Goal) in retirement?

The Level I Goal of financial diversification in retirement involves buying or otherwise acquiring just one rental property. I liken the Level I Goal to an insurance policy or backup plan to protect yourself against the many unknowns of the future. Between the often-unpredictable stock market, the shaky Social Security system, and the very real threat of simply outliving your savings, the Level I Goal offers a degree of safety provided by adding a layer of authentic diversification to whatever is in your current retirement picture.

The Level II Goal offers an additional level of financial comfort in retirement. It involves acquiring a couple of rental properties, or one multi-family home, to create a cushion beyond what the Level I Goal provides. Those who achieve the Level II Goal will have enough monthly rental income, after the mortgages are paid off, such that, when added to their other expected sources of monthly income (pension, Social Security, retirement distributions, etc.), their monthly income needs are satisfied.

The Level III Goal gets you to complete financial self-sufficiency, but requires more work and greater cash reserves. It involves owning enough rental property such that, once all mortgages are paid off, you can retire on the rental income. Your rental income will fully fund your life, with other sources of income and savings being icing on the cake.

The Level II and III Goals can come later and in accordance with your needs, wants, motivation, and resources. However, I strongly believe that the modest degree of financial safety offered by owning even just one rental property should not be an optional goal. This is why I'll show you a number of ways to achieve this very attainable Level I Goal. The moves that are best for you will depend on where you are in life in terms of your age and level of resources, among other considerations. I've included a special chapter called "Hatching Your Plan" to help you develop the right strategy based on your circumstances. Finally, by taking action on your strategy, and by using the right moves for your situation, you will experience the unparalleled pride of knowing that you have protected your retirement dreams and late-life financial security, as well as the financial security of generations to come, with the powerful and time-tested tool of real estate.

How to Read This Book

This book is really two books in one: the why, and the how. The "why" portion sets the stage, and the "how" portion is about going out onstage. Imagine jumping onstage without preparing. Sure, you might do fine, but you also might freak out, forget why you were out there in the first place, run off, and never get out there again.

This is why I strongly recommend reading this book from start to finish.

But . . . of course some readers will be eager to just roll up their sleeves and dive right into Part Three, *How to Protect Your Retirement Dreams with Real Estate,* side-by-side with its companion workbook, the *R.O.R.E. [Retire on Real Estate] Blueprint for Success: A Step-by-Step Companion Guide,* which is available on my website (www.GetaChicken.com). If this describes you, you are obviously ready to get moving on building your truly diversified retirement plan. Nonetheless, I encourage you to double back and read Parts One and Two of this book, before too much time passes. Part One explains the motivational *urgency* for getting started and Part Two provides the motivational *techniques* for crossing the finish line and achieving your Goal.

This book can be read on your own or with others. There are several topics presented in Part One that you may want to discuss with a friend, a relative, a co-worker, or even a small group, rather than absorb in isolation. Working with others can also provide motivation, accountability, and be a great forum for exploring ideas and opportunities, especially as you get into the strategies and action steps presented in Part Three.

As you read this book, keep in mind that I've included a glossary on my website, www.GetaChicken.com, which I've specifically designed to accompany this book. After all, where else will you see "chicken" in a glossary of real estate or retirement terms? As you read, I encourage you to look up unfamiliar terms on my website. Finally, please note that there is a References section in the back of this book that contains the citations and website locations for the multitude of facts and statistics that I've included throughout this book, which are also excellent resources for further exploration.

INTRODUCTION

One evening, while enjoying a delightful dinner with some friends, a dark cloud came over the room. The conversation had shifted to retirement, a topic that should have been exciting! And yet the sense of anxiety and dread in the room was palpable. Like the majority of adults these days, my friends were terrified that their later life story would be a "choose your own adventure" type with only one of two possible outcomes: work for all their living days, or retire with the risk and ever-present fear of running out of money. As I listened to my friends, two sets of feelings stirred inside me. The first was a deep, but almost guilty, knowing that—with a handful of properties— my wife and I will indeed retire, and that we will retire in comfort and with complete financial self-sufficiency. The second feeling was a newfound sense of urgency and responsibility to my friends, and to society at large, to share what I've learned about real estate, and the retirement industry in general, so that others can take steps now to protect their late-life financial prospects and retirement dreams as well. This is why I wrote this book.

This is *not* a "get rich quick" book, nor is it a "get out of the rat race" book or a "become a millionaire" book. Instead, I advocate for an authentic rebalancing of your retirement portfolio so that it includes at least one tangible, cash-flowing rental property held for the long term. While you may become an accidental millionaire in the process, that is not the purpose of this book. Again, my goal is to show you how to create a retirement that is financially safe, comfortable, and/or even completely self-sufficient by diversifying what you have to include real estate.

Are you excited by the idea of retirement? Do you long for the days when you control your own time . . . and have plenty of it? Time to bask in the sun. Time to travel. Time to enjoy the company of family and friends. *Time to do whatever you want.*

Or do you fear retirement? Are you paralyzed by questions like:

"Will I outlive my savings?"

"Will I end up having to live in my kid's basement?"

"Will I spend my last living days destitute and on the streets?"

"Will I have to work for the rest of my life?"

If you are like most working adults, chances are that your answer is "Yes!" to both the excitement and the fear. You are excited by the idea of retirement, yet you are terrified that you won't have enough saved to last all your living days. Sadly, these conflicting feelings can tarnish the excitement and dampen the celebration of one of life's most anticipated milestones.

We cannot solve our problems with the same thinking we used when we created them.

ALBERT EINSTEIN
Quintessential genius and winner of the Nobel Prize
in Physics, 1922 (1879–1955)

If you are worried or confused, you are not alone. Many people are afraid. And if they aren't, they should be. This book serves as a wake-up call, exposing the truth behind the retirement industry and why your fears are absolutely justified. It also provides hope and concrete action steps to safeguard your retirement dreams.

This book's purpose is twofold: to make the case for owning at least one rental property as part of a *truly* diversified retirement plan, and to show you exactly how to do it, no matter what your age or circumstances may be. This book shows you the benefits and techniques of leveraging rental property to create cash flow forever, to catapult your net worth, and to secure for yourself a financially safe, comfortable, or even completely self-sufficient retirement. I will show you how you can do this—even if you have little to no savings to your name and even if you've already stopped working.

Which came first, the chicken or the egg? Well, in this book, the egg comes first, then the nest, then the chicken. In other words, Part One is *The Egg: Why the "Nest Egg" Idea Is Seriously Cracked.* Part One explains why we are facing a retirement crisis individually and as a society. I then weigh the full spectrum of risks and rewards of real estate, and make the case for owning at least one rental property as part of one's long-term plan. I encourage readers to "think beyond the nest egg and get a chicken," with the chicken being a metaphor for a rental property since rentals provide income month after month just as chickens provide eggs day after day.

Part Two, *The Nest: Setting Yourself Up for Success,* reveals a new way of thinking about assets, liabilities, saving, and spending. I also offer what I hope is a unique perspective on setting and achieving goals of any kind, and I propose one Ultimate and three Primary Goals that are specific to building rental property into your truly diversified retirement plan.

Part Three, *The Chicken: How to Protect Your Retirement Dreams with Real Estate,* shows you a range of powerful techniques and clever strategies that you can use to shatterproof your nest egg with rental property. Part Three shows you how to acquire a rental property, or otherwise generate income using real estate, even if you are starting from nothing. I include strategies that are specific by age group and level of resources so that you can develop a custom plan that meets your own needs, desires, and current situation.

Finally, there is Part Four, which you can access on my website at www.GetaChicken.com. Part Four is the *R.O.R.E. [Retire on Real Estate] Blueprint for Success: A Step-by-Step Companion Guide,* which walks you through each of the methods described in Part Three, along with many of the calculations and exercises from earlier chapters. This *R.O.R.E. Blueprint for Success: A Step-by-Step Companion Guide* provides a detailed manual for finding, evaluating, and purchasing the right property. It leads you through the essentials of property management, starting with how to find an awesome tenant! The *R.O.R.E. Blueprint for Success: A Step-by-Step Companion Guide* also shows you how to find and hire a trustworthy and responsible property manager in the event that you want to let someone else handle[11] day-to-day work of managing your rental property.

This book references a number of appendices that are located on my website for your convenience. Online Appendix A includes my story of how I got started in real estate (also available in the back of this book). Online Appendix B is the complete set of stories of individuals and couples I call "not-chickens." They are not-chickens because they were literally not chicken. They were not afraid to take the plunge by buying or otherwise acquiring one or more rental properties for their long-term investment portfolio. Each story is fascinating and contains a wealth of additional unique tips and "lessons learned." I strongly encourage you to read these stories and learn from them! Online Appendix C, *Recommended Reading and Other Resources*, provides a list of my favorite books, websites, and other resources to help you get started and to help you become as successful as possible. Online Appendix D is a glossary of terms, both technical and slang, that are used throughout this book.

Many of the examples provided throughout this book draw from my copyrighted Cash Flow Analysis (CFA) Tool, which is downloadable for free at www.GetaChicken.com. This CFA Tool has two components. The first component consists of the twelve scenario-based templates of varying terms (down payment, mortgage interest rate, length of mortgage, and whether the property will be managed by a property manager) for a hypothetical property with a purchase price of $100,000. While this purchase price may not be attainable in every market, I chose it because it is an easy, uncomplicated number that works well for demonstration purposes.

The second component of the CFA Tool consists of a modifiable template that you can use for your own analysis of potential properties, whatever the price tag may be. You can use this template to see how the cash flow and cash-on-cash return change as you modify different pieces of financial information related to the property or the mortgage.

On my website, I also provide the complete version of my Anderson Inspection Method (AIM) Tool to use on your initial property walk-throughs. To take full advantage of this simple, but revolutionary, personal inspection worksheet, simply download the app or print a hard copy from www.GetaChicken.com for your own use. The AIM Tool allows you to *quickly* assess the general quality of a property and necessary repairs and upgrades. It also helps you remember various aspects of a given property at a later time, as well as differentiate one from another if you see multiple properties within a short span of time.

I wrote this book based on the knowledge and experience I've gained as a landlord and real estate investor for over a decade. I am not a lawyer, accountant, real estate agent, or financial planner, and my thoughts are not offered as professional advice. They are offered solely in a spirit of generosity. Use the information contained herein at your own risk. I recommend that you run the strategies, clauses, and tax information by a trusted professional in the relevant field. The best advisers are those who own rental property themselves or specialize in real estate investment law, accounting, etc.

As a final disclaimer, the methods I share in this book are for purposes of diversification. I am not against stocks, bonds, REITs, or even mutual funds or financial planners. I am all about balance that includes all of these investment vehicles, as well as rental property. That said, I do have a problem with mutual funds and commission-based financial planners who charge excessive, undisclosed fees. Chapter 1 shows you how to assess your own situation and how to ensure that you aren't being robbed by the financial industry writ large.

Do you remember that dinner-table conversation I shared with you in the beginning of this section? It was that unsettling conversation that compelled me to write this book in the first place. My goal here is to inspire people to revisit the way we've been trained to prepare for retirement. In spreading the word (and with your help) I imagine—for all of us—a different type of dinner-table conversation in the future. In fact, I envision many glorious conversations, a couple of decades from now, with my friends—*and you with yours*—in which we celebrate the brave moves of our younger years. Since success is more fulfilling when shared with others, I envision laughing, toasting, and telling stories about how we made it. I see enthusiastic sharing of new interests and volunteer activities. We are remembering shared travels and even times at our respective vacation homes. And, together with our friends, we are overcome with gratitude for having had the courage, many years earlier, to build rental income for our safe and secure retirements. And yes, no matter what your age happens to be at this very moment, those younger years I refer to are now . . . right now.

PART ONE

THE EGG

Why the "Nest Egg"

Idea Is Seriously Cracked

1

IT WAS NEVER MEANT TO BE THIS WAY

A Brief, Fascinating History of Retirement
Options and the Current Landscape

My parents worked hard to build up their nest egg. They were self-employed, so they knew there would be no pension to rely on once they stopped working. They put four kids through college and worried about money . . . a lot. But they did build what they felt was a fairly sizable egg. Then my dad died suddenly and unexpectedly, leaving Mom both devastated from the loss and paralyzed by questions like: "Will our savings be enough for me to retire? And when??" In fear, she kept working. Now, fifteen years later, she is seventy-five years old and still working part-time. Yes, she has a nest egg. But is it large enough to last her? Will she ever be able to retire with the peace of mind to know that she'll never run out of money?

The answer that she and my three siblings and I have come to is: Who knows?! And this is precisely the problem with the current nest-egg model of saving for retirement. It's not that the stock market might tank and remain low in the years she needs her money the most . . . though it could. It's not that her assets could be wiped away in an instant by identity theft . . . though they could. It's not even that fees of 2 percent or more could have wiped out more than half her account value over four decades of investing . . . though they did. It's that she will never, ever know for sure if she has enough money saved up to last all her remaining days.

If you really sit down and think about the "nest egg" model, it just doesn't make sense. The whole premise is that you build up as much money as you can over your whole life, in order to draw down from it in retirement. Then, you cross your fingers and hope, wish, and pray that it will be enough to last you. And that's terrifying. And the older you get, the more terrifying it becomes. And this is where my mom is right now.

This model is in stark contrast to the system it replaced: the pension. With the pension, workers were guaranteed income for life. They didn't have to worry about whether the money would last. By definition, it would.

Take my parents-in-law, for example, both of whom were teachers in the public school system and are now comfortably retired. But their comfort doesn't depend on one risk-laden, finite sum of money saved over the course of their lives. In addition to their savings, and Social Security benefits, they have pensions that promise to pay them monthly incomes for life.

Pensions and retirement accounts operate on two entirely different playing fields. Ideally, you would have both, plus Social Security to boot. Pensions operate on the monthly-income playing field. They provide monthly income for life, just as a salary provides sustainable income during one's working years. In contrast, a retirement account, or "nest egg," operates on a totally different type of playing field. It doesn't operate on a monthly basis. By definition, a nest egg is limited or finite. It can be used up. And there are so many factors that go into the old "how long will it last?" question that it is nearly impossible to answer with any degree of confidence.

There is an interesting history as to how this all went down, which I'll get into shortly. For now, let me say that pensions are nearly extinct. Almost all workplaces have either partially or completely eliminated the pension and have replaced it with mutual fund–based retirement accounts, a national trend that shows no signs of stopping or slowing down.

This means that, if you were to time-travel a couple decades or more into the future, you would find that the vast majority of our population will, without a doubt, wind up in my mom's precarious situation, not my in-laws' more stable one. And for those with less in savings, Social Security could be their only source of income, as it currently already is for many individuals without savings or pensions. What this means is that, without a pension, you could be forced to downsize significantly in your older years, possibly dipping into poverty, unless you are able to continue working for the rest of your life. That's without considering any physical, mental, or cognitive health challenges that may arise as you get older.

There is another option: Create your own "pension." Take matters into your own hands. The way to do this is through rental property. Because of rental property, my wife and I are optimistic about retirement. The same goes for the millions of others who own rental property. You, too, can get to that same place of optimism. This is because *rental property is like a pension plan for those who don't have a pension.* Rentals that are well maintained and well managed provide consistent income, month after month . . . for life.

God grant me the serenity to accept the things I cannot change, the courage to change the things I can, and the wisdom to know the difference.

Prayer adopted by Alcoholics Anonymous and authored by
Reinhold Niebuhr, theologian

There is a well-known prayer that goes: "God grant me the serenity to accept the things I cannot change, the courage to change the things I can, and the wisdom to know the difference." This serenity prayer pretty much sums up my book. You can't change the fact that you don't have a workplace pension, or that you have a very small pension, or whatever the case may be for you. Yet, you do have the ability to create a pension-like plan for yourself, through real estate. It's up to you to understand this difference and take action.

A BRIEF, FASCINATING HISTORY OF THE 401(K)

The 401(k) was never meant to be our only retirement vehicle outside of Social Security. And yet, without ever having been planned, or tested, or modeled as such, it has gradually become just that.[1]

What many of us don't realize is that, when measured against the extent of time that civilized society has been around, the 401(k) is just a baby! In fact, it was born in my own lifetime. The birth of the modern-day 401(k) can be attributed to Ted Benna, who, in 1980, asked the U.S. Department of the Treasury to slightly modify the Revenue Act of 1978. At the time, Benna's goal was simply to help his company, The Johnston Cos, an employee-benefits consulting firm (not to be confused with Johnson & Johnson, Inc.), improve its bottom line and pay less in taxes.[2]

In its early days, the 401(k) was not relevant to lower-paid workers because most could not afford to set aside funds for later. They needed their wages for their more pressing day-to-day living expenses. (This struggle to save is really no different from how it is today, especially with stagnant wages and ever-escalating living expenses.) The difference, however, is that back in those days, lack of participation in the 401(k) was not particularly concerning for those individuals who knew they would have a pension to rely on in their older years.[3]

You see, in its early years, the 401(k) was never meant to replace the pension. It was meant to simply add to the pension and Social Security as a sort of three-legged stool, for those who could afford it.[4] Then, after only a few years into its life, the role of the 401(k) began to shift. The investment vehicle that had originally been built to shield the income of the highest-paid employees began morphing into the main retirement option for the vast majority of workers.

The momentum for this shift picked up speed in the 1980s as pensioned places of work increasingly sought to improve their bottom line by cutting costs. In 1986, Congress dramatically lowered the pension benefits offered to employees of the federal government and added the option of enrolling in a 401(k)-type plan called the Thrift Savings Program (TSP). Interpreting this massive transition as a sort of government endorsement, the private sector quickly followed suit. Companies found the 401(k) to be infinitely cheaper than the pension. Rather than paying retired workers a good-sized portion of their salaries for life, the 401(k) allowed companies to chip in a small "match" during the employees' working years, only. This pleased company shareholders, drove up profits, and fueled a surge in the entire mutual-fund industry. This then marked a heyday for mutual-fund companies, as they discovered how to take advantage of this relatively new product called the 401(k). By forging relationships with businesses, these mutual-fund companies could gain instant and exclusive access to all of a company's employees and a consistent cut of their weekly or biweekly paychecks.

In spite of being originally developed to help the bottom line of companies, or perhaps because of it, the 401(k) took off in the United States, and eventually spread to other countries under different, or sometimes surprisingly similar (like the "Japan 401[k]"), names. Benna claims he had no idea that the 401(k) would take off the way it did. He told *Workforce Management* magazine, "I knew it was going to be big, but I was certainly not anticipating that it would be the *primary* [italics mine] way people would be accumulating money for retirement thirty plus years later."[5]

Progress is impossible without change, and those who cannot change their minds cannot change anything.

GEORGE BERNARD SHAW
Irish playwright and winner of Nobel Prize in Literature, 1925
(1856–1950)

THE CURRENT LANDSCAPE

As I've mentioned, most people's retirement plans consist of any or all of the following three elements:

1. Social Security
2. Pensions
3. Retirement accounts (such as stocks, bonds, and mutual funds held in a 401(k), 403(b), 457, TSP, or IRA)

Some people might literally add "the lottery" to this list, a sign of how desperate we have become for help. Instead, I offer a better and more reliable #4: rental property. After spending some time on Social Security, pensions, and retirement accounts in this chapter, the rest of the book covers, at length, rental property, the fourth, most vital, and most neglected element of a truly diversified retirement plan.

There is no security in life, only opportunity.

MARK TWAIN

Great American author (1835–1910)

Social Security

Social Security is a program that has been helping elderly individuals and persons living with disabilities since 1935. At that time, the United States was just beginning to recover from the Great Depression and millions were still out of work. Social Security was established in response to great societal concern for the nation's seniors, disabled individuals, and those in need of unemployment insurance.*

---

* Unemployment Insurance (UI) is now provided by a joint state/federal (Department of Labor) program, rather than by the Social Security Administration.

Social Security is still available to 90 percent[6] of seniors. It is most desperately needed by those who are poor and living on the edge of poverty. Without Social Security, 22.2 million American seniors[7] (44.4 percent) would be living below the poverty line, as compared to the 9.1 percent who actually do. Social Security's critical role is even more pronounced among women, minorities, and the very elderly.[8]

And while Social Security is desperately needed among the poor and near-poor, it has become increasingly vital for the middle class as well. For the vast majority of adults in the United States, retirement literally equates to Social Security. In fact, Social Security is the *only* source of income for a quarter of current retirees and it is the *primary* source of income for nearly three quarters of retired people.[9, 10]

According to Jonathan Peterson, Executive Communications Director at the American Association of Retired Persons (AARP) and author of *Social Security For Dummies*, "Social Security is incredibly important for the middle class, as well as the less affluent. In a world where defined-benefit pensions are increasingly scarce, savings rates are low, home values have fallen, stocks are volatile, and older workers often struggle in the labor market, Social Security income is indispensable for the middle class."[11]

Even so, Social Security payments aren't nearly as generous as people expect them to be. These days, Social Security payments range from one quarter to one half of individuals' pre-retirement salaries.[12] The average Social Security payment for retired workers in January 2016 was $1,341 per month.[13] That comes out to $16,092 for the year, barely over the Federal Poverty Line (FPL) for a single person in the United States.

In other words, while Social Security might be one part of your retirement picture, you can't count on it being your entire picture. Those who rely on Social Security benefits alone have income—and corresponding lifestyles—that are significantly lower than they had while working. As an example, someone earning $50,000 should expect to receive somewhere between $1,000 and $1,300 per month in Social Security benefits, depending on birth year.[14]

You can calculate your own projected Social Security benefits on the online calculator at the Social Security Administration website:

www.ssa.gov/OACT/quickcalc/index.html. You can also register on the www.ssa.gov website to find your precise individual retirement benefits based on your actual income history. Keep in mind that these projections are based on current policy and may not reflect any future cutbacks to Social Security benefits.

Speaking of cutbacks . . . this is the second reason not to put all your eggs in the Social Security basket. The Social Security Administration (SSA) has stated that additional reductions in benefits and increased taxes on those benefits may be necessary in the future.[15] In other words, there is a good chance that current workers will receive less in retirement than what retirees currently receive.[16]

Furthermore, the age at which people are allowed to receive Social Security benefits has been increasing (see Table 1.1) and may continue to increase.[17,18] You can see that for those born before 1938, the Social Security retirement age was and continues to be age 65.

TABLE 1.1. SOCIAL SECURITY ADMINISTRATION RETIREMENT AGE BY BIRTH YEAR

BIRTH YEAR	SSA RETIREMENT AGE*
1937 and prior	65
1938	65 and 2 months
1939	65 and 4 months
1940	65 and 6 months
1941	65 and 8 months
1942	65 and 10 months
1943–54	66
1955	66 and 2 months
1956	66 and 4 months
1957	66 and 6 months
1958	66 and 8 months
1959	66 and 10 months
1960 and later	67

*This information comes from the Social Security Administration website at: www. ssa.gov/OACT/ProgData/nra.html.

However, in 1983, because of improvements in the health of older people and increasing average life expectancy, Congress passed a phased-in change to the SSA retirement age (as well as the percentage of benefits to be taxed).[19,20] For those born in 1960 and later, the retirement age is now up to 67 years old. It is not unlikely that the Social Security retirement age will be pushed back even further over time.

The bottom line is that, when our time comes, we should not expect too much in terms of Social Security benefits. We could very well be working longer, for less in return from the government. We certainly shouldn't *rely* on Social Security as our primary retirement strategy or even our *only* safety net. We need to build something else.

Pensions

The traditional pension, or "defined benefit plan," is a plan in which retirees receive monthly income for life from their former employer based upon number of years of service and salary. The pension has been wonderful for workers. What's not to love about a steady source of monthly income flowing endlessly into your bank account after you've stopped working?

The problem is that the pension is gradually becoming extinct. Over the last twenty-five years, public- and private-sector employers have been rapidly abandoning the pension in favor of investment vehicles such as the 401(k) and 403(b) plans.[21] In 1983, almost two thirds (62 percent) of workers with an employer-sponsored plan had the "defined benefit" classic type of pension; by 2011, this number had fallen to 7 percent.[22] This shift has silently been reshaping the retirement prospects for my entire Generation X cohort, as well as Millennials (Gen Y), and future generations.

Disturbingly, even those who are currently receiving pension benefits are not necessarily safe. While most companies have simply shifted away from offering a full pension to new employees, some companies have actually frozen or reduced the pensions of those who have already retired and who have come to depend on them. An example of this is the case of retired employees of the city of Detroit, who, in 2015, saw their pensions slashed 6.7 percent and were then required to pay additional taxes and return the excess interest that they had received.[23]

Some experts predict that most private-sector pension plans will be frozen in the next few years and eventually terminated.[24] What this means is that in addition to not providing the pension benefit to new employees, current pension participants are at risk of having their benefits terminated when a freeze occurs.[25] Needless to say, this adds a new level of fear and insecurity for those who have already retired and who currently depend on their pension for their day-to-day expenses.

Related to the issue of pensions is employer loyalty. It is becoming increasingly clear that we *all* need to develop self-sufficiency more than ever (even those who have a pension). We cannot rely on our employers to look after us. The eight million U.S. adults who were laid off right when times were the hardest—during the Great Recession of 2008—need no reminder.[26] Neither do the thirty million adults (20 percent of the U.S. working population) who were laid off some time over the subsequent five years, between 2009 and 2014.[27] In addition to layoffs, nearly one million federal employees were furloughed in 2013,[28] and millions of individuals working in state and local governments experienced furloughs, shortened workweeks, reductions in pay and benefits, frozen cost-of-living-adjustments (COLAs), and layoffs over the years following the Great Recession.[29, 30, 31, 32]

*You are the master of your destiny. You can influence,
direct, and control your own environment. You can
make your life what you want it to be.*

NAPOLEON HILL
Author of *Think and Grow Rich* (1883–1970)

Retirement Accounts

As I've mentioned, the 401(k) is an employer-sponsored retirement plan that has largely taken the place of the pension. Similar retirement plans for nonprofit organizations are called the 403(b) and 457(b). The Thrift Savings Program (TSP) is the equivalent for federal employees. From this point forward, I will use the term "401(k)" to refer to all types of employer-sponsored mutual fund–based retirement plans. (Separately, there are also self-purchased retirement accounts such as the Individual Retirement Account [IRA] and the self-employed, or "Solo," 401[k] that mirror the employer-sponsored accounts in many ways.)

The technical terms for the pension and the 401(k) are confusingly similar, something that I suspect is not accidental. "Defined benefit" refers to the good old-fashioned pension, just discussed. "Defined contribution" refers to the 401(k). Here's an easy way to remember the difference. Which would you rather have? Fixed, ongoing, "defined" *benefits* (to you), or fixed, ongoing, "defined" *contributions* (from you)? The choice is obvious.

With the exception of accounts that are invested exclusively in bonds, 401(k)s are based on the stock market and are—by definition—based on market risk. This market risk is entirely shouldered by the employee/retiree. To make matters worse, this risk also extends to decisions of whether or not to contribute, how much to contribute, and how to allocate investments. If things go wrong, the blame lands on us, even in spite of having received little-to-no training on how to best manage a mutual-fund portfolio in the first place. Table 1.2 summarizes the differences, which are stark, between the pension and the 401(k).

TABLE 1.2. THE PENSION AND 401(K), COMPARED

PENSION ("DEFINED BENEFIT")	401(K) ("DEFINED CONTRIBUTION")
Income like a stream (like eggs from a chicken)	Savings as a pool of funds (also called the "nest egg")
Income for life, barring any change to pension benefits	Income until it runs out
Risk is on the employer	Risk is on the worker
Income is predictable (fixed, inflation-adjusted monthly amount)	Income is unpredictable (depends on the timing of the stock market)
Not subject to fees	Subject to fees
Subject to income tax	Subject to income tax (non-Roth: at time of withdrawal; Roth: at time of contribution)

In 2009, the 401(k) came under fire by *Time* magazine.[33] This assault was followed by similar tirades in the *New York Times, CBS News*, the *Huffington Post, Mother Jones*, PBS *Frontline*, and *National Public Radio*, among other news outlets. In its groundbreaking piece, *Time* asserted that "the 401(k) is a lousy idea, a financial flop, a rotten repository for your retirement reserves," and that "44 percent of Americans are in danger of going broke in their postwork years." There are a number of reasons for the scathing criticism of the 401(k) and similar retirement plans, which I will fully dive into in chapter 2. The remaining pages of this chapter go into the basics about mutual fund–based retirement plans, as well as some of the drawbacks and benefits.

RETIREMENT ACCOUNT RULES AND RESTRICTIONS

There are many rules and restrictions attached to the various types of traditional retirement accounts . . . which is not surprising, considering that the 401(k) was named after a piece of tax code. While we must, of course, live within these parameters, and while these accounts can be indispensable to your long-term retirement plan, this also means that *broadening* your plan to include real estate can give you some added flexibility, especially when it comes to when, why, and how you want to access your money.

Minimum Age at Withdrawal

Do you own your retirement savings? The answer is definitively "no." Well, not until you reach age 59½, that is . . . unless you want to pay the 10 percent penalty.

However, if your retirement investments include real estate in addition to a traditional retirement account, then you have more flexibility. When you own real estate, you don't need to be a certain age to access your money. Granted, selling a house is not nearly as easy as simply selling shares or closing an account, but you are free to do so, no matter your age. If you find a better opportunity, you can sell your rental and buy another investment property (as discussed in chapter 8) without tax consequence. Also in chapter 8, I share strategies for buying and selling real estate using a self-directed IRA or 401(k), at any age, and strategically using retirement money between the specific ages of 59½ and 70½ to purchase real estate.

Settling for crumbs doesn't keep you fed—
It keeps you starving.

DANIELLE LAPORTE
Author of *The Desire Map*

Taxes

We've become so accustomed to paying Uncle Sam every April that it barely occurs to us to question it. However, if you stop and think about it, we spend about three to four months of every year working purely for the government (assuming a 25-to-33-percent tax bracket). I appreciate the benefits of taxes to society. After all, tax revenues keep our traffic lights running, our public education systems working, and our streets safe. Plus, taxes compassionately ensure that children and families living in poverty receive health care, school-time meals, and housing subsidies, as they should.

That said, when it comes to calculating how much money we'll need to retire, many of us forget to factor in taxes. The fact is, when we withdraw funds from our retirement accounts, after age 59½, we won't get to keep it all. We will owe income tax on both the amount we contributed as well as the amount that the accounts grew over time.

That is, unless you have a *Roth*-type retirement account. In 1997, Congress began offering the Roth IRA retirement savings vehicle. The Roth IRA allowed both contributions and earnings to be withdrawn *tax-free*, after age 59½ and as long as the account has been open at least five years. In 2006, Roth versions of the 401(k), 403(b), and governmental TSP also became available. In all Roth-type accounts, you are taxed on the contributions when you first make them, rather than being taxed on both your contributions *and earnings* at the end, as you would with a traditional, non-Roth type of retirement account.

This makes the Roth a no-brainer for younger people, who are typically in lower tax brackets earlier in life and who have more time for their accounts to grow. Plus, Roth-type accounts can serve as a *last-resort* emergency fund, throughout the life span, since contributions (not earnings) can be withdrawn penalty-free at any time, for any reason.

The Roth can be less advantageous for those in higher income/ higher tax bracket situations or in periods of life where an up-front tax deduction is preferred, as may be the case for some individuals in their second half of life. That said, there are still benefits that you may want to discuss with your accountant or tax adviser as you decide which type of account is best for you. For example, Roth-type retirement accounts have no age limit for making contributions, there are no forced withdrawals, and they can be passed down to heirs without tax consequence to them.

Forced Withdrawals at Age 70½

Most retirement plans, with the exception of the Roth IRA, require you to start withdrawing your funds beginning at age 70½, *whether or not you want to or need to*. This requirement is technically called the required minimum distribution (RMD), though you will also see it referred to as the minimum required distribution (MRD).

The amount you are required to withdraw is based on your account balance and the government's idea of your maximum life expectancy. The formula is relatively simple and can be found on the IRS website at www.irs.gov/pub/irs-tege/uniform_rmd_wksht.pdf. As mentioned in the previous section, you should plan to pay income tax on your non-Roth account withdrawals, but not on your Roth-type accounts. Be sure to consult an accountant for the specifics related to your personal situation.

The problem with the RMD is a control issue. For instance, imagine a situation where the stock market takes a horrific nosedive just as you turn 70½ or any time thereafter. This happened to millions of seniors in 2008. Those turning 70½ at the downturn in the stock market were required to begin withdrawing a portion of their earnings. Even beginning investors understand that when it comes to stocks and mutual funds, the goal is always to buy low and sell high, not the other way around. With the RMD, if you are age 70½ or older, the government doesn't care whether the market is up or down. You must withdraw regardless of whether the selling price of your shares is higher or lower than what it was when you bought into the fund.

Those with the insight and diligence to immediately reinvest their withdrawn funds into another mutual-fund account can get around this issue, even though each time you sell and buy, there are fees you must pay. However, this is yet another instance in which the money we have worked so hard to earn, save, and grow over our lifetimes is not *really* ours. We do not have ultimate control over it, even after reaching age 59½. Within chapter 8, in the section called "Tap Your Retirement Account after Age 59½," I share other ways the RMD requirement can hurt you and some strategic moves that you can use to lessen its impact.

BENEFITS OF MUTUAL FUND–BASED RETIREMENT ACCOUNTS

In spite of some of the limitations, there are, of course, many benefits to the mutual fund–based retirement accounts. These vary by the type of retirement account. Again, the Roth products (the Roth-401[k], Roth-403(b), Roth-IRA, and governmental Roth-TSP) are excellent ways to invest in the stock market over a long stretch of time, without having to pay income tax on the account growth when you tap into those funds after reaching age 59½.

Growth in Value

An obvious benefit of mutual funds is the growth potential within the stock market, barring any sustained crash, recession, or depression. Another benefit is that the inside buildup of the assets that make up the account—such as the accumulation of earnings (dividends, interest, and capital gains)—is not taxed.

To demonstrate the growth potential in the stock market, consider the example of Haley, a 30-year-old teacher who makes $50,000 per year. With every paycheck, Haley contributes 5 percent of her salary until she reaches her official SSA retirement age of 67. At this point, she will have contributed $92,500 over her lifetime. Assuming her account earns an average annual rate of return of 7 percent, her contributions will have more than quadrupled to $415,878. However, as you will see in chapter 2, this money is not all hers. Depending on the fee structure of her account, and irrespective of market risk, she could lose up to half, *or more*, of her own hard-earned money to fees alone. And that's before factoring in taxes.

Life shrinks or expands in proportion to one's courage.
ANAÏS NIN
Author elected to the National Institute of Arts and Letters,
1974 (1903–1977)

Free Money

Another benefit to employer-sponsored retirement plans is company matching. If you work for a company that provides matching, this is a way to make money from nothing. With every paycheck, your employer essentially gives you a bonus, provided you also invest a certain minimum amount in the plan. In Haley's case, if her employer's policy is to match up to the first 5 percent of her contributions, at 50 percent of whatever amount she contributes, her $415,878 account balance would actually be $623,828, again before fees and taxes are factored in. This is free money and Haley would be a fool not to take advantage of such a benefit.

Autopilot

Another benefit to employer-sponsored retirement plans is that, typically, your contributions are automatically withdrawn from your paycheck. Putting your investing on autopilot is what many personal finance experts refer to as "paying yourself first." The more technical term for this is "dollar cost averaging," so named because you contribute regularly and systematically, irrespective of whether the market is up or down. You aren't attempting to time the market. This system makes it effortless to save money because it is invested before you even have a chance to see it . . . or spend it. It is particularly effective if you have a low fee plan (see chapter 2 for more on this!) and if your employer contributes matching funds to your account.

Loaning Money to Yourself

Lastly, my favorite benefit of employer-sponsored plans is the ability to loan money to yourself. This can be an excellent way to leverage your own retirement funds to purchase rental property. Indeed, I've done this a couple of times myself! Please bear in mind that I do not believe in tapping your retirement savings for "stuff," or even experiences, that will put you further behind in the long run (e.g., travel, home renovation, a new car). However, using this money as leverage to achieve a more diversified retirement portfolio is an excellent strategy to cast yourself further ahead in life, and in retirement. Part Three will go into significant detail on how to best take advantage of money that you already own in your various types of accounts— money that is otherwise inaccessible—to create a balanced retirement portfolio with real estate.

In wrapping up, the 401(k) appears to be here to stay. In spite of its many obvious benefits, it is important to understand, as I've shown in the earlier part of this chapter, that we got here by accident, not by design. There are some serious flaws, which will be the subject of chapter 2. Not understanding these flaws, and relying blindly, *and solely*, on the 401(k), could be a setup for disaster. And with that, I invite you to take a breath and turn the page . . .

2

VERY REAL THREATS TO A VERY FRAGILE EGG

Running Out of Money, Risk, and Fees

"Nest egg." What a strange phrase this is! According to the Merriam-Webster Dictionary, the official definition of "nest egg" is: an amount of money that is saved over a long period of time in order to pay for something in the future.

These days, the term "nest egg" usually refers to our life savings for our hopeful, one-day retirement. However, there is evidence of the term being used as far back as the late 17th century to refer to saving money for any specific long-term goal. The term comes from the practice of leaving a real or fake egg in a hen's nest in order to induce her to continue laying her own eggs there.

I find it fascinating that something as crucial as saving for retirement, or for our older years in general, has become metaphorically attached to something as fragile as an egg. Can you think of anything more fragile? This is why the "egg-drop challenge" is so popular for kids' science classes and why the "egg-toss" game is so fun (and messy!).

We've all had the experience at some point in our lives of accidentally dropping a raw egg on the floor. One of my most vivid middle-school memories has to do with just that. I was in "home ec," which really meant cooking and sewing. (Strange, now that I think about it, that "home economics" didn't involve classes on money management, budgeting, or economics. But anyway, I digress.) One day in home ec, we were cooking something that involved eggs when one of the girls in my class left her egg on the counter, and . . . off it rolled. Splat! I remember this so well because the teacher chastised her loud enough for the whole class to learn a lesson from her apparently unforgivable mistake. The teacher boomed, "An egg is fragile! You must protect your egg!"

You must protect your egg. But what if it's your nest egg, and it's exposed to the threats that are seemingly beyond your control? In this chapter, I will show you what these dangers are so that you can be more aware and motivated to take the steps necessary to protect your own fragile egg. The rest of this book, including strategies in this chapter, are about protecting your nest egg and retirement prospects. The three biggest threats are:

1. Running out of money
2. Risk
3. Fees

Truth will ultimately prevail where there are pains taken to bring it to light.

GEORGE WASHINGTON
Founding Father and first president of the United States (1732-1799)

THREAT #1: RUNNING OUT OF MONEY

Over the course of your life, how many times have you been advised or even admonished to save for retirement? These days, we're bombarded from all sides with warnings to build our nest egg. Whether it's through advertisements from financial institutions, general stories in the news, or pop-culture financial "gurus," the message is consistent: we're doing a terrible job of saving and we need to do better, or else . . .

However, there's an elephant in the room that nobody seems to want to talk about. The problem is this: When it comes to saving for retirement, there simply is no way to *really* know how much you will need. There are countless retirement calculators out there, but no matter how sophisticated they are, these calculators are likely to fail you.

For starters, it is simply impossible to know exactly how long you will live. You could look forward to retirement your whole life, only to have a sudden illness or accident rob you of all that you've stashed away, and all the time and forsaken lattes and dinners out that these savings represent.

On the other hand, you could outlive your savings. Since people are generally living longer than ever before, your nest egg will need to stretch further in retirement than it would have had to for our parents and grandparents (those of whom who were without pensions, that is).

If you are worried, you are not alone. In fact, the degree to which feelings of uncertainty are plaguing us is evidenced by the following stats. (The stats vary somewhat, but the gist is consistent.) A poll by the AARP found that 61 percent of adults feared running out of money in retirement more than death itself.[1] This poll also found that the majority of people between ages 44 and 54 are worried that they won't be able to cover basic living expenses once they retire. More than a third of those polled had no idea whether, at the end of the day, their savings would be enough. Similarly, the 15th Annual Transamerica Retirement Survey by the Transamerica Center for Retirement Studies found that 70 percent of female and 63 percent of male workers believe they could work until age 65 and still not have enough money saved to safely retire.[2] A recent survey by the Employee Benefit Research Institute found that 82 percent of working adults believe they won't have enough money to live on comfortably throughout their retirement years; 71 percent feared not having enough money to take care of their basic expenses in retirement.[3]

Adding to this fairly endemic level of concern, there is no way to *really* know what your standard of living or necessary expenses will be once you stop working. Many financial advisers make certain assumptions in their calculations. For example, many assume you will spend *less* in retirement than you do now. In reality, retirees frequently find that with more time on their hands, they tend to spend more, whether it's on travel, dining out, or doing things they enjoy that cost money. As people age, they also tend to have more health-related expenses, sometimes many more. As our homes and vehicles age, we can expect more of these unexpected expenses, not less. Retirement calculators are not crystal balls, and yet they are often treated as such when it comes to planning for life after leaving the world of steady income. While we can take some measures to try to safeguard our financial future, we can't ever fully plan for the unexpected. Unforeseen expenses *will* come up.

I can't change the direction of the wind, but I can adjust my sails to always reach my destination.

JIMMY DEAN
American country-music singer (1928–2010)

A Million Dollars?

Many people assume that a million dollars is the golden ticket for retirement. However, this number has no real meaning, especially given the uniqueness of everyone's circumstance and lifestyle. According to popular investment advice, retirees can live on $40,000 per year if they take out 4 percent of their one million dollars each year.[4, 5] However, according to Jeff Sommer, a *New York Times* financial columnist, even if that million bucks is invested in so-called risk-free municipal bonds, your chance of outliving your savings is a whopping 72 percent.[6]

But most people don't have a million dollars. Not even close. It's just too hard to save. Plus there is the ever-present reality of mutual-fund and financial-adviser fees, which you will read about under Threat #3 later in this chapter.

In 2015, the U.S. Government Accountability Office (GAO) conducted a study and found that half of adults ages 55 and older have no retirement savings whatsoever and one quarter have less than

$148,000.[7] The Economics Policy Institute found that the average person with a 401(k) is on track to retire with only 20 to 40 percent of what they need to maintain their current standard of living.[8]

The problem is that we are approaching the idea of retirement from the wrong angle. It's just not practical for many individuals to save enough to safely retire, especially when there's no way of safely knowing how much is enough.

From this point forward, rather than feeling bad about how you're doing in this department, and instead of burying your head in the sand and hoping it will all turn out okay, I encourage you to start thinking outside the box. Think beyond the nest egg.

Most people cannot save their way to retirement today.

KIM KIYOSAKI
Author of *It's Rising Time*

THREAT #2: RISK

Whether it's a first date or a wedding, there's always a chance that things might not go as planned. This is risk. When we hop in the car to drive to the post office, there is risk. Even if it's quite small, we risk getting in an accident on the way there. And if we do get in an accident, our risk of suffering injury or death can be dramatically lessened by buckling up. Risk speaks to the unknown.

This section will go into the three main risks associated with mutual fund–based retirement accounts:

1. The stock market
2. Financial advisers
3. Electronic and cyber-related risks

Keep in mind as you read this section that, in spite of these risks, I'm not proposing we stop contributing to our retirement accounts. Indeed, we *should continue* to fund our retirement accounts for many of the reasons explained in chapter 1, in the section "Benefits of Traditional Retirement Vehicles," just as we *should continue* using our car to do whatever we need to do. I'm simply suggesting that you understand the risks and wear your seat belt. And in this area of life, diversification is your seat belt. Diversification is about doing something completely different from what you are currently doing, in addition to doing what you *are* currently doing, in order to lessen risk as you prepare for the future. Simply said, it is about not putting all your eggs in one basket.

Anyone who thinks there's safety in numbers hasn't looked at the stock market pages.

IRENE PETER
American writer

Risk #1: The Stock Market

We all know there is risk in the stock market. We've seen our accounts plummet (and then bounce back sooner or later). We understand that recession is a normal part of the business cycle. We understand the risk.

And while the stock market does tend to trend upward over time, the question is: *What if . . .* What if *all* your retirement savings are tied up in the stock market? What if the market drops just when you plan to retire? What if it drops later on, like in your seventies, when you are mandated to take withdrawals regardless of the price of your stock? What if the dip is major and long-lasting?

When it comes to the stock market, risk is defined as the chance that an investment will do worse than expected, or that we will lose money. This is because the entire system is built on the premise of buying shares at one price and selling at a higher price. And, as much as we like to reassure ourselves that the market always bounces back, the truth is that we're playing with risk. This is why financial advisers ask you about your "risk tolerance," and why we have low-, medium-, and high-risk stocks.

Risk in the stock market is not about *whether* it will bounce back. Risk is about timing. Because the stock market is intimately tied to risk, and because it naturally moves in up-and-down cycles, the stock market has an odd way of working when it comes to retirement. Not completely unlike the lottery, it creates winners and losers at random. The difference is that winning and losing in the stock market depends largely on your timing. If you are retiring and the market is up, and stays up, you're a winner. If the market falls after you've stopped working, you're not.

To compound the issue, the inherent risk in the stock market is actually greatest for those who are closest to retirement. Even those with moderate to substantial amounts invested are subject to this risk. In the words of Stephen Gandel, author of *Time* magazine's seminal article on the retirement crisis:

> In what must seem like a cruel joke to many, the accounts proved the most dangerous for those closest to retirement. During the market downturn, the 401(k)s of 55-to-65-year-olds lost a quarter more than those of their 35-to-45-year-old colleagues. That's because in your early years, your 401(k)'s growth is driven mostly by contributions. You control your own destiny. But the longer you hold a 401(k), the more market-exposed it becomes. It's a twist that breaks the most basic rule of financial planning.[9]

The financial industry has attempted to convince us that our 401(k) plans will make us wealthy by the time we are ready to retire, certainly wealthy *enough* to retire. And yet in October 2008, when the stock market tanked, triggering what is known as the Great Recession, more than seventy million Baby Boomers on the brink of retirement lost vast sums of their life savings. In fact, nearly everyone with a 401(k) saw their accounts tumble by 25 to 50 percent overnight, depending on how they had their investments allocated.[10]

As I described in chapter 1, our society has simply veered into this nest-egg way of planning for retirement; it was never planned, researched, modeled, or tested. So in essence, at the expense of those early Baby Boomers who happened to be without a pension, the Great Recession constituted a test drive of the 401(k).

And sadly, the road test failed for those retiring in or around 2008. Many people were forced to delay their retirements or cancel them altogether, depending on circumstance, while others were forced out of their jobs and thrust into "early retirement" as companies trimmed down their workforces. It is a cruel reality that when the economy suffers, companies can be quick to let go of workers, and often older workers are the first to go. Losing one's job late in life—but earlier than planned—can mean losing nearly everything at once: daily routine, community of friends and co-workers, and pride. This also comes with the possible loss of promised pension benefits and retirement account values.

The main purpose of the stock market is to make fools of as many men as possible.

BERNARD BARUCH
Stock market financier and adviser to Presidents Woodrow Wilson and Franklin D. Roosevelt (1870–1965)

The last thing to point out here is that as Baby Boomers continue to retire over the next couple of decades, they will collectively be pulling vast sums of money out of the stock market. This will occur in part by choice, part by necessity, and part by mandate (see the section on the RMD from chapter 1). Do with this information what you may; however, in the sage words of Robert Kiyosaki, author of *Rich Dad Poor Dad*: "You do not need to be a rocket scientist to know that it is hard for a market to keep going up when more and more people are getting out."[11]

The point of this section is not to scare you off from investing in your 401(k), IRA, or other type of retirement account or mutual fund. The point is to help you become aware of the risks of investing *solely* in these vehicles in the hope of your accounts appreciating in value. Just as you might have a fire extinguisher in your kitchen for an event that may never happen, you need a backup plan for retirement. A retirement portfolio that is truly diverse includes types of assets that entail completely different types of risk from each other, as you'll see in the next chapter.

October: This is one of the peculiarly dangerous months to speculate in stocks. The others are July, January, September, April, November, May, March, June, December, August, and February.
MARK TWAIN

Risk #2: Financial Advisers

Since this section is about risk, it would be a disservice not to mention financial advisers here. After all, we collectively entrust our advisers with billions of our dollars each year. In other words, we delegate risk to them in the hope that they will know more about investing than we do. Many of us may even expect them to "beat the market."

We'll cover fee structures of financial advisers and fee-related risk in the next section. However, it is worth mentioning here that you need to *really* trust your financial planner. By trust, I mean having confidence in both their level of competence and their honesty. I don't mean the warm, fuzzy feeling that comes from their enthusiasm, friendliness, and apparent interest in your kids or favorite sports team! Nor does it mean the sense of confidence inspired by their no-nonsense professional disposition. *Good eggs and bad eggs look the same on the outside.* This goes for your financial planner, too. Unethical, unscrupulous, or simply bad financial planners present themselves just as well as the ones who are knowledgeable, impartial, and honest.

Financial planners have a range of education, experience, and expertise. Some are trained by the companies they represent, while others are independently credentialed as a Certified Financial Planner. Some receive a percentage of your investments whether or not they go up or down in value, while others provide investment advice on an hourly basis.

If your investment adviser claims that he or she can "beat the market," run away fast. It is now widely accepted that advisers are not able to outperform the market. In fact, given the often-exorbitant fee structure charged by some advisers, John Bogle, founder of Vanguard, and other finance experts, assert that most people would be better off investing in a low-fee index fund, themselves, than investing with a financial planner.[12,13] The last section in this chapter, "Threat #3: Silent but Deadly Fees," is a must-read because it shows you exactly why millions of people are being robbed by retirement-account companies and financial planners . . . and how to find out if you are one of these unlucky ones.

The difference between playing the stock market and the horses is that one of the horses must win.

JOEY ADAMS
Comedian and *New York Post* columnist (1911–1999)

A Word About Unscrupulous Financial Advisers

When it comes to unscrupulous financial advisers, the name "Bernie Madoff" often is the first to come to mind. After all, he destroyed the financial security and retirement dreams of thousands of individuals by swindling them out of billions of dollars collectively. He also wiped out charitable organizations and their beneficiaries, owners, and employees of small businesses, and customers of the banks that had invested with him.[14,15,16] Madoff ran the largest and most infamous Ponzi scheme in history.

While the scale of Madoff's scam is unparalleled, and while we may be inclined to think that this kind of crime only happens to "other people," the undeniable truth is that smaller-scale and potentially less obvious financial scams are around us all the time. In fact, roughly one Ponzi scheme was uncovered every six days in the United States in 2015.[17]

In an effort to help everyday investors like you and me, the U.S. Securities and Exchange Commission (SEC) has published a list of Ponzi-scheme red flags, as shown below:

1. Promises of high returns and little to no investment risk
2. Overly consistent returns
3. Investments that are not registered with the SEC or state regulators
4. Sellers that are unlicensed (either companies or individuals)
5. Secretive and/or complex investment strategies
6. Issues with producing timely statements
7. Errors and/or inconsistencies on statements
8. Difficulty receiving payments
9. Pressure to "roll over" gains into other investments[18]

Scam artists can be unscrupulous financial advisers, insurance brokers, and annuity salespeople. I spoke with an elderly widow, whom I will call Charlotte, who had been conned by her annuity salesman into buying a policy with a well-known insurance company. After seemingly elite treatment, a physical exam, and an extensive application, the company required $20,000 up front, plus another $20,000 each year thereafter. Charlotte moved forward and generously enrolled in this policy so that her grown kids would not have to pay taxes on her estate upon her death. Her problem was that this $20,000 annual price tag would have substantially dented her limited nest egg and jeopardized her chances of outliving her own money or even having anything left in her estate to be taxed on at all.

Risk #3: Electronic and Cyber-Related Risk

This section on risk was not fun to write. I'm sure it will be equally depressing to read. However, back to the analogy of the fire extinguisher in your kitchen, it is important to acknowledge that having all your money in virtual accounts, with online accessibility, comes with a certain level of risk. There are many different types of electronic and cyber-related risks, and the lines between them are fuzzy. However, there are three general categories:

1. Identity theft and "ransomware"
2. Cyberterrorism and cyberwarfare
3. Technology errors and frozen accounts

Any mutual-fund manager or investment adviser will tell you that you need to diversify. They will inform you about high- and low-risk stocks. They will tell you about bonds. But what most won't tell you, what most may not even recognize, is that diversification must go beyond virtual accounts. True diversification requires diversifying across both electronic and non-electronic accounts. What is a non-electronic account? It is real estate. It is a house or building that you can walk into, touch, and improve with your own hands.

Identity Theft and Ransomware

According to the U.S. Federal Bureau of Investigation, identity theft is one of the fastest growing crimes. It entails the fraudulent acquisition and use of a person's private identifying information for financial gain. Just as your bank accounts and credit cards are at risk of being wiped out by a malicious computer hacker, your retirement accounts are also at risk. While the hacking of retirement accounts currently seems to be relatively rare as compared to credit card and bank accounts, their very online nature and virtual existence make them prime targets. Recognizing this, Steve Vernon of *CBS Money Watch* has provided a resource for safeguarding your retirement accounts at the following website: www.cbsnews.com/news/how-to-protect-your-retirement-savings-from-identity-theft-and-internet-fraud/.[19] In addition to the tips he provides on protecting your retirement accounts from identity theft, think about building something separate, something tangible, something that is not vulnerable to a computer hacker at all.

Ransomware is a whole new breed of computer hacking. It involves a type of malicious software designed to block the owner's access to a computer system until a sum of money is paid as a ransom. It can be aimed at individuals, businesses, and governments. According to a National Public Radio segment, fourteen hospitals in the United States were targeted with ransomware in the spring of 2016.[20] The medical files were literally held hostage, compromising patients' health, until a large sum of money was paid for their release. Similar incidents have been reported by a police department in Massachusetts, a café in Maryland, and an incident that affected over six thousand Mac computer users.[21] In each case, the malicious hackers demanded, and received, money for the release of files.

Cyberterrorism or Cyberwarfare

There are numerous examples of hacks into governmental and nongovernmental computer networks by foreign governments or entities. For example, there was the foreign infiltration of the U.S. electrical grid in 2009.[22] There was the attack on Sony Pictures' computer system in 2014 in which personal employee information was leaked to the public.[23] And there was the massive attack on the U.S. government with the stolen identities of an almost unfathomable 21.5 million federal employees in 2015.[24]

Cyberterrorism and cyberwarfare involve threats to our national security and stability. They are malicious acts by terrorists or nations to penetrate computers or networks for the purpose of causing massive disruption. The concern, which is not insignificant, is that a large-scale cyber-attack could seriously damage the financial-services industry or other aspects of our national infrastructure.[25,26]

Technology Errors and Frozen Accounts

Let's face it. Computers are fallible. They break down. Software sometimes does funky stuff. And on occasion, they are attacked by malicious viruses. When it comes to our own computers, technology breakdown—in one form or another—is not only possible, it is almost inevitable. In fact, we've almost come to expect it. This is why we go to great lengths to protect ourselves from our own computers. We back stuff up. We download the latest anti-virus software. We buy a new computer every few years (usually after our last one crashes!).

Banks, mutual-fund companies, and even the New York Stock Exchange (NYSE) all deal with the same issues, but on a larger scale. They have more (way more!) stuff at risk. They have better (way better!) anti-virus software and firewalls. And they have more bad guys (way "badder") trying to hack into their systems. What this means is that, even at the level of the NYSE, things have the potential to go awry.

On August 1, 2012, tens of thousands of accidental stock trades flooded the stock market. This major "oops" moment was caused by a simple software glitch at a high-speed electronic trading company, Knight Capital, in which legitimate stock trades were each multiplied accidentally by one thousand. The error was detected and halted within forty-five minutes, but it caused the company's stock price drop from $10.33 to $2.84 per share.

This was not the only time a technical issue sent the stock market flying into a tailspin. In July 2015, the NYSE shut down for nearly four hours. At this writing, it was still unclear whether the shutdown was in response to a technical error or cyberthreat.[27]

Simultaneously, on the other side of the Atlantic Ocean, the citizens of Greece saw their bank accounts essentially frozen by the government in an attempt to fix the Greek government debt crisis. Banks and the stock market were shuttered, with ATMs being the only source of cash. Greeks were limited to withdrawals of 60 Euros ($66) per day.[28,29] While these "capital controls" were only expected to last a couple of weeks to a month, two years later, these ATM withdrawal limits and other capital controls were still in effect and are expected to remain so indefinitely.[30]

You take so many measures to protect your own computer and personal information. Yet, because of cyber-related risks beyond your control (identity theft, ransomware, cyberwarfare, technology snafus, and frozen accounts), it must be acknowledged that virtual assets do come with a certain level of risk. And having *all* your money—from your bank account to your retirement account—residing electronically escalates your level of risk. Failing to diversify into tangible assets (like real estate) is like driving without a seat belt or having no fire extinguisher in your kitchen. And in this technology-dominant era, the best safeguard is one that is not, also, technology-based.

THREAT #3: SILENT (BUT DEADLY) FEES

The third threat goes beyond risk into the land of certainty. What you're going to read next will floor you. Seriously, if you are not sitting on the floor right now, you might want to take a moment to get there in order to prevent injury.

Have you ever heard that saying about casinos? "The house always wins." Well, when it comes to your retirement accounts, there are good ones and, well . . . let's just say, there are casinos.

The fees you pay to your retirement or mutual-fund company can be devastating. If you add up all the fees and if they are under one half of 1 percent, then you can feel confident that you have a really good plan.[31] If you are between half a percent and 1 percent, then you have an okay plan. If your plan's fees are between 1 and 2 percent, then you are losing money. Anything more than 2 percent and you're being robbed.

While fees that add up to a couple of percentage points may not sound like a lot, they translate into big bucks. Really big bucks. In an attempt to help consumers understand whether their plan is a good egg or a bad one, the U.S. Department of Labor (DOL) published information, in 2013, on the topic at www.dol.gov/ebsa/publications/ 401k_employee.html#section9 and explained the impact of fees by way of the following example:

> Assume that you are an employee with 35 years until retirement and a current 401(k) account balance of $25,000. If returns on investments in your account over the next 35 years average 7 percent and fees and expenses reduce your average returns by 0.5 percent, your account balance will grow to $227,000 at retirement, even if there are no further contributions to your account. If fees and expenses are 1.5 percent, however, your account balance will grow to only $163,000. The 1 percent difference in fees and expenses would reduce your account balance at retirement by 28 percent.[32]

This is just one example. The impact of the fees depends on how long you invest, whether you continue to make contributions, and your average rate of return. And of course, more than anything else, the impact depends on the fees that are charged by your plan.

John Bogle, the aforementioned founder of Vanguard and author of many investment-related books, has been aiming to get the word out about fees for a while. On the PBS *Frontline* episode "The Retirement Gamble," he said:

> What happens in the fund business is that the magic of compound returns is overwhelmed by the tyranny of compounding costs. It's a mathematical fact. There's no getting around it.

He gives an example of a mutual fund with a 7 percent average return and a 2 percent annual fee. Over fifty years of investing, the fund will have lost almost two thirds of its value![33]

The impact of seemingly small fees boils down to simple math. In this example, the 7 percent rate of return will have been essentially reduced to a 5 percent rate of return. The remaining 2 percent rate of return goes directly toward your company's bottom line. From the consumer's perspective, the 2 percent loss is not even noticeable. It just quietly comes out of the balance each month, often not even showing up as a line item.

As James Ridgeway, former *Wall Street Journal* and *Mother Jones* journalist, states: "Fees have always been one of the built-in scams of mutual funds." He quotes Representative George Miller (D-California), chairman of the House Committee on Education and Labor, as saying during a February 2009 hearing on retirement security,

> Wall Street middlemen live off the billions they generate from 401(k)s by imposing hidden and excessive fees that swallow up workers' money. Over a lifetime of work, these hidden fees can take an enormous bite out of workers' accounts.[34]

In other words, the mutual-fund and retirement-account companies with high fees are literally banking on your not paying attention.

The 401(k) mutual fund is one of the only products
that Americans buy that they don't know the price of.
It's also one of the products that Americans buy that
they don't even know its quality or know how to judge
its quality. It's one of the products that Americans
buy that they don't know its danger.

PROFESSOR TERESA GHILARDUCCI
Professor of Economics at The New School and author of
When I'm Sixty Four: The Plot Against Pensions and the Plan to Save Them,
on PBS *Frontline* (April 23, 2013)

An Example of How Fees Work

As another example of how this works, let's assume that three triplet siblings (let's call them Amy, Bill, and Chris) just celebrated their 40th birthdays together. Toward the end of the bash, and feeling slightly uninhibited, they ended up talking money with each other. As they shared their situations, it dawned on them that their retirement-savings situations were shockingly similar. That is, all except for one small detail hidden in the fine print of their companies' prospectuses. The amounts they were paying in fees to their companies were

1, 2, and 3 percent, respectively. Other than the varying fees, Amy, Bill, and Chris each had retirement account balances of exactly $50,000, were invested in mutual funds with a 7 percent average rate of return, planned to make no additional contributions, and hoped to retire at age 67.

Table 2.1 and Figure 2.1 show the impact of the different fees on Amy's, Bill's, and Chris's future account balances at age 67. For Amy, the 1 percent in fees will dent her ultimate retirement savings by 22 percent (one fifth). She was pretty depressed about this until she learned that Bill's 2 percent in fees will eat up 40 percent of his entire account balance in the end. Chris, on the other hand, left the party thoroughly depressed (though enlightened). Chris realized that if he stays with his current plan, the fees of 3 percent will consume *more than half* of his total savings by the time he hopes to retire! You can see from Table 2.1 that—in the end—the mutual-fund company will actually make more money than Chris will . . . when it was Chris's money to begin with! And when Chris was the one shouldering all the risk! It's almost unbelievable.

The next day, Chris took action to find an index fund with a new company with fees, at less than 1 percent, that were even lower than

TABLE 2.1. TOTAL RETIREMENT SAVINGS AND TOTAL LOST TO FEES BY AGE 67
(Assuming $50,000 Balance by Age 40, No Additional Contributions After Age 40, And a 7% Average Rate Of Return)

	AMY: FEES TOTALING 1%	BILL: FEES TOTALING 2%	CHRIS: FEES TOTALING 3%
Total amount they would have saved (assuming no fees)	$310,692	$310,692	$310,692
Amount that is actually theirs (by different fee amounts)	$241,116	$186,672	$144,168
Amount lost to fees	$69,576	$124,020	$166,524
Proportion of total that is attributable to the fee itself	22%	40%	54%

FIGURE 2.1. DIFFERENCE BETWEEN THE AMOUNT SAVED WITHOUT FEES VERSUS SAVED WITH FEES RANGING FROM 1% TO 3%

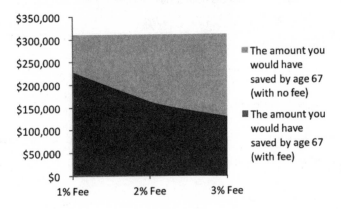

Amy's. Being the good brother that he is, he quickly informed his sibs and they all made the change together to the consumer-friendly mutual fund.

Table 2.1 shows exactly how the 401(k) and IRAs are failing workers, using our hypothetical triplets as an example. Figure 2.1 is a graphical representation of the same information. This graph shows the difference between what Amy, Bill, and Chris would have accrued after twenty-seven years with no fee (the solid and striped sections, combined, at $310,692), compared to the amount they would have built up with fees of 1, 2, and 3 percent (shown as the solid section on the graph). Another way of looking at this graph is that the striped section represents the total amount of money that Amy, Bill, and Chris would have lost to their mutual-fund companies under their different fee scenarios (ranging from $69,576 to $166,524).

I should note that if Amy, Bill, and Chris had continued making contributions to their plans until age 67, rather than stopping at age 40, they would have each amassed much more money (in spite of also bringing in more money for the mutual-fund companies). In fact, as you can see from Table 2.2, each of their total account values, as well as the amounts that they would have been able to keep for themselves, would have more than doubled.

TABLE 2.2. TOTAL RETIREMENT SAVINGS AND TOTAL LOST TO FEES BY AGE 67

(Assuming Continued Contributions of $5,000 per Year After Age 40)

	AMY: FEES TOTALING 1%	BILL: FEES TOTALING 2%	CHRIS: FEES TOTALING 3%
The total amount they would have saved (if no fee)	$683,112	$683,112	$683,112
The amount that is actually theirs (by different fee amounts)	$559,646	$460,018	$379,589
The amount lost to fees	$123,466	$223,094	$303,523
The proportion of total that is attributable to the fee itself	18%	33%	44%

Table 2.2 is good evidence for the importance of continuing to make contributions to your retirement plan or mutual fund. However, it is equally good evidence for the importance of taking a close look at your accounts to ensure that you are in a low-fee plan. Find out the annual operating expenses (also called the expense ratio) and all other fees, using the method in the next section, and make any necessary changes to ensure that you are in a low-fee plan, as soon as humanly possible.

Figure Out Your Plan's Fees and Their Impact

You can determine the damage that fees will have on your own mutual fund and retirement accounts. To do this, you need to gather your numbers and simply plug them into the calculator at the following website: www.401kfee.com. The hard part will be gathering your numbers. Some companies make it almost impossible to determine your fees, while others make it a bit easier. Sometimes these fees are either not disclosed, disclosed only to your employer, or disclosed in such a confusing way that they can be impossible to interpret.[35,36]

You have a few options when it comes to finding out what your fees are. First, you can go through the mutual-fund-company prospectus that comes in the mail. Look for a number that is expressed in the form of a percentage. Once you've found the percentage, check to see if this is called an "expense ratio" or "annual operating expenses." If it is, you've found the right number. These annual operating expenses may not encompass all the fees that you might be subject to with your plan; however, they are a good starting point.†

A second option is to call the company to ask about the fees. However, don't put too much weight on anything they say over the phone. Ask them to send you the prospectus or some other document so you can see it in black and white.

Finally, you can look up the fees online. There are at least two free resources for checking out many plans' fee structure. The company Brightscope is an independent financial information and technology site aiming to bring "transparency to opaque markets." Their site (www.brightscope.com/ratings/) provides the expense ratios for different funds. For comparison, it also provides information on how your fund compares to others in the same category.

The Financial Industry Regulatory Authority (FINRA) also provides assistance in determining fees through its site: http://apps.finra.org/fundanalyzer/1/fa.aspx. On this site, fees are called "annual operating expenses." FINRA also lists any front-end, back-end, or redemption fees that may be associated with your plan. However, the site also discloses that "the results do not reflect the application of other fees that may apply, such as ETF commissions, exchange fees, or account maintenance fees. Had these fees been considered, your costs would be higher and account values lower."

It is important to note that the fee information from both sites also does not account for any fees that your financial planner charges, if you have one. I'll go into this redundancy a bit more in the next

---

† The range of fees can include any of the following: back-end load (also known as deferred sales charge or redemption fee, when shares are sold), bookkeeping fees, finders' fees, front-end load (when shares are purchased), insurance-related charges, legal fees, management fees (also known as investment advisory fees or account maintenance fees), revenue sharing, rule 12b-1 fees (ongoing), sales charges (aka: loads or commissions), shelf space, soft dollars, surrender and transfer charges, stewardship fees, transactional fees, trustee fees, wrap fees.

section. For both websites, when you enter the ticker symbol for your fund, you receive instantaneous results. Note that the results from the two sites will probably not be identical, so it is a good idea to look at your fees both ways, and go with the higher one, knowing that some fees never make it into the calculations.

Finally, it is worth noting that if you are unable to locate your plan's fees, either through a prospectus or either of the above websites, you may have a dud of a plan. Meaning, as I discuss in the next section, *get out.*

Getting the Best Return on Your Retirement Accounts

The simple exercise that I proposed in the last section will either reassure you that all is well with your accounts, or it will arm you to take action. If you have one retirement account, you can evaluate whether you want to stay, or switch to a lower-fee plan. If you have more than one plan, say from past and present employers, you could save potentially tens of thousands of dollars in redundant fees alone by consolidating your funds into the one with the lowest fees. Or, if none of your plans have fees under 1 percent, find a plan that does and move all your accounts into that new plan. There is no need to "diversify" across different fee amounts. It is always best to ensure that you are in the lowest-fee plan possible. Talk to an accountant before moving your funds across plan type (Roth, non-Roth, 401[k], IRA, etc.) to understand any taxes or penalties based on your own personal situation.

Your retirement account is a critical part of a diverse retirement plan. The key is to make sure you are in the right one. As I shared in chapter 1, there are several benefits to employer-sponsored retirement plans. The direct-deposit feature makes it almost effortless to save money. If your workplace provides matching funds, then this is essentially free money for your account. Finally, as I share later in this book, once your account builds to some value, you can leverage those funds to purchase income-generating real estate if you like, and then pay yourself back, with a net result of two asset classes (your retirement account plus a rental property) rather than simply your one retirement account. Again, for all these reasons, the take-home point from this chapter is this: Don't ditch your 401(k) or other retirement plan, and don't stop your contributions, but *do* make sure you are invested in the right one.

Fees and Your Financial Adviser

Many people swear by their financial adviser. After all, most of us don't have the expertise—or even the interest—to safely make our own investment or retirement-planning decisions. And while this may be true, especially when it comes to understanding the technicalities related to the stock market, bonds, annuities, and the like, there are two very important concepts that everyone should understand. How do financial planners get paid? And, to whom are they are loyal? This section goes into these two critical questions.

As you read this section, also keep in mind another critical question. I will share the answer with you toward the end, but for now, just see if the answer bubbles up on its own. The question to contemplate is this: Why don't most financial planners ever talk about investing in real estate?

According to the U.S. Securities and Exchange Commission, there are true investment advisers and there are "broker-dealers" who are, quite literally, *salespeople*. It is difficult to tell them apart because both types go by the term "financial adviser" or "financial planner," and both types market themselves in ways that emphasize the financial-advisory aspect of their services.[37] Where it gets confusing is that, under U.S. law, broker-dealers are not required to make their customers aware of any conflict of interest that could bias their recommendations.[38] This means that, by law, broker-dealers are allowed to be secret salespeople with no legal obligation to act in the *best* interests of their clients. They are merely required to find investments that are "suitable" *enough*.

Helaine Olen, author of *Pound Foolish* and former personal finance columnist for the *Los Angeles Times*, stated on the PBS *Frontline* episode "The Retirement Gamble" (April 23, 2013) that the term "financial adviser" is "a term that means almost nothing. It is somebody who might be a financial planner, or it could be a broker who is really a salesperson."

We have a system today where anybody can hold themselves out as an expert. They call themselves retirement planners, financial planners, advisers, et cetera. We don't have a standard way that the consumer can figure out who has the expertise to provide advice.

PHYLLIS BORZI
Assistant Secretary of Labor, 2013, U.S. Department of Labor,
on PBS *Frontline* (April 23, 2013)

At roughly 85 percent, the vast majority of "financial advisers" are registered as broker-dealers.[39,40] These salespeople usually represent one or more companies, and they are paid by commission to sign you up for certain products even if those products are not necessarily in your best interest, as long as they are suitable enough.[41,42] Their decisions can be swayed by the product types that offer the best commission, or by the products that have sales-target incentives in terms of the number of customers they enroll.[43]

A 2015 White House report titled *The Effects of Conflicted Investment Advice on Retirement Savings* found that the advice provided by broker-dealers is estimated to cost individuals an average of 1 percent in fees, translating to a 25 percent loss in total portfolio accumulation, on average.[44] Now that you understand the impact of fees (from earlier in this chapter), you can see that this additional 1 percent in fees due to conflicted investment advice is on top of the mutual-fund fees that were just discussed in the examples of Amy, Bill, and Chris.

On top of that, have you ever wondered how your financial planner makes his or her money? If your adviser is a broker-dealer, you can be fairly certain that they are taking a slice of your annual return in the form of fees. Again, take Amy, Bill, and Chris. Their mutual-fund fees were 1, 2, and 3 percent, respectively, and their rates of return were—in truth—6, 5, and 4 percent, respectively (not the 7 percent that was advertised). Now imagine that, instead of either enrolling in an IRA or mutual fund on their own, or enrolling in their work-sponsored plan, they had enlisted the help of a financial adviser to invest their money in a mutual fund for them. If that adviser charges 1 percent in fees, then in the end, Amy would actually be getting Bill's earlier rate of return (5 percent); Bill would be getting Chris's rate of return (4 percent); and Chris? Poor Chris would have a rate of return of only 3 percent (7 percent initial return minus 3 percent in plan fees minus 1 percent in fees from his financial planner). Finally, once we add in the cost of conflicted advice, just discussed, Amy's, Bill's, and Chris's returns drop again to 4, 3, and 2 percent, respectively. Yikes.

The problem is that the investor puts up 100 percent of the money, takes 100 percent of the risk, and receives only 20 percent of the profits (if there are profits).
ROBERT KIYOSAKI

The truth is that in spite of the holiday cards, free dinners, and apparent interest in your life, many broker-dealing financial advisers don't necessarily have your best interests in mind. Some may, of course. But for some, the lure of lifelong commissions is simply too powerful. And this also brings to light the answer to the question I posed at the beginning of this section: Why don't they typically encourage real estate investing? It's simple . . . they would have no piece of the pie, no commissions, no way to collect money on those types of investments. Plus, you would have less money to invest in their products that are laced with commissions and bonuses.

So, if roughly 85 percent of financial planners are broker-dealer types, what about the other 15 percent? These "fiduciary" financial planners are a completely different breed. These are true advisers, or "fiduciaries," because they tend to be *exclusively fee-based*. In this context, fees are a good thing. What this means is that you pay your adviser either a flat fee or an hourly fee in exchange for their wisdom and guidance. These advisers represent their clients, only, rather than trying to walk the fine line between their clients' best interests and their companies' quotas and tempting commissions and bonuses. Since exclusively fee-based advisers do not receive commissions, they have no conflicts of interest. And, if there are any conflicts of interest, they are required by law to divulge them. Since they are free agents, they are *true advisers* rather than salespeople.

The one drawback of some exclusively fee-based advisers, however, is that their expertise may be limited to non-tangible (virtual or electronic) assets such as stocks, bonds, mutual funds, and real estate investment trusts (REITs). This lack of diversification into the world of tangible real estate is potentially problematic due to Threat #1, the danger of running out of money, and Threat #2, risk, as discussed earlier in this chapter. When selecting an adviser, you should always interview a few, *before selecting one*, to get a sense of how their ranges of expertise compare to each other. Pay attention to whether they bring up real estate on their own. If they don't, be sure to ask questions to probe their comfort level with real estate investments.

By design, mutual fund companies, managers, and financial advisers (who are not exclusively fee-based) are set up to make lots of money, risk-free for themselves, while we shoulder all the risk. Since they make money in fees that are often collected as a percentage of their clients' account balance as time goes on, they make actual money whether the accounts go up or down in value. In contrast, we only make theoretical money when the account value goes up, and we only make actual money if the investments are sold at a higher price than when they were purchased. This also means that, even though fund managers may be well meaning and may sincerely *want* their portfolios to do well, they don't have a truly *vested interest* in their performance because it is not their skin in the game. In addition, the often-touted method of dollar cost averaging keeps our money flowing into the system and it keeps mutual-fund companies, managers, and advisers paid, one way or another, even when our accounts are losing value.

A SPECIAL NOTE FOR WOMEN

This is a special note for women, and men who care about their wives, mothers, daughters, sisters, and women in general. As you probably know, women tend to live longer than men. This means that if a woman retires at the same age as a man, she will probably need to stretch her savings further. On top of needing her nest egg to last longer, women typically reach retirement age at a disadvantage. This is due to many factors. It is well established that women continue to earn only 78 percent of men's pay for comparable work.[45] This means that, assuming men and women save the same proportion of their income each year, and since women typically make less than men, they also save less. For easy math, consider the example of a woman making $78,000 and a man making $100,000, both of whom sock away 5 percent each year in their retirement accounts. Five percent for the woman equates to $3,900, while five percent for the man is $5,000. Over thirty years, at 6 percent interest, the compounding effect of this (assuming no pay raises for either) adds up to a whopping $74,247 difference!

Unfortunately, however, this was a best-case scenario. The reality is that we can't assume women and men save at the same rate. Research from the Transamerica Center for Retirement Studies (TCRS) found that among employees of medium to large companies, fewer women than men work for employers that sponsor a 401(k) plan and, of those who do, women are less likely to participate.[46] Furthermore, among those who do participate, women tend to auto-invest smaller percentages of their paychecks than men.[47] A study by the Employment Benefit Research Institute found similar results among Individual Retirement Account (IRA) holders, with the female–male gap in savings being greatest among those who are closest to retirement age.[48] There are probably many reasons for the lower savings rates among women, including the finding from the TCRS survey that female employees are focused on "just getting by" while more male workers prioritize "saving for retirement."[49] Taken together, these smaller percentages saved on lower amounts earned can add up to significantly lower savings by retirement age for women as compared to men.

What this means is that unless you do something radical, right now, surviving retirement as a woman may mean substantial sacrifice. You either sacrifice now (by forcing yourself to save more and living with less money and the risks described earlier in this chapter) or you sacrifice later (by adopting a lower standard of living in retirement or not retiring at all). Alternatively, you can use the strategies in this book to jettison yourself out of the limited-nest-egg way of thinking and into a sustainable cash-flowing asset . . . one that will never be used up and that will pay you every month, now, throughout your retirement, and "beyond" in the form of an inheritance for your heirs.

3

WHY YOU NEED
A "CHICKEN"

The Rewards and Risks of Rental Property

S o, what's with all the talk of chickens and eggs? Well, it's simple. Just as chickens provide eggs day after day, income-producing rental properties provide cash flow month after month. If you aim to retire one day, and if you won't have a pension to provide stable monthly income, you are going to need some monthly eggs. Sure, one big fat nest egg would also be nice, if you have that luxury. But as we've already discussed, you can never be totally sure how long that nest egg will last you. This means living in constant anxiety of the possibility that it could run out, as well as possibly having to live with the consequences of it actually running out. Best-case scenario, it doesn't run out during your lifetime, but you may have little left over to pass on to your surviving spouse or your kids.

■

*Rental property is the "pension" for those
who don't have a pension.*
K. KAI ANDERSON

On the other hand, if you have little (or big) eggs streaming into your bank account every month, then you know exactly how long they will last. Those eggs will last until you sell your chicken. They can literally last *forever*.

Once you pay off your mortgages, the monthly income is available to use any way you like. If you pay off your mortgage sooner, the income could be your college savings plan, as it is ours. It could also mean early retirement, which is also part of our plan!

As with any type of investment, there are benefits as well as risks to owning rental property. After spending a moment to stress the importance of diversification, this chapter delves into the benefits and risks related to investing in real estate. In addition, since the risks are of a different breed than the risks in the stock market, I will also share some tips for how to reduce their chances of occurring and how to bounce back if they do.

BENEFITS OF RENTAL PROPERTY

There are many benefits to investing in real estate for the long term. While you must wait for some of these benefits, you get to enjoy many of them right away. The benefits you often enjoy right away include lowering the amount of income tax you currently pay (depending on your income) and creating a small amount of cash flow (after paying your mortgage principal, interest, and other expenses) to save, live off of, or reinvest. These aspects will be covered in detail in the following section of this chapter. The other benefits are less tangible. They include pride in ownership and the confidence that comes with that. They also include the peace of mind in knowing that you have created—with your own work—a safety net for your retirement and your older years in general.

In terms of the benefits you enjoy later on, the main one is serious cash flow resulting from having paid off your mortgage. Add to that the possible scenario of escalating real estate values and upward-trending rental rates over time. For a nominal entry fee on your part, you can eventually own—*free and clear*—an asset that is worth a serious chunk of change that provides steady income month after month. These now-and-later benefits are listed in Table 3.1.

TABLE 3.1. NOW-AND-LATER BENEFITS OF OWNING RENTAL PROPERTY

NOW	LATER (ONCE MORTGAGE IS PAID OFF)
Modest cash flow	Serious cash flow
Lower current income taxes	Increased net worth
Ownership of an asset that can be refinanced, to extract money, if needed	Ownership of a non-liquid asset to sell or refinance if/when needed
Pride in ownership	Diversification beyond virtual bank accounts and virtual assets
Peace of mind from having created a retirement safety net	Diversification beyond stock market–based retirement accounts

Benefit #1: Rentals Are a Way to *Not* Put "All Your Eggs in One Basket"

Diversification is the number one reason for owning at least one rental as a part of your long-term plan. The myth of mutual funds is that you are diversified. It may be true that you are somewhat diversified across different dividend- and non-dividend-paying stocks, bonds, and REITs. However, keep in mind that if all your savings are in virtual assets that rely on buying at one price and selling at a higher one to be profitable, then you are not *truly* diversified. To be truly diversified, you need to think beyond Wall Street. You need to think Main Street, or First Street, or even Pickle Street. In other words, think real estate.

Rental property is important to diversification for many reasons. For starters, the up–down cycles in real estate values don't always line up with those of the financial markets. In fact, using data from the 1800s to the present, many economists agree that—while difficult to measure—real estate cycles often last about eighteen years.[1,2,3,4] If this is accurate, then the next great dip in real estate values can be expected in roughly the year 2025. Meanwhile, opinions and theories on stock-market cycles are more variable with theorized cycles ranging from just a couple of years to roughly seven years to many years.[5,6,7] Stock-market "day traders" can often see four or more cycles in a day.[8]

Owning rental real estate can protect you, and even help you thrive, regardless of what happens in the economy. More importantly, real estate is tangible. People will always need homes, meaning that the rental market demand will endure even if housing values go down. The long-term investors with tenants were relatively spared in the real estate crash that began in 2007. In fact, many landlords claim that the rental market had never been stronger. The sad truth was that during these hard times those who lost their homes to foreclosure were suddenly in need of rental housing.

Those who suffered the most when the real estate bubble popped fall into three main groups. The first group includes new-home buyers who were deemed "subprime" by mortgage companies but were given so-called "creative" mortgages anyway. They were deemed subprime because they would not have been able to afford their homes using a conventional thirty-year mortgage. As graphically demonstrated in the movie *The Big Short*, these individuals were intentionally and deceptively lured into mortgages with low and seemingly affordable initial payments, which escalated to unaffordable levels after a period of time. See chapter 8 for more information on these dangerous types of mortgages.

The second group of people who suffered in the housing crisis were existing homeowners who had tapped their home equity by refinancing or opening up lines of credit to purchase items or experiences. The burn came when some kind of hardship, like job loss or divorce, made it difficult to make the higher payments required by their new mortgage. Then, once home values plummeted below the amount financed, it became impossible for homeowners to sell those properties.

The third group who suffered in the crashing real estate market were the "flippers" and the "fix-and-flippers." These are the individuals who had purchased a house either in hopes of riding the tide of appreciation or with plans to renovate and sell (i.e., fix and flip). They purchased at one price and hoped during those intoxicating days of double-digit appreciation that they would be able to sell a short time later at a higher price. Unfortunately, this plan was similar to those who buy a stock or mutual fund at one price and hope to sell for a higher price not too far down the road. When the music of the real estate market stopped, and especially if the home was midway through renovation and not rentable in its current state, these individuals were left holding the hot potato and got burned.

All three sets of people who suffered the most in the housing crisis were banking on appreciation. When you invest in real estate in the form of rental property held for the long term, you don't bank on appreciation. Appreciation is a nice fringe benefit; however, the golden eggs are the cash flow, which brings us to Benefit #2.

Benefit #2: Rentals Provide Golden "Eggs" as Cash Flow

As we discussed in chapter 2, the number one threat to the nest-egg way of planning for retirement is the threat of running out of money. And the number one advantage of rentals is the antithesis of this threat: Rentals provide a steady, indefinite stream of income for you, month after month. Well maintained and well managed, they never run out.

In preparing for retirement, we are almost always asked to estimate the total amount of money that we think we'll need once we stop working. The answer to this often-overwhelming question is usually calculated from a formula that is based on many different assumptions and questions. If you are using an online calculator, you may end up guessing the answers to these questions. For example, how are we to know what the *actual* rate of return will end up being on our investments? And should that number account for the impact of mutual-fund and financial-adviser fees, taxes, and conflicted financial advice as discussed in chapter 2? How are we to know what the rate of inflation will be after we stop working? And can we possibly know exactly how long we will live or how much we'll need to spend on our health, housing, and leisure needs in retirement? With all this ambiguity, the expectation that we could get within a realistic ballpark estimate of our ideal retirement age, or the amount of money we'll need to safely retire, is almost preposterous.

The thing is, these calculations are based on taking our projected life expectancy and working backward according to how much we expect to spend in the latter third of our lives, and how much we expect to have saved up at different points. The end result, our optimal retirement age, can be quite depressing.

Obstacles are those frightful things you see when you take your eyes off the goal.

HENRY FORD
Industrialist and originator of the five-day
workweek (1863–1947)

Instead of working backward, try working forward. As Kim Kiyosaki, author of *Rich Woman* and *It's Rising Time,* recommends, try thinking about your "number" in a new way. Instead of calculating backward from death to retirement age to present day, calculate forward to see how long your money will last if you had to stop working *right now.*

Suppose you have $30,000 saved up in your 401(k) and $3,000 worth of expenses per month. To figure out how many months you could last on these savings, simply divide $30,000 by $3,000/month and your result is ten months. Ouch! This example shows, in plain numbers, the problem with the nest egg. If you are going to stop earning a paycheck, then you are going to need your money to last longer than ten months . . . a lot longer.

Even if you've saved up $300,000, if you spend at the rate of $3,000 per month, your money will last you only a hundred months, or a mere 8.33 years! If you have a million dollars, $3,000 per month in spending will last you 27.78 years. In this last scenario, if you retire at age 62, then your funds will expire just before you turn 90. Then what? Note that these calculations are rough and do not factor in any growth (or loss) if the funds are held in the stock market, nor do they adjust for inflation or the time value of money.

Now let's calculate in a forward direction how much you'll really need. Add up all your sources of monthly income that you expect to receive after you stop working: Social Security, pension, RMD, dividends from any dividend-producing asset, and anything else that might be a part of your unique picture. To assist with the Social Security and RMD lines, simply refer back to the online resources that I provided in chapter 1.

Keep in mind that it is best not to use the "Other" line to divide up your savings into a monthly amount, because the point of this exercise is to calculate the amount of reliable monthly income you can expect to receive, *even if you were to live forever.* The only way to get monthly income from savings would be to know how long you'll live in order to know how to divide the number. Plus, keeping your savings out of this calculation will give you a conservative sense of the monthly income you'll need, allowing you to reserve your savings for emergencies and larger purchases. See Figure 3.1.

Add up the income streams to get the total income that you expect to receive each month and enter this on the "Total Income" line. On the "Total Expenses" line, simply use your current monthly income or your current monthly expenses as a rough guide for what you will need in retirement. Even though you may be inclined to subtract your home mortgage payment from this amount (if you expect to have it paid off by the time you plan to retire), you may want to be conservative and keep it in. The reason: There's always something. Even if your mortgage is paid off, you may have some other expense in its place, like another mortgage, long-term care expenses, and so forth.

FIGURE 3.1. CALCULATING TOTAL EXTRA NEEDED (PER MONTH)

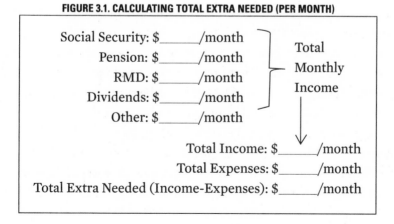

Social Security: $_____/month ⎤
Pension: $_____/month ⎥ Total
RMD: $_____/month ⎬ Monthly
Dividends: $_____/month ⎥ Income
Other: $_____/month ⎦

Total Income: $_____/month
Total Expenses: $_____/month
Total Extra Needed (Income-Expenses): $_____/month

Finally, subtract your "Total Expenses" from your "Total Income" to come up with your "Total Extra Needed." This is the amount of additional monthly income you will need in order to achieve financial comfort in retirement. You'll learn about this in chapter 5; however, this is what I call the "Level II Goal." Also in chapter 5, I share the notion of the "Level III Goal" of complete financial self-sufficiency once the mortgages are paid off. To set yourself up for the Level III Goal, you'll want to enter "0" on the Total Income line. This makes all of your other expected sources of income a *bonus*. If any of these sources dry up or vanish, for any reason, then you will still have the monthly income from your rental properties.

Once you determine the amount of cash flow you need, you can play around with the modifiable Cash Flow Analysis (CFA) Tool at www.GetaChicken.com. Table 3.2 shows a static example of the CFA Tool. The specific number of properties for the Level II or III Goal depends on how much monthly income you expect to need in retirement and how much income you expect your properties to produce. The Level II Goal has the added variable of how much income from other sources you expect to receive.

As an oversimplified example, imagine that your calculation informs you that to be comfortable (the Level II Goal), your "Total Extra Needed" is $2400 per month, and that the properties you are able to buy will generate $803 each month after all expenses, but not including mortgage principal and interest (the "NOI" line on Table 3.2). In this example, assuming the mortgages are paid off by the time you retire, you will need three properties (or one multi-unit property) that generate $2400 per month in cash flow, to complement your other sources of income and provide the degree of financial comfort you seek. Keep in mind that property types and income-generating potentials vary by geographical region, so be sure to do your research using numbers that are relevant to your own market.

Just as cash flow wins the game of Monopoly, cash flow will also help you win the game of retirement. Money coming into your bank account every month is the key to reducing both worry and hardship, especially when it comes to leaving the workforce and giving up your

TABLE 3.2. CASH FLOW ANALYSIS TOOL ($100,000, 20% DOWN, 30-YEAR)

			25% DOWN 30-YEAR TERM SELF-MANAGED		25% DOWN 30-YEAR TERM PROPERTY MANAGER
Purchase Terms	PURCHASE PRICE		100,000		100,000
	Down Payment	20%	25,000	20%	25,000
	Total Mortgage Amount		75,000		75,000
	Total Closing Costs	4%	4,000	4%	4,000
	Updates & Repairs		2,000		2,000
	Cash (Out of Pocket)		31,000		31,000
Monthly Operating Expenses	MONTHLY INCOME				
	Monthly Rent Expected		1,200		1,200
	Vacancy	5%	60	5%	60
	Effective Gross Rent (EGR)		1,140		1,140
	MONTHLY OPERATING EXPENSES				
	Management Fee	0%	0	10%	$ 120
	Insurance		50		50
	Maintenance/Repairs	10%	120	10%	120
	Other Expenses		-		-
	Property Taxes	2%	167	2%	167
	Total Operating Expenses (TOE)		337		457
NOI	Monthly Net Operating Income (NOI = EGR minus TOE)		803		683
Cash Flows & ROI	Monthly Payment (Principal + Interest) @	4%	358	4%	358
	Monthly Cash Flow		445		325
	Annual Cash Flow		5,343		3,903
	Cash-on-Cash Return		17%		13%

salary for good. In fact, if you own rental property, you are not giving up your salary; you are merely trading the salary you receive from your employer to a salary that you receive from your property's tenants.

No other investment has had as consistent and powerful an effect on the average person's net worth as real estate ownership.
GARY KELLER
Founder of Keller Williams Realty and
author of *The Millionaire Real Estate Investor*

Benefit #3: Rentals Help You Build Your Net Worth

Net worth is defined as the sum of your assets minus the sum of your debts, though, as we discuss in chapter 4, not all debts are the same. Credit card debt and other "bad debt" must be deducted from your net worth. But "good debt," for example a mortgage on a cash-flowing investment property, is more complicated. The way I see it, when it comes to good debt, net worth is like energy.

Do you remember learning about the two forms of energy back in your school days in science class? Not to give you an unpleasant flashback, but do you remember potential and kinetic energy? As a refresher, potential energy is stored energy (before being released) and kinetic energy is energy of motion (after being released). Potential energy results from work being performed against an object, like when you compress a spring. When the spring is released, the potential energy turns into the powerful kinetic energy of motion.

How does this connect to real estate and why is it so important? Well, imagine that you buy a cash-flowing rental property using the good debt of a mortgage. Like compressing a spring, you must do physical work to acquire and maintain that potential energy. During this time, the mortgage prevents the cash flow from being all that great. The length of time you hold that spring depends on the length of your mortgage. More rentals equate to a higher total value (and more work!) and greater levels of stored, potential energy. As you continue holding the spring, and as you gradually pay down the mortgage, this potential net-worth energy waits quietly for release. The moment the mortgage on a property is completely paid off is the moment that the passive net-worth energy is released and kinetic net-worth energy—the liberated cash flow—is experienced.

Benefit #4: Rentals Create Equity

Equity is defined as the difference between the amount a property is worth and the amount of debt you have on it. In shorthand, it is the property's "value" minus your mortgage balance, or "principal." It is an odd concept because it is based in part on hard numbers (the actual amount you owe at any given point in time) and in part on soft numbers (the amount you think it is worth at the same point in time).

When you first buy a property, you may have very little equity in it. However, as time progresses, your equity will gradually grow through the combined forces of paying down your principal and appreciation (assuming your property value does appreciate). As this happens, your actual net worth grows while your potential net-worth energy becomes closer to being released, as discussed in the previous section.

Even though equity is not actual money in your bank, more equity is always better because of the flexibility it affords. You can refinance to purchase more property. You can sell to make another large purchase, such as a vacation home. And, of course, once you own a property without a mortgage ("free and clear"), you can keep this new-kinetic net-worth energy as an uninhibited source of income.

Figure 3.2 and the corresponding Table 3.3 show an example of how this works over time. As you look at Figure 3.2, focus on the spread between the solid line and each of the two dashed lines. The line that curves upward shows hypothetical appreciation of 4 percent per year. Remember that appreciation is to be considered a fringe benefit, not a guarantee. It's the icing on the cake, but it is not the cake.

The two lines that arc downward are based on the hypothetical situation of paying off a $100,000 fixed-rate mortgage over fifteen years at 4 percent interest.‡ The lighter dashed line assumes a down payment of 20 percent. The darker dashed line assumes either that no down payment was made or that the property was purchased at roughly 20 percent below market value.

As you move along to the right, you can see that as you pay off your mortgage and assuming the property value increases at an average of 4 percent per year, the spread between the upper line and the two lower lines becomes quite wide. This spread represents your equity in the property. *In the end, the property that you proudly and boldly took ownership of for twenty thousand dollars, or less, will have grown into a solidly income-producing asset worth $180,000 after fifteen years.* (Note that in the situation of flat or even negative appreciation, you still come out as a winner due to the equity gained through debt pay-down.)

Before closing this section, I want to stress the dangers of interest-only mortgages, which are in part to blame for the housing and mortgage crisis of 2008. Interest-only mortgages come with substantial risk in the event that you need to refinance or sell due to changing priorities or circumstances in your life. For example, in Figure 3.1, with an interest-only mortgage your safety and/or gain would be completely reliant on the upper arc of appreciation. The lower two arcs would be nonexistent since you would not be paying down any of the principal. This might be fine in a world of guaranteed appreciation. However, remember that appreciation is not guaranteed. If the market becomes such that it is impossible to sell or refinance when you need to, and if all your equity depends on the upper arc of appreciation, then you would be in trouble.

As you'll see in chapter 5, the Ultimate Goal is to pay your mortgage off completely and get to the end of one of the two lower arcs

---

‡ Note that Figure 3.2 and Table 3.3 do not include expenses such as mortgage interest, taxes, insurance, and other operating costs. Please see Risk #6 in this chapter for a discussion on mortgage interest and other expenses.

shown in Figure 3.2. The upper appreciation arc is largely out of your control but can be enhanced by maintaining and upgrading your property over the years.

FIGURE 3.2. NET RESULT OF ACTUAL DEBT PAY-DOWN ($100,000 MORTGAGE AMORTIZED OVER 15 YEARS AT 4% INTEREST) AND HYPOTHETICAL APPRECIATION ACROSS TWO DOWN PAYMENT SCENARIOS (0% AND 20%)

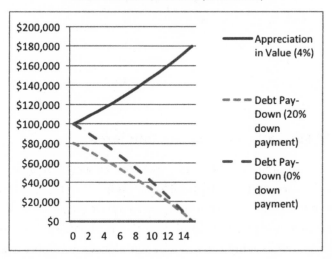

TABLE 3.3. ACTUAL DEBT PAY-DOWN ($100,000 MORTGAGE AMORTIZED OVER 15 YEARS AT 4% INTEREST) AND HYPOTHETICAL APPRECIATION ACROSS TWO DOWN PAYMENT SCENARIOS (0% AND 20%)

YEAR	APPRECIATION IN VALUE (4%)	DEBT PAY-DOWN (20% DOWN)	TOTAL EQUITY (20% DOWN)	DEBT PAY-DOWN (0% DOWN)	TOTAL EQUITY (0% DOWN)
0	$100,000	$80,000	$20,000	$100,000	$0
1	$104,000	$76,027	$27,973	$95,033	$8,967
2	$108,160	$71,891	$36,269	$89,864	$18,296
3	$112,486	$67,588	$44,898	$84,485	$28,001
4	$116,986	$63,109	$53,877	$78,886	$38,100
5	$121,665	$58,447	$63,218	$73,059	$48,606
6	$126,532	$53,596	$72,936	$66,995	$59,537
7	$131,593	$48,547	$83,046	$60,684	$70,909

Table continues

YEAR	APPRECIATION IN VALUE (4%)	DEBT PAY-DOWN (20% DOWN)	TOTAL EQUITY (20% DOWN)	DEBT PAY-DOWN (0% DOWN)	TOTAL EQUITY (0% DOWN)
8	$136,857	$43,292	$93,565	$54,115	$82,742
9	$142,331	$37,823	$104,508	$47,859	$94,472
10	$148,024	$32,131	$115,893	$40,164	$107,860
11	$153,945	$26,208	$127,737	$32,760	$121,185
12	$160,103	$20,043	$140,060	$25,054	$135,049
13	$166,507	$13,627	$152,880	$17,034	$149,473
14	$173,168	$7,516	$165,652	$8,687	$164,481
15	$180,094	$0	$180,094	$0	$180,094

Benefit #5: Rentals Can Lower Your Taxes

When you work for a living, you pay taxes. However, in many situations, when you own rental properties, Uncle Sam pays you. Depending on your income, buy-and-hold real estate investing is one way you can actually reduce the amount you pay in income tax from your work, even while being taxed on the rental income you receive.

There are two ways owning a rental can help you at tax time. The first is through tax deductions. You can deduct your property taxes and mortgage interest, just as you can on a personal residence. Plus, you can write off all operating and maintenance expenses related to your property in the same way that a business owner can write off expenses related to running his or her business. Deductible expenses include property and landlord umbrella insurance, maintenance, repairs, marketing, and even meals over which you discuss the state of affairs with the rental. Remember to keep your receipts, track your expenses, and work with a good accountant to be sure you capture all your allowable deductions. Be sure to discuss these concepts with your CPA, too, so that you don't miss out on any deductions. Also talk with your CPA because these benefits do not affect everyone equally; they vary by personal circumstance and income.

The second way investors benefit at tax time is through "depreciation." Depreciation might sound like a bad thing: After all, it can mean the opposite of appreciation. However, in IRS language, it means tax break . . . whether or not your property goes down in value. Depreciation is a powerful, and—believe it or not—mandatory, tax incentive for owners of investment real estate to deduct the hypothetical wear and tear of the property (the structure, appliances, many of the materials such as tile, etc.). Land is not depreciable. I've provided a practical example of how depreciation works in the section on "Taxable Income" in the *R.O.R.E. Blueprint for Success: A Step-by-Step Companion Guide* available at www.GetaChicken.com.

There are other tax advantages to owning rental property. For example, if you sell a property at a loss, you can take this as a deduction against your other earned income. This is different from selling stocks at a loss because these stock-related losses can only be applied to similar stock-related income. If all your stocks go down, and you don't have income to report, you are limited in the extent to which you can take deductions.

Real estate also offers tax advantages over your typical savings account. If you happen to receive interest on your savings (though this hasn't been possible in many years), you pay taxes on this growth at the same tax rate as your ordinary earned-income tax bracket. With real estate, as long as you've owned the property for at least a year, if you decide to sell your property you may pay a lower capital-gains rate than you do on your ordinary income taxes, though you have to pay back the amounts deducted in depreciation over the years. Another advantage is that you can use the advanced tax strategy called the "1031 Exchange" to trade up into a new investment property without having to pay taxes on the capital gains from the sale. See the section "Put Your Chickens to Work" in chapter 8 for more information on this and other advanced moves related to buying, selling, and trading property.

If you want to read all the tax rules yourself, right from the IRS, you can find them in the government document www.irs.gov/pub/irs-pdf/p527.pdf.[9] However, for a much easier and more enjoyable read, check out Amanda Han and Matthew MacFarland's book, *The Book on Tax Strategies for the Savvy Real Estate Investor.*

Benefit #6: Rentals Protect You from Inflation

Many of us were raised with the advice to save our money. I was, too. As a young teen, back when most banks were small, local banks, my parents took me on an adventure to our town bank, to open up my very first savings account. I had discovered the profession of babysitting and I was beginning to make some real money. It was the early '80s, and there was actually an interest rate attached to my account. I remember literally watching my savings grow, dollar by dollar, even without adding extra money to the account!

Not so these days. As of the writing of this book, the United States has had near zero-percent interest rates on savings accounts for many years. Even certificates of deposit (CDs) are essentially useless in terms of growing your money over time.

This is where inflation comes in. Inflation is a term that quantifies the extent to which prices escalate from one year to the next, in the general economy, in a given country. It can be highly variable between countries and over time. For example, while prices of consumer goods in the United States inched up only 1.6 percent between 2001 and 2002, they skyrocketed 13.5 percent between 1979 and 1980.[10]

On average, prices tend to increase each year by about 2 to 3 percent over the year before.[11] What this means for savings accounts these days is dire. If you put your money in a savings account that earns no interest, then this translates to a real-world interest rate of roughly *negative* 2 to 3 percent per year.

In contrast, consider rental property. Rental property that you purchase with a fixed-rate mortgage is a great way to protect yourself against inflation. This is because your payments are locked in place at the time you purchase or refinance your property. Your monthly payment stays constant as time goes on and as inflation is at play in the economy. Relative to the increasing costs of all your other expenses, your fixed-rate mortgage payment will, in essence, be going down.

Benefit #7: Rentals Boost Your Return on Investment (ROI)

Return on investment is a measure to help you decide how to get the biggest bang for your buck when you have money to invest. It can be helpful when you are trying to decide between a couple of different properties (as shown in the property evaluation section of the *R.O.R.E. Blueprint for Success: A Step-by-Step Companion Guide* available at www.GetaChicken.com). It can also be useful if you are trying to decide between buying a rental property and putting money somewhere else—like in a stock, mutual fund, certificate of deposit (CD), or savings account. In this section, you will see how rental property compares with these other ways that you can invest your money, and even the old-fashioned method of hiding it under a mattress. Table 3.4 shows profoundly different rates of return based on the different ways you can hold your money.[12] Table 3.4 also shows the impact of hypothetical 3 percent inflation on each savings method. While these are just annual rates of return, you can imagine the impact of these rates over many years.

Annual Cash-on-Cash Return is one measure of ROI. It is defined as the amount of money the asset generates in a year divided by the total amount paid out of pocket for the asset. For real estate, the "amount made" is your total annual *cash flow* (income-expenses). The "amount paid" is the total amount that you paid to acquire the property, including the down payment, closing costs, and expenses for repairs and upgrades.

Cash-on-Cash Return = Amount made/Amount paid

Recall from your middle school math lessons that the smaller your denominator (the amount paid), the larger your result. What this means is that the less you invest out of your own pocket, the higher your cash-on-cash return. Recall also that you can't divide by zero;

otherwise, the result shoots to infinity. What this means is that if you were to pay absolutely nothing for the property (including closing costs and repairs), then your cash-on-cash return would technically shoot the moon. This type of no-down-payment scenario is rare, but technically does occur when you convert a primary residence into a rental.

A money market may be the ultimate risk because it will likely lag inflation.

JOHN BOGLE

Founder of Vanguard and author of

The Clash of Cultures: Investment vs. Speculation

Financial risk is defined as the probability of losing money. This means that even though it may *feel* like the safest thing to do with your money would be to stuff it under the mattress or lock it away in a savings account, this is actually the further thing from the truth *when it comes to growing your money*. In comparison with other investment strategies, saving your money in a non-interest-bearing account is actually the "riskiest" strategy. And yet, as a side note, don't confuse this method of saving with holding a stash of cash as an emergency fund for your rental properties and life in general. This is essential, and is covered in depth under Risk #4, later in this chapter.

Similar to a savings account, a money market account is, in theory, supposed to be a very low-risk investment, with the principal staying at its cash value. However, there are times when this is not the case. In 1994 and again in 2008, a phenomenon called "Breaking the Buck" occurred, in which a money-market fund's investment income became so low that it did not cover its own operating expenses or investment losses, and the value of the account actually became worth less than the amount of money originally invested. It is called "Breaking the Buck" when the net value of one dollar in a money-market fund falls below one dollar.

TABLE 3.4. AVERAGE RATES OF RETURN BY INVESTMENT WITH AND WITHOUT ADJUSTMENT FOR 3% INFLATION*

INVESTMENT TYPE	APPROXIMATE RATE OF RETURN	INFLATION-ADJUSTED RATE OF RETURN
Cash under the mattress	0%	–3%*
Cash in the bank	0%	–3%*
Money Market Funds	0%	–3%*
Certificate of Deposit	1%	–2%
Bond	4%	1%
Low Risk Stocks	5%	2%
Medium Risk Stocks	9%	6%
High Risk Stocks	15%	12%
Real Estate (25% down)	17%	14%
Real Estate (20% down)	19%	16%
Real Estate (0% down)	Infinite	Infinite

*For the purpose of this table, the inflation rate is assumed to be 3 percent.[13] Real estate purchase assumptions include purchase price of a $100,000, thirty-year term, self-managed property. See the Cash Flow Analysis (CFA) Tool in Table 3.2 and at www.GetAChicken.com. Rates do not reflect the impact of fund or broker fees (see Threat #3 in chapter 2, "Very Real Threats to a Very Fragile Egg"). Table data source: http://www.smareserves.com/why-3-inflation/.

RISKS OF INVESTING IN REAL ESTATE

As you can tell by now, I strongly believe that owning one or more cash-flowing rental properties is an important—*if not essential*—part of a truly diversified plan. Chapter 2 went into the many threats and risks of relying *solely* on retirement accounts and savings accounts. Now that we're at this point, you're probably wondering, "But what about all the risks involved with rental property? Surely real estate is risky, too!"

I'll go into the risks and general downsides in this section. But before I do, I want to mention that risk in real estate is different from throwing your money into a mutual fund, closing your eyes, and hoping things turn out peachy. This is because you have a certain amount of control to *prevent* risks from manifesting in the first place. And if they do arise, you have a certain amount of control to recover, provided you have emergency funds and/or undesignated income from your salary that you can fall back on if necessary. That element of control might be daunting, but it can also be incredibly empowering. Read on and you'll see exactly what I'm talking about.

Risk #1: The Tenant from Hell

Just as we can lessen our risk of developing some chronic diseases by eating well and exercising, we can lessen our risk of having a terrible tenant destroying our precious investment by doing a thorough tenant screening. And if we do wind up with the tenant from hell—like the one who fails to pay the rent on time, fails to clean, collects pets like others collect stamps, whose cats are apparently unable to find a clean litter box to do their business, and whose poor dogs were never taken out on walks so they did all their business in the basement (yes, we had that tenant!)—there are measures we can take to recover.

When this happened to us, we lost two months of rent during the time it took to clean and repair the property and re-rent it, though we had a security deposit for one of those months to lessen the sting. We had to hire someone to pull out all the carpet and refinish the hardwood floors underneath. And we—with the help of a clearly very dear friend along with my very loving mother who happened to be visiting at the time—pinched our noses and removed seemingly infinite amounts of dog and cat poop from the basement and back yard. Unbelievably gross, yes. But we were able to recover. And in the end, we possessed not only an upgraded property, but also an improved landlording IQ! We had become smarter about doing tenant screenings, and we had become stronger and more assertive as well. We learned to "just say 'No'" to requests for "just one more cat"—or any cat, for that matter. In the end, we continued to own this incredible cash-flowing asset with a fifteen-year mortgage that will be paid off in time to cover our daughter's college tuition before supplying us with a chunk of our future monthly retirement income. But from that point forward, we learned to never cut corners on the tenant screening process again.

The problem arose because I was excited by the fact that the potential tenant seemed "really nice." Thanks to my disillusioning experience with this individual, I came up with the phrase: *"Good eggs and bad eggs look the same on the outside."* The lesson here is to never be swayed by someone's positive appearance or friendliness. Being taken advantage of isn't always limited to the work of ill-meaning scam artists (who, by the way, often present themselves very well, too!). It can also happen when you cross paths with well-meaning people who find themselves taking on more rent (or pets!) than they can afford. Always do credit and background checks. For added layers of protection, use a month-to-month lease with the right to terminate, for any reason, with thirty days' notice.

Unfortunately, it is this kind of situation that spreads the fear of landlording. I'm pretty sure we grumbled about our situation as it was unfolding, and as we did, others latched on to it as the reason they would never want to be a landlord. However, what most people don't understand is that property owners recover from these situations, go on to find great tenants, and continue paying down their mortgage until the house is paid off and becomes virtually pure revenue. A situation like this forces you to draw upon inner strength that you may not know you possess, and it can require you to dip into your emergency funds to cover the repair expenses or the mortgage while it is unrented; but the point is, you can recover.

The other takeaway is that you don't have to learn the hard way. You can usually line up a quality tenant if you conduct a thorough screening, which I go into in depth in the *R.O.R.E. Blueprint for Success: A Step-by-Step Companion Guide* available at www.GetaChicken. com. If you don't want to take on this task yourself, you have options. For example, you can do what Kevin and Andrea do and simply enlist the services of a professional property manager. Check out their story, among others, in the Online Appendix B, *True Stories of "Not-Chickens."*

To recover from a bad tenant situation, you have a couple of options. You can either evict, or do a "soft eviction." I much prefer a soft eviction, because it allows the tenant to leave with pride intact and it is much quicker and less expensive than an eviction. In a soft eviction, you have a one-on-one, face-to-face meeting and, in a friendly but assertive way, share the reasons why the situation is not working out. I had to do this for one of our house-share tenants after the other three tenants came to me in a desperate plea. In my meeting with the fourth tenant, I came armed with a few rental listings that seemed equally desirable and even more affordable than her current lease with me. It was an emotional meeting, and I had to stress repeatedly that I liked her as an individual, but it was just not a good match. I refunded her entire security deposit to help her get started in another place. If your main goal is to get someone out of your property and return things to normal as quickly as possible, then sometimes a small amount of sacrifice is necessary to prevent a larger-scale and more lengthy legal fight.

If you absolutely must evict a tenant, you must have just cause and you must follow specific procedures, which vary by state. These typically include providing a specific type of written notice to the tenant and giving the tenant a chance to turn things around before proceeding with the eviction. Consult a real estate attorney to ensure that you follow the correct procedures. If you do end up having to go through a legal eviction, remember that, in the end, you will get your property back, you will recover financially, and you will be stronger and smarter because of the experience.

Risk #2: Plunging Property Values

Another common real estate fear is the risk of crashing property values, as occurred in the housing meltdown beginning in 2007. When this happened, "buy-and-hold" rental property owners were often completely unaffected by their properties' plunging values. The values were only on paper. It was the rental income that mattered.

The difference for us in 2007 was that we were not trying to buy low and sell high. When the values of our properties plummeted, as they did for most homes virtually everywhere, we continued to rent them out just as we always had. In fact, as people started losing their life savings and their homes, we had more people interested in renting from us than ever before. What we and other property owners experienced was consistent with findings from a Harvard University study on rental housing trends in the United States. This study found an increasing proportion of renters and a decreasing proportion of homeowners across all income levels and household types in the five years following the recession that began in 2008.[14]

So, rather than selling their properties in the downturn, many individuals, including ourselves, decided to buy more property. It is terribly sad, but also undeniably true, that the housing meltdown provided an unending stream of discounted, bank-owned ("REO") properties, as well as new renters for those properties.

Before you buy a rental or convert an existing home into a rental, you can take preventive measures that will help safeguard you against the risk of plunging property values. These measures are cures for Risk #3, the Risk of Vacancy, as well. First and foremost, you need to buy with cash flow in mind by ensuring that the property's rental income is greater than the mortgage and other expenses combined. Second, you need to make sure that your property is in an area that people want to live in so that it is easy to rent. On a related note, the area should be one that is as bulletproof as possible to future downturns in the economy. In other words, invest in an area where people will be able to continue living if the economy tanks. For example, areas near universities are usually safe bets, whereas areas that are solely dependent on one factory or one major business are more risky. If that business lays off workers or if that factory shuts its doors, people will lose income and/or leave town, and your property could be in trouble.

Another way to prevent plunging property values from causing your demise is to stay away from fix-and-flip deals. The reason for this is that if property values take a hit while you are in the middle of a renovation, you could be stuck with a house and no way to sell it. See Risk #7 for more on the perils of fix-and-flip deals.

A funny thing happens in real estate.
When it comes back, it comes back up like gangbusters.
BARBARA CORCORAN
Founder of the Corcoran Group, Inc., author of *Shark Tales*,
and *Shark* on ABC's *Shark Tank*

Risk #3: The Risk of Vacancy

There's no question that you need paying tenants in your property to cover the mortgage and other expenses and to make a little profit. As with all real estate risks, the emphasis is on preventing the issue and having the financial resources to recover gracefully if or when the issue does arise.

There are certain preventive measures you can take to ensure that you rarely have a vacancy. The first preventive measure has to do with the actual property you purchase. It is imperative that you have a property that people want to live in. This boils down to the general area, the precise location, and the quality and cleanliness of the property itself.

The second preventive measure has to do with property management, whether you do it yourself or hire someone else to do it for you. It is important to always anticipate vacancy. This even applies to new purchases. When you put a property under contract to purchase, ask the seller to grant you permission to show it to prospective tenants before settlement, in order to line up renters right away. We do this with all properties we purchase. Ideally, you will get a key (or the combination to the lockbox) so that you have access to the property yourself. If someone is currently living in the home, you'll need to give them the courtesy of twenty-four hours notice before showing it to a potential tenant.

Go to any and all lengths to line up your tenant before settlement. Not only will this guarantee no vacancy from day one, it will also give you a feel for the rental market, the rent you can charge, and the amount of rental demand. If there is not enough demand to support the rent that you need to make the numbers work, you can still get out of the contract. If you do find a tenant for a property that you don't own yet, be sure to add a clause to the rental agreement indicating that it is contingent on your taking ownership of the property.

If you already own the property, it is equally important that you or your property manager anticipate vacancies. Require that your tenants notify you two months before the lease ends if they plan to leave or renew. You can offer an incentive to your current tenant if he or she finds a replacement tenant. However, don't rely on that tenant to do the work for you. In my experience, it is incredibly rare for a tenant to find a next tenant even if they are breaking the lease themselves. But if they do, be sure to go through the entire tenant-screening process yourself, as detailed in the *R.O.R.E. Blueprint for Success: A Step-by-Step Companion Guide* available at www.GetaChicken.com.

You'll want to start advertising the property as soon as you receive notice that your tenant is moving out. The sooner you start showing it to prospective tenants, the sooner you find a quality replacement. The *R.O.R.E. Blueprint for Success: A Step-by-Step Companion Guide* has more information on marketing your property. Again, if these tasks are not exactly your cup of tea, you can outsource them to a property manager. You can also hire a less-costly tenant finder, someone whose job it is to find and screen tenants, but who does not take on full property management services.

Finally, you can prevent vacancy by thoroughly screening your potential tenants, as I also go into in the *R.O.R.E. Blueprint for Success: A Step-by-Step Companion Guide*. Doing thorough tenant screenings will lessen your chances of having to go through a later vacancy due to eviction. When you have a quality tenant, you'll be more likely to keep him or her by proactively keeping your property nice and promptly responding to their requests and concerns. You can also keep a quality tenant by not raising their rent. In fact, we rarely raise the rent on our existing tenants. We usually only raise rents when there is turnover between tenants.

Risk #4: The Risk of Costly Repairs

The risk of having to make a costly repair from time to time is actually more of a guarantee than a risk. After all, it's a known fact that stuff breaks down over time. These expenses should be anticipated, not feared. Every now and then, you *will* need to repair or replace a leaky roof, switch out an appliance, or deal with water in the basement. It's a fact of life for any property owner. When something major needs to be repaired or replaced, this is called a capital expense, or "CapEx" for short. CapEx refers to larger repair expenses that come up less frequently but have a significant financial impact when they do.

There are several measures you can take to prevent costly repairs from destroying you or even occurring in the first place. The first occurs after you are under contract but *before you purchase* a property. (Read closely the "Evaluate Your Potential Property" in the *R.O.R.E. Blueprint for Success: A Step-by-Step Companion Guide.*) You can lessen your risk by getting both a professional inspection coupled with estimates from contractors or service providers for repair costs.

You should also obtain the manufacture dates from your inspector and/or the seller's paperwork for *all* appliances, heating and cooling systems, hot-water heater, and roof. If any system is beyond its life expectancy (see Table 3.5), and if you still think the property makes sense to buy, then it's not too late to negotiate the contract with the seller. Ask to have the outdated system replaced before settlement, or request cash back from the seller at settlement to apply toward replacing the system yourself. Both of these options are preferable to simply lowering the purchase price, because that would still require you to pay for the replacement or repair out of your own pocket while only having a minuscule effect on lowering your mortgage.

The second—and essential—preventive step is to know how you will pay for repair expenses when they do arise. There are as many methods for this as there are ice cream flavors. And, as with ice cream, some methods are better than others, but they are all good. The worst flavor is none at all, an empty cone, and that is true for your backup plan as well. You need a flavor.

Some investors have an emergency fund, while others prefer to rely on a line of credit or surplus employment income. Investors also vary as to whether they set aside a certain percentage of the rental income, a percentage of the principal owed on the mortgage, a flat amount each month, or simply the minimum to maintain a given amount for each property owned. Some investors use a home warranty for repairs while others see this as a waste of money and prefer to use lower-budget handymen and secondhand appliances. Still others prefer to use larger companies that offer low-interest monthly payment plans, which they incorporate into their cash-flow analysis as a recurring line item until it is paid off, seeing this as an affordable way to replace something major like a new roof or heating system.

In spite of this real-life variation, it is widely regarded that the best strategy is to have an emergency fund set aside from the moment you purchase the property. The most conservative method—which is what banks like to see when you are applying for a loan—is six months of expenses that are "liquid" or easily accessible. Banks don't usually care if these funds are in a retirement account or a savings account; but when it comes to your emergency fund, it is best to have this money separate from and in addition to your retirement savings. One method is to set aside an amount that is equal to your mortgage payment (principal, interest, taxes, and insurance, or "PITI") plus 50 percent of your total projected rental income for six months for each property you own. So, as an example, if your monthly mortgage payment is $700, and if your rental income is $1200, then you'll want to set aside at least $8400 ($4800 + $3600) as your emergency fund or "cash reserve" for this property.

Because you will be dipping into these funds for small and large expenses alike, you'll need to replenish this account continually.

When you run your numbers *before deciding whether to purchase the property* (see Cash Flow Analysis Form at www.GetaChicken.com), you should budget a certain amount of your rental income every month to go into this account.

While many people put in somewhere between 5 and 10 percent of the rental income, Brandon Turner of www.BiggerPocket.com, the go-to resource for articles and online discussion forums on all things real estate, uses a flat amount of roughly $200 per month on many of his single-family homes. He reached this number by listing out all the systems, their total replacement costs in his area, and the average life expectancy of each. He then calculated the average cost per month of replacing each item (see Table 3.5). This comes to roughly $2,400 each year, though this could be more for homes that are older, have older components, or have more deferred maintenance.[15]

TABLE 3.5. EXPECTED LIFE EXPECTANCY AND COST BREAKDOWN, PER SYSTEM FOR A TYPICAL SINGLE-FAMILY HOUSE

CAPITAL EXPENSE	TOTAL REPLACEMENT COST	LIFESPAN (YEARS)	COST PER YEAR	COST PER MONTH
Roof	$5,000	25	$200	$16.67
Water Heater	$600	10	$60	$5.00
All Appliances	$1,000	10	$100	$8.33
Driveway/Parking Lot	$5,000	50	$100	$8.33
HVAC	$3,000	20	$150	$12.50
Flooring	$2,000	6	$333	$27.75
Plumbing	$3,000	30	$100	$8.33
Windows	$5,000	50	$100	$8.33
Paint	$2,500	5	$500	$41.67
Cabinets/Counters	$3,000	20	$150	$12.50
Structure (foundation, framing)	$10,000	50	$200	$16.67
Components (garage door, etc.)	$1,000	10	$100	$8.33
Landscaping	$1,000	10	$100	$8.33

Source: www.biggerpockets.com/renewsblog/2015/10/13/real-estate-capex-estimate-capital-expenditures/.

The third preventive measure to lessen the occurrence of major repair issues is to stay on top of routine maintenance and to address small issues before they become big ones. For example, the seemingly small issue of a broken or clogged gutter can lead to water leaking through walls, destroying drywall, and inflicting mildew and mold. Yikes! Stay on top of the little stuff and the big stuff will stay away from you.

There is a risk with the small stuff, too, of course. The risk is that you won't want to deal with these things and your procrastination could lead to larger repair issues or tenant frustration, followed by vacancy. There are a couple of different approaches to this risk. The first is to adjust your attitude. While I don't particularly enjoy receiving calls about mice in the kitchen, I remind myself that an occasional house or tenant issue is the small price I pay now for a secure and even early retirement once the mortgages are paid off. I figure I can make this kind of time in order to ensure my family's long-term financial security.

As one sows, one shall reap.
And I know that talk is cheap.
But the heat of the battle is as sweet as the victory.

BOB MARLEY
The "King" of Reggae

That said, the second option is to do what we do as much as possible with our local properties, and what Jen and Rachel do with all of their long-distance properties. (See Online Appendix B for their story.) We simply ask the tenants to help. Whenever possible, I ask the tenants to be available to meet the handyman or service contractor, and I schedule accordingly. This is far less intrusive on my own family time and usually just as effective, especially if the tenants are home anyway. Jen and Rachel, with long-distance properties, actually build into their rental leases a provision indicating that the tenant is responsible for meeting the maintenance and repair service providers at the property, as needed. (You can read about their experience managing rental property from a distance on my website at www.GetaChicken.com.)

The third option, of course, is to hire a property manager to take care of the details. If the monthly cash flow affords it, this can be an excellent way to own property for the long term and to not have to deal with the work involved in owning it. Many people choose this hands-off method, including couples Amanda and Matt, and Kevin and Andrea, whose stories I've included in Online Appendix B. Amanda's story is definitely worth your time to read. She shares some lessons learned the hard way about unscrupulous property managers and how to identify them. My *R.O.R.E. Blueprint for Success: A Step-by-Step Companion Guide* available at www.GetaChicken.com will also help you avoid bad property managers and find a good one, remembering once again that: Good eggs and bad eggs look the same on the outside!

Risk #5: Funds Are Not "Liquid"

Many individuals in the finance industry would say that a downside of investing in real estate is that your money is not as "liquid" as it would otherwise be in a retirement or savings account. This means that you can't access your money as easily, since you would have to sell or refinance your property to retrieve your equity in the form of cash.

I would argue that as long as you also have funds in a retirement account and an emergency fund, this is not actually a downside. With real estate, your funds are protected from identity theft, incompetent financial advisers, and the risk inherent in the stock market itself. And most importantly, with real estate your funds are protected from *yourself.*

When you have money invested in stocks and mutual funds, it can sometimes be way too convenient to cash them in. If the stock market takes a dip, the fear of a great loss may trigger the impulsive part of your brain to sell, even if at a loss. It's just too easy to have instant access to your dough. But if you pull your money out on the downswing and then the market eventually rebounds, then you've locked in your losses by missing out on the rebound. The people who were most hurt in the Great Recession beginning in 2008 were those who sold their mutual funds and stocks during the downturn. And, sadly, among those who did so, those who were oldest in age were especially hard hit because they have had less time to start over in rebuilding their savings.

Just as those who held on to their plummeting stock and mutual fund investments were able to survive the crash by waiting for the rebound, those who kept their overvalued properties after the housing crash also survived. In fact, many thrived. As an example, there are countless people who decided to buy a second property in the downturn, move, and convert their first home into a rental. Many of these "accidental landlords" were simply aiming to avoid selling their property at a loss or losing it to foreclosure. And, in the process, many used the opportunity to fulfill a long-awaited desire to own rental property. This was the case of Kevin and Andrea, as well as Beth and David (see Online Appendix B for their stories), two couples who converted their homes into rental properties because their values were too low to sell without taking a loss. Ironically, simply by seizing the opportunity to add even just one rental property to their investment mix, the housing crash helped these couples, and many others, lock in a more diverse and secure long-term financial plan.

Don't wait to buy real estate, buy real estate and wait.

T. HARV EKER

NY Times No. 1 Best-selling author of *Secrets of the Millionaire Mind*™

Risk #6: The Expense of Mortgage Interest

Mortgage interest is the monthly (tax-deductible) fee that you incur as a part of your monthly mortgage payment for the privilege of having been given a loan to purchase a property. From your lender's perspective, it is how they get paid for providing you a mortgage.

Table 3.6 shows how the cost of a mortgage over the life of a loan varies by interest rate and term. In this example of a $100,000 mortgage, the amount you would pay in mortgage interest can range from

$15,873 to a whopping $189,664, a fee equaling almost two times the original mortgage amount!

TABLE 3.6. THE TOTAL INTEREST PAID (BY YOUR TENANTS) OVER THE LIFE OF A $100,000 MORTGAGE, BY VARYING TERM LENGTH AND INTEREST RATE COMBINATIONS

	MORTGAGE WITH 3% INTEREST	MORTGAGE WITH 5% INTEREST	MORTGAGE WITH 7% INTEREST	MORTGAGE WITH 9% INTEREST
10-year term	$15,873	$27,279	$39,330	$52,011
15-year term	$24,305	$42,343	$61,789	$82,568
20-year term	$33,103	$58,389	$86,072	$115,934
30-year term	$51,777	$93,256	$139,509	$189,664

From this table, it is clear that lower interest rates for shorter terms are best. However, while the mortgage interest may be daunting, don't let this scare you away from investing in real estate. Mortgage interest is more of a perceived risk than an actual one. Unlike when you purchase a home for your personal residence, it is not actually you who will be paying these interest-related fees—or your principal, taxes, insurance, or other expenses, for that matter. The reality is that, if you've done your cash-flow analysis right, before taking ownership of the property, then the rent from your tenants will cover everything until your mortgage is paid in full.

Yes, it's true that the less you pay in mortgage interest, the greater your cash flow and the closer you are to owning your property free and clear. However, mortgage interest is not a reason to not invest in rental property. It is a means to an end. The bottom line is that your tenants pay the mortgage interest on your behalf, as a part of their rent, for the privilege of living in your home, so in that sense it doesn't much matter if the mortgage interest is $15,873 or $189,664.

The impact of the mortgage interest depends on whether the property is your personal residence or whether it is a rental. When you buy a home or car or boat or anything else that comes with an interest rate (even small stuff on your credit card, if you don't pay it back right away), you need to factor the total amount in interest over the life of the loan into the total cost of owning that item. This interest that you pay on your mortgage, loan, or credit card adds up over the years and is *real money*. On the other hand, when it comes to purchasing an income-producing asset like a rental property, if you've done your initial calculations right, then, for the reasons just described, these costs are more *theoretical*.

Risk #7: Investing in Higher-Risk Real Estate (In Other Words: What Not to Buy)

People often lump real estate investing into one group, not realizing that each of its many varieties are unique. The focus of this book is

TABLE 3.7. WHAT NOT TO BUY (AND WHY NOT)

WHAT NOT TO BUY	WHY NOT?
Condo	No control over escalating condo fees and assessments
Cheap home with very low rent	Capital expenses will consume a higher proportion of the total income (thereby lowering the cash flow) than they would be on a home with high rental income
High-end expensive home	Rents not commensurate with property sales prices, thereby lowering the cash flow potential
Major fixer-upper	Challenging, expensive, and risky in the event of a downturn in real estate market
Raw land	Risky in the event that value does not increase. No monthly income (unless there is a business purpose for the land)
REIT	"Buy low, sell high" type of investment risk that moves with the overall market. No control over specific investments. No personal tax advantages
Property in an undesirable or dangerous area	Difficult to rent or sell, and/or unpleasant or unsafe to manage
Property with potentially negative cash flow	Can be draining on existing resources and risky in the event of a change in your salaried income
Property purchased "sight-unseen"	Issues that you wouldn't know about without physically touring the property yourself
Timeshare	No control over annual expenses (taxes and maintenance), special assessment fees and no resale value
Ugly house or neighborhood	Difficult to rent to people who will help maintain the property and pay rent on time
Vacation property	Subject to vacancy if there is a sustained downturn in the economy

residential rental property. There are some other types of investments that are higher-risk for the beginning investor, as listed in Table 3.7 and described in this section. Some require advanced levels of training and experience. Some just don't make sense from a cash-flow perspective.

Still others are rooted in the risk-based premise of buying at one price, crossing your fingers, and hoping to sell at a higher price down the road. This "capital gains" method of investing typically involves significantly more risk because, like investing in stocks and mutual funds, you may or may not be able to sell for a higher price when you need your money. It can be risky because the market could change dramatically after you get in but before you are able to get out, as happened to so many people in the housing bust beginning in 2007. This type of short-term investing is more akin to gambling. Long-term goals require a long-term plan, and the safest and most sustainable long-term plan is to patiently own and hold real estate for a long duration.

Properties That Are Purchased "Sight Unseen"

If there was one thing I learned from my father about investing in property, it was this: Never, *ever* buy a property without seeing it first. My dad learned this the hard way. When I was a kid, he decided it would be a good idea to purchase a charming little piece of land in the middle of woodsy New Hampshire. He lined up a mortgage for this parcel and made the purchase. After signing the stack of papers, he loaded up the whole family into the car for a very exciting trip up north to see our new property. Unfortunately, we were in for quite a surprise! That sweet little parcel of land, *that we now owned,* was directly across the street from the county dump! This was a brutal awakening for him and a lesson that my three siblings and I will never forget.

Always, always, *always* inspect your property. You don't *necessarily* need to do this before putting it under contract, as long as you have a good "out" clause; however, you absolutely must see the property yourself before you go through with the purchase.

I've included an extensive segment on property evaluation and inspection in the *R.O.R.E. Blueprint for Success: A Step-by-Step Companion Guide* to this book. Also, to help with your initial walk-through, I've developed the quick-and-easy Anderson Inspection Method (AIM) Tool, which is downloadable for free on my website, www.GetaChicken.com.

Houses That Are Too Expensive or Too Cheap

For different reasons, you may have the most success if you stay in the middle price-range when buying a rental. For example, expensive homes often do not have rents that are commensurate with higher mortgages, thereby lowering your chances of attaining positive cash flow. As Gary Keller explains in his book *The Millionaire Real Estate Investor*, the best deals can often be those that are in the low end of the middle of any market.[16] These so-called "bread and butter" homes constitute the largest market where the most people in the population are buying and renting homes.

Cheap houses are also dangerous when you consider the financial impact of making occasional major repairs. (Refer back to our discussion on capital expenses, or "CapEx," under Risk #4 in this chapter.) The risk stems from the combination of the age of the property and its components, as well as the fact that many systems tend to cost roughly the same amount whether they are installed in an expensive house or a cheap house. As Brandon Turner, of www.BiggerPockets.com, explains:

> Just because a house worth $400,000 is ten times more expensive than one that is $40,000, that doesn't mean a roof, windows, paint, or anything else will also be ten times more expensive. What this means is that CapEx is a much greater percentage of the income when dealing with lower-priced properties. On a home that rents for $2,000 per month, the CapEx of $200 per month is 10 percent of the income, but on a home that rents for $600 per month, the CapEx of $200 per month will be a whopping 30 percent of the rent.[17]

Condos

Buying a condo might seem like a safe, worry-free investment strategy, but from a cash-flow perspective they can actually be rather risky. It's a control issue: You have no control over the condo fees and the extent to which they can escalate each year. In addition, on occasion, a condominium building can also incur a very high expense for upgrades or extensive repairs that are not within budget. When this happens, and if there are insufficient funds in the reserve account, the condominium board will pass these so-called "special assessment fees" on to condo owners. These fees can be extremely expensive, ranging from $1,000 to $20,000, or more, per unit.

Between the rising condo fees and special assessment fees, the cash-flow situation on a condo can shift from positive to negative, overnight. In addition, many condo associations prohibit rental units or they charge extra fees to owners who rent out their units, a lesson that I learned when I rented out my condo (my very first rental property!).

In spite of these cash-flow downsides, you may be attracted to the seemingly lower maintenance involved in owning a condo. If so, keep in mind that, for the sake of your cash-flow *stability* over the long term, you may actually be better off buying a house in a middle-class neighborhood and hiring a property management company to take care of it for you.

Gambling on House Flipping (Don't Flip the Bird!)

Fixing and flipping involves buying a run-down house, doing repairs and renovation, and then selling it at a price high enough to recoup your purchase price and renovation costs while making a little profit for your efforts.

Buying at one price and hoping to sell at a higher price is inherently risky. There are just too many ways to get burned . . . for example, by underestimating repair costs, over-improving a house, neglecting to consider holding costs (loan payments, utilities, taxes, etc.), failing to take into account short-term capital gains tax, and so forth. Plus there is the risk of unpredictable repair and renovation costs, contractors' escalating quotes once a job is under way, disappearing or dishonest contractors, and new repair issues that arise once you look inside the walls, among other issues. It's not that these things *might* happen; I know from experience that they *will* happen.

If you are just starting out and have no renovation experience, I strongly recommend staying away from fix-and-flip deals. One bad fix-and-flip experience could ruin you financially and turn you off to long-term real estate investing with properties that are closer to "move-in ready."

After you become experienced with purchasing property, becoming a landlord, and attending to the more minor-league repairs and upgrades, you may (or may not) decide that this is something you eventually want to pursue. Fix-and-flips, done successfully, can help expedite your goals if you put the proceeds toward the balance of your existing mortgage(s) or apply them toward the purchase of a new rental or rental emergency fund. However, fix-and-flips and their many risks are way beyond the scope of this book.

It is unfortunate that so many people associate real estate investing with rehabbing rather than the safer variant of investing, which is holding property for the long term. I believe this is partly due to the rise of popular shows like *Flip This House,* among many others. These shows make fix-and-flip deals seem adventurous and highly profitable; however, the reality is that these kinds of deals can sink you. Again, buying for cash flow is the cure to this risk.

Gambling on Raw Land

Another area that can be confusing is that of raw land. If you purchase raw land in hopes of selling it for a higher price down the road, you are gambling, not investing. Raw land by itself is not technically an asset, as defined in chapter 4, because it does not typically provide cash flow. If you have a mortgage on this raw land, and no income, then it is actually a liability. (My Dad's land by the dump was a double liability!) On the other hand, if you have a plan to create income from your land, perhaps by renting it to a valet car company (in the city), a farmer (in the country), or a fast-food restaurant or gas station (anywhere in between), then this land could become a powerful asset with high income potential and minimal property management. Take a look at Heather's story in Online Appendix B. She purchased raw land and then strategically put the pieces together to lease it to a fast-food restaurant.

Purchasing raw land in hopes of making a profit when the price goes up is playing the dangerous game of speculation. However, if you are strategic, owning land as part of an income-generation strategy and leasing it to an individual or business can be an effective means of generating monthly income with potentially very little ongoing maintenance on your part. As you'll see in chapter 4, the bottom line to remember is that an asset is only an asset if it puts money into your bank account every month. However, if something regularly takes money away from your bank account (like a mortgage on unutilized land), it is a liability.

Gambling on a Real Estate Investment Trust (REIT)

A real estate investment trust (REIT) is similar to a stock, except that you are investing in the real estate industry rather than a publicly traded company. An "Equity REIT" invests in commercial property (like shopping malls, office complexes, apartment buildings, hotels, etc.). A "Mortgage REIT" finances commercial loans. In both cases, when you are investing in a REIT, you are investing in a virtual asset.

REIT investing can be as easy as typing the right ticker symbol into an online stock trading site like E-trade. And yet, while this is obviously a ton simpler than finding the right property and managing tenants, there are downsides. For one thing, while REITs are thought to offer some diversification to the stock market, it's not much. For example, if you compare the Vanguard REIT Index (ticker symbol VNQ) to the Dow, Nasdaq, or S&P on a site such as Yahoo Finance, you will see that all four generally move in tandem with each other. What this means is that if we experience another major stock market crash, it is likely that REITs will crash right along with the rest of the market, as they did in 2007. In contrast, and as I've mentioned earlier, many investors who owned rental property in the right areas, held for the long term, were able to do well because they continued to collect rent and pay their mortgages on time.

To the individual investor, REITs also lack many of the benefits that are inherent to brick-and-mortar real estate. You don't get the tax benefits. You don't get the cash flow, unless you have a dividend-paying REIT. And you don't have the ability to use the leverage of a mortgage to your advantage to receive strong returns on investment. Most importantly, you are playing the role of a gambler when you buy something at one price with hopes that the price will go up over time. And yet, just like the stock market and house-flipping, this is just what many people are doing when they invest in REITs.

Gambling on a Timeshare

Is there any worse investment? Seriously, if you want to get ahead financially, I strongly recommend that you avoid timeshare pitches, even the ones that come with a free weekend at a tempting resort. Timeshare salespeople are paid big bucks to sound very convincing. The problem is that these things become worthless as soon as you sign on the dotted line. There is literally no resale value at all. Plus, in addition to the hefty initial sales price, there are ongoing annual taxes and maintenance fees—over which you have no control—which make timeshare ownership a costly endeavor. A timeshare is a liability to the nth degree. Trust me. I know this from experience. We got suckered into a timeshare long before we started purchasing rental property, and we've been stuck with it, and paying for it, ever since!

In Summary

Investing in real estate is not without risk. However, when you own residential rental property for the long term, it is a different kind of risk. Unlike the market and cyber-related risks of stock market–based retirement accounts—risks that are mostly out of your control—risks in real estate are more tangible, and as a result more preventable and controllable. Most longtime landlords and property owners have at least one horror story. We do, too. However, there are steps you can take to minimize your risk and help you manage things when the unexpected does strike. It all comes down to ensuring that you have funds to fall back on, buying the right property, and finding the right tenant. In the end, we recover from sour events, become empowered in the process, persist in owning the property, and continue paying down the mortgage until it is owned free and clear.

Many people fear the risks involved with owning rental property. You could choose to avoid all the potential suffering by never owning a rental property. But then you would never experience its benefits. Just like life, owning rental property entails some work and some lessons learned along the way. And yet if you don't get into the game due to fear of whatever lessons you might have to learn along the way, then you will also miss out on the financial benefits and sense of empowerment that come with owning rental property.

PART TWO

THE NEST

Setting Yourself Up

for Success

4

PREPARE THE NEST

Rethinking Money, Debt, Assets, and Liabilities

RETHINKING MONEY

I was raised to believe that money was a bad thing. Well, not money itself, but the pursuit of money. Every now and then, I still find myself downplaying the importance of money. And yet I know that money is a necessary thing, an enjoyable thing, and, when used right, even a very loving, generous, and charitable thing.

Money is good for the good it can do.
GARY KELLER

At the most basic level, money is a necessity. It provides food, clothing, and shelter. It gives us wheels and heat and medicine. It gives us the freedom to get on an airplane to explore this beautiful world or to reconnect with loved ones living long-distance. Money can be used for good, loving purposes. It can be used to help out a friend. It can be donated to charity. It can help a homeless family start over. And it can literally buy time, in the form of time off of work, especially if you are self-employed or in retirement.

According to the book *Retire Happy* by Richard Stim, there are four essential ingredients to a happy retirement: money, health, a network of family and friends, and having engaging and enjoyable activities. However, superseding all of these factors, His Holiness the Dalai Lama asserts in his book *The Art of Happiness*, co-authored with Howard Cutler, that one's state of mind, perspective, or outlook is—hands down—the most important determinant of happiness. Our outlook on our circumstance is indeed critical. After all, the very *quality* of our financial situations, our states of health, our networks of family and friends, and our activities are all quite literally *defined by our perceptions and our appreciation of them.*

However, since we live in the real world, and since our outlook doesn't pay the bills (at least not by itself!), I believe that there are two key ingredients to a happy retirement that can help or hinder the success of all the others. These are our money and our mindset. I've portrayed these ingredients in relation to each other in Figure 4.1.

FIGURE 4.1. FOUR ESSENTIAL INGREDIENTS TO HAPPY RETIREMENT

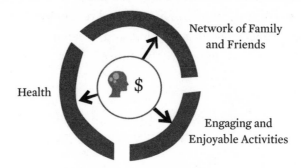

In the center of the diagram, our state of mind is represented by the picture of the head, and our state of financial health is represented by the dollar sign. Around the outside are Stim's remaining ingredients: our network of family and friends, the activities we find engaging and enjoyable, and our state of health.

Money and mindset affect everything. Money allows us to go out and enjoy time with friends (without being a burden on them!); our mindset helps us enjoy those friendships. Money allows us to travel, to visit long-distance loved ones, and to vacation, while our mindset makes it possible to take the initiative and appreciate these experiences. Money allows us to participate in whatever recreational activities we enjoy—or try new ones—and mindset allows us to be up for the adventure. Money is essential for maintaining our health as we get older—be it for copays or vitamins, acupuncture or exercise, long-term care insurance or walkers. And equally important, we need a positive state of mind in order to be simultaneously grateful for whatever our current state of health happens to be, as well as to be willing to do whatever is necessary to maintain or improve that particular state of health.

RETHINKING ASSETS AND LIABILITIES

Robert Kiyosaki teaches that an asset is something that brings money into your life on an ongoing basis, like a rental property. I completely agree with him. I also believe that assets go beyond this strict definition into other areas. For example, what about your friend who encourages you to follow your dreams and achieve your goals? Is this person an asset? What about your state of mind? Could positivity and motivation be considered assets?

I believe they are. These things, among other intangibles, are what fuel us. They are vital to our lives, to our success in achieving our dreams and goals, and ultimately to our happiness in this thing called life. As I see it, there are three overarching categories of assets: those of the heart, those of the mind, and those of the pocket. I developed Figure 4.2 to show how these asset classes fit together.

These three classes do not stand on their own. They are interdependent, with each affecting the others in a number of ways. The sweet spot is that spot right in the middle where all three asset classes are in effect. The heart feels alive, the mind is positive and proactive, and the pocket is enjoying positive cash flow through rental property or another type of passive income.

I'll go into these three asset classes next. Note that it may appear that this section veers a bit off the point of my message of diversifying retirement planning with rental property. However, as you read this section, you will see how nurturing the assets of the heart and mind

FIGURE 4.2. ASSET CLASSES FOR THE 21ST CENTURY

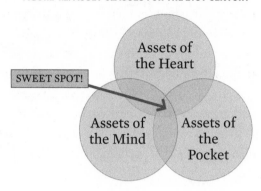

will boost the assets of the pocket and your eventual success in protecting your late-life financial security and retirement dreams.

A stranger is just a friend I haven't met yet.
WILL ROGERS

Assets of the Heart

Assets of the heart include all the positive relationships in your life. These include your relationships with your spouse or partner, your kids, other family members, and your neighbors, friends, co-workers, and business associates. Even your relationships with total strangers count here. Assets of the heart include laughter, pleasure, romance, leisure, play, and good times in general. Assets of the heart also include conversations, activities, and interests that ignite your passion.

Investing in assets of the heart means prioritizing time for the people in our lives who matter most. This includes being present with our loved ones, listening to them, holding them, snuggling and cuddling and having fun with them. It means reaching out to friends to keep those friendships alive and healthy. It also includes being helpful and pleasant to others, whether it is volunteering for a cause, helping someone out in need of a favor, or simply sharing a smile or friendly exchange with people you encounter throughout the day. For many people, investing in assets of the heart means being a part of a religious or spiritual community. It may also mean being a part of some other kind of group, like a rock band, hiking group, book club, soccer team, or whatever it is that *you* enjoy.

Liabilities of the Heart

The opposite of an asset is a liability. It is something that brings you down, zaps you of energy, or sucks money from your life. In the case of the heart, liabilities include relationships that have become unhealthy, unhappy, or toxic. However, before you are too quick to blame your significant other, remember that our relationships can be strained by our own negativity, criticism, and/or the inability to let go of stress, anxiety, or the need to work. It is important to learn to keep those traits in check and to let yourself, or even force yourself, to be lighthearted and fun at times.

Other liabilities of the heart could include friendships that don't lift you up or bring out your best. Liabilities could also include the absence of friendships or activities outside of your work and family. Rather than coasting on autopilot through life, take a close look at who and what is in your life and, as with your primary relationship, pump some new energy into those friendships and activities that make you a better, happier, and more interesting person.

Assets of the Mind

Assets of the mind include things such as positivity, grace, courage, willingness to learn from mistakes, eagerness to continue learning, being daring, and taking action. It takes work to foster these qualities in one's own mind, especially when faced with work demands, personal stress, and negative input from the world at large. However, again, like the assets of the heart, you have the right, and the responsibility to yourself (and to your loved ones), to do so.

There are so many ways to continually foster the assets of your mind! As with the assets of the heart, one way is to surround yourself with positive people, such as those who are striving toward their own personal goals or working for the good of humanity in some way. Other ways include meditation or prayer, journaling, reading, exercise, dance, playing music, or whatever it is that works for you to help you clear your mind. Reading spiritual, motivational, or psychological self-help books is also an excellent way to foster and nurture the assets of the mind. There are so many excellent books. As a place to start, I highly recommend Napoleon Hill's groundbreaking classic on the power of the mind, *Think and Grow Rich*, which I reference later in chapter 6.

Emancipate yourselves from mental slavery, none but ourselves can free our minds!

BOB MARLEY

Liabilities of the Mind

Liabilities of the mind include paralyzing fear, procrastination, inaction, laziness, avoidance, delusion, and ignorance. We are all victims of the liabilities of the mind at times, but succumbing to them for extended periods of time can have a very negative effect on you, your loved ones, and your future financial prospects.

As a side note, if you think you might be one who overindulges in drinking, drugging, eating, gambling, gaming, watching back-to-back Netflix shows, or some other behavior that lessens your ability to reach your full potential, then these could have very harmful effects on your state of mind (and body) over time. Left untamed, these patterns can become addictions, and addictions can spread like a cancer to affect other assets of your mind, heart (your relationships and passions), and pocket (your financial security and retirement dreams).

Whether it is the cost of booze or smokes, Starbucks or Coke, lottery-playing or day-trading, these patterns of behavior, which are the domain of the mind, ultimately also hurt our bottom line, which is our forever line. I say "forever line" because one day leads to the next, and the next, and so on. If we maintain unhealthy patterns, then we will one day wake up to find ourselves in exactly the same place—or even further behind. If this is your situation, I encourage you to find a private therapist or check out a 12-Step program that is relevant to your situation to take back the reins of your life.[1]

Assets of the Pocket

I've put assets of the pocket last, not because this category is the least important: To the contrary, it is *essential* to the subject of this book! I've included this last in order to avoid trivializing how very important the assets of the heart and mind are to a successful, happy, and even financially abundant life both before and during retirement.

The category I've called "Assets of the Pocket" refers to your "financial house" (or free-range chicken yard!) and the extent to which it is in order (or has at least one egg-laying chicken!), especially in preparing for retirement. Assets of the pocket actually have little to do with your job, because you won't have that when you retire. Assets of the pocket have nothing to do with the resale value of your car or jewelry, because it is unlikely that you could sell these things for anywhere close to what you originally paid for them. And they have little to do with the size of your bank account or retirement accounts, because no matter how much you have, there is no way to *really* know how long your funds will last you in the end.

Assets of the pocket have everything to do with owning one (or more) sustainable asset that brings passive income into your life on a regular basis, thereby setting you up for a worry-free retirement. It's all about getting that chicken! Not just any chicken—one that will lay eggs for you month after month in perpetuity. One that you can eventually pass to your loved ones when you die.

So how do you go about getting this chicken? Well, this is the subject of the rest of this book. However, the most basic answer is that you use a mortgage. In fact, mortgages were invented to help the vast majority of us buy homes that we wouldn't otherwise be able to afford. Robert Kiyosaki, author of the game-changing book *Rich*

Dad Poor Dad, explains that if a mortgage is used to purchase a cash-flowing rental property, then this mortgage is "good debt." Good debt is debt that improves your financial situation in both the near term and the long run, while bad debt worsens it in both. As he famously says, "Good debt puts money in your pocket."

Liabilities of the Pocket

Like assets of the heart and mind, assets of the pocket also have their villain: the liabilities of the pocket. Again, according to Robert Kiyosaki, if something takes money from you every month, then it is a liability. This will be doubly true once you retire, since you will no longer be able to rely on income from your job to sustain the cost of that liability.

Liabilities of the pocket basically equate to bad debt that you take on when you purchase things that don't create income. Bad debt is money that you must pay back every month while getting nothing in return (except for whatever it is that you purchased). Bad debt usually takes the form of credit card debt but also can include car loans, personal home mortgages, and lines of credit. While you may feel that some liabilities are necessary, like your home and car, be careful not to fool yourself into buying a more expensive home or car by calling these things assets. They are still liabilities; and the greater the purchase price, the greater your monthly liability tends to be.

Your home is not an asset.
ROBERT KIYOSAKI

Anything that must be sold to recapture its value does not count as an asset for retirement-planning purposes. After all, who in the world is going to buy that flat-screen TV off you for the same price you paid, when they can just go to a store and get a new one off the shelf, on sale, instead? And what if you can't find someone to buy your house for at least the amount you paid for it? We're all way too familiar with that scenario from the housing meltdown beginning in 2008.

Most people factor their home into their retirement picture. After all, you've certainly heard it said that our home may be the largest investment, or asset, we ever purchase. But is this really the case? To cut to the chase, the answer is, well . . . it depends. Before the mortgage is paid off, it is just a liability. After you pay off the mortgage, it depends on your operating expenses (utilities, taxes, insurance, etc.) and whether your home can make you any money. According to Kiyosaki's definition, technically speaking, if you rent out the garage or a room in the house, and if the rent covers your operating expenses, then your home becomes an asset.

Whether or not you decide to rent out space in your home, it is widely accepted that a key component to any retirement strategy is to live mortgage-free in your own home. There are other benefits to owning your own home. For one thing, it's your home, your abode. Also, at tax time, you get to deduct your mortgage interest, your homeowner's insurance, and any points you may have paid at closing.[2] Finally, as you'll see in chapter 8, if you buy a property with an investor's mindset (as detailed in the *R.O.R.E. Blueprint for Success: A Step-by-Step Companion Guide* at www.GetaChicken.com), then, at any age or stage in your life, you can move out and turn your home into a cash-flowing rental property.

In general, what the three asset classes (heart, mind, and pocket) boil down to is this: In the different areas of your life, are you being filled up, or depleted? Fed, or starved? Every now and then, I like to take an inventory of these different areas of my life and make adjustments where necessary. I believe this is vital for both day-to-day and long-term happiness and fulfillment.

Never say "Poor me." Saying "Poor me"
only makes you more poor.
K. KAI ANDERSON

How to Turn a Liability into an Asset

What to Do with an Existing Negative Cash-Flowing Rental Property?

Rental properties fall into the liability trap when they are not "cash-flowing"—that is, when they cost you more money each month than they bring in. The number one way to avoid a bad-debt rental property is to buy the right property at the right price. (See the *R.O.R.E. Blueprint for Success: A Step-by-Step Companion Guide* and the free Cash Flow Analysis [CFA] Tool on my website at www.GetaChicken.com.)

If you currently own an investment property that has zero to negative cash flow, you need to find a way to turn your rental liability into a rental asset. There are a few ways to do this. One method is to enroll in the governmental Section 8 program. Landlords with Section 8 property often report that they can achieve market rent with the added security of being paid every month by the government.

Another way to improve your cash flow is to refinance your mortgage to achieve a lower monthly payment. Refinancing involves replacing your current mortgage with one that has better terms in order to achieve one of three goals: lower your payment, slice off time until payoff, or take out additional funds. If your goal is to improve the cash flow on a property, then you'll want to lower your monthly payment, of course. This may be possible if you can get a lower interest rate or if you shift from a lower-term mortgage to a higher-term one: for example, going from a fifteen-year to a thirty-year mortgage.

We've found that, hands down, the absolute best way to boost the cash flow on a property is to turn it into a house-share and rent by the room to responsible individuals. The details of this are shared in chapter 7, "Borrow a Chicken." For example, for a little extra work on our part, converting one of our single-family properties into a house-share boosted the total rental income from $1,350 to $2,400 per month. Plus there is the unmatched feel-good benefit of providing affordable housing to several individuals, rather than attempting to raise the rent on one tenant.

Other ways to increase cash flow are to have the tenants pay their own utilities if they are not already doing so, charge extra for on-site parking, and install coin-operated laundry or vending machines or another amenity. Using one of these methods (or raising the rent) should be done cautiously, however, as they could cause excessive financial burden on your tenants or cause them to seek housing elsewhere.

If you are losing too much money on a rental that you already own, and if you've already exhausted all of these methods, then it may be best to sell that property and start over. Other factors in your decision should be the length of time until the mortgage is paid off, the anticipated repair needs of the property, and whether you can afford to float the negative portion of the cash flow from your regular income source until things shift or until the mortgage is paid off.

Remember that a decision to bail should be about cash flow, not property value. When your rental is cash-flow positive, and if you are in it for the long term, it won't matter so much what the property value is. You can weather any storm or turbulent real estate market, as long as you have rent-paying tenants.

Your Home

In getting on top of finances, one goal should be to take a good look at all of your liabilities and then convert them into assets wherever possible. Even though your home is not an asset, you may be able to make it work for you, at least a little. For example, if you have extra space in your home, you can rent it to someone for a little extra money each month, or list it on www.Airbnb.com. With your landlord's approval, you can do this even if you don't own the home yourself.

Chapter 7, "Borrow a Chicken," goes into this in depth. However, I will briefly mention here that we rented space in our home for a period of time, and it was a win-win-win. Two very responsible college gals rented our finished basement (and shared our kitchen and living space); we benefited from $800 in monthly income; and our young daughter fell in love with them! They loved her back and, as any parent knows, life is often easier when there are other fun, loving, trustworthy adults in the home. Needless to say, if you have children—and even if you don't—trustworthiness is essential!

Your Other Stuff

More than ever, you have opportunities to make money off your liabilities—that is, your existing stuff and your space. For example, you can rent out your car through sites like www.Turo.com (formerly known as RelayRides), www.carclub.easycar.com/home/carowners, and www.getaround.com. A growing company called FlightCar (www.flightcar.com) allows you to make money on your car when you drop it off at the airport, rather than paying for airport parking. The car-sharing revolution has gone international with Germany's www.mitfahrgelegenheit.de, France's www.drivy.com, and Australia's www.drivemycar.com.au, among many other companies across many other countries.

You can make money off of your other stuff too. You can rent out space in your home through www.Airbnb.com. You can rent out your parking pad or parking garage through sites like www.JustPark.com. You can rent out extra land to gardeners and farmers through www.SwapItShop.com or, in Canada, www.SwapSity.ca. If you are a dog lover, you can take in someone's dog while they are on vacation through sites like www.DogVacay.com and www.Rover.com. You also can rent out your skis and bikes and other recreational equipment through www.SpinLister.com. In fact, through sites like www.us.Zilok.com (www.uk.Zilok.com in the UK, etc.), you can pretty much rent out anything you own!

RETHINKING SPENDING

This book is about using rental property to boost the income in our lives, especially as we prepare for retirement. And, just as the cash flow of a property involves money coming in and money going out, the same is true for our personal lives. This means that it is important to get a grip on our outgoing money just as much as the incoming. That said, I recognize that there are tons of books on saving and budgeting, so I will try to offer a brief, fresh perspective on the subject in the remaining pages of this chapter.

Goals are theoretical, habits are actual.
DANIELLE LAPORTE

I believe most of us have patterns or daily habits that keep each of us at a given, unique, and relatively stable state of being. We stay at that state until we change some element of our behavior (either positive or negative, large or small) on a consistent and even daily basis. Starting a new daily pattern is like adjusting the temperature on our own personal thermostat. Once we begin our new pattern, things start to shift . . . until we land at our next thermostat setting, or "temperature," or state of being.

This is what I call the Thermostat Change and Results Theory, or just Thermostat Theory for short. As a disclaimer, my theory is *scientifically untested*, as far as I know; however, you can try it out in your own life and share with me, anecdotally, how it goes for you. To all research psychologists and physiologists, have at it!

Thermostat Theory is a way of shifting your life by shifting your metaphorical temperature setting. It can be applied to anything in our lives: finances, friendships, clutter, health . . . you name it. In fact, while this book is about retirement planning using real estate, Thermostat Theory is probably easiest to understand in the context of weight control.

Consider the example of Mary, portrayed in Figure 4.3. Mary is fifty pounds overweight. If she makes one small positive change, on a daily basis, she will start to make progress in the right direction, perhaps without even seeing it herself. Her weight will shift until it lands on that invisible new setting and will remain stable as long as she maintains that change. For example, in Figure 4.3, you can see the impact of her replacing her daily sugared soda at lunch for ice water

FIGURE 4.3. THERMOSTAT THEORY (AS APPLIED TO HEALTHY HABITS)

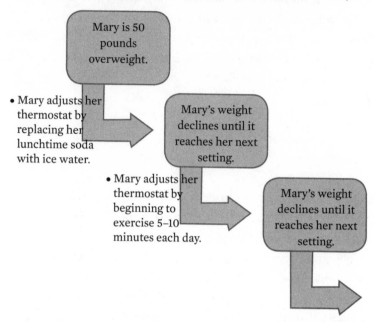

with lemon. By doing this, she has essentially changed the setting on her invisible thermostat.

If Mary maintains this first change and then makes yet another small change, such as adding five to ten minutes of exercise to her morning routine, things will shift ever so slightly again until she lands on her next setting. And so on, until she reaches a healthy weight. At that point, if she maintains the daily habits that brought her to her healthy new setting, she will be able to enjoy her new state of well-being indefinitely.

Thermostat Theory works in the opposite direction as well. In fact, I am convinced that this is how people go from healthy to unhealthy without even realizing what happened. Little by little, the incremental changes we make and maintain on a daily basis pile up. Of course, the impact of this phenomenon may be especially pronounced at key periods in our life, such as when our body's metabolism is naturally changing as we get older. In the same example of Mary, if she had added a second Coke to her day, rather than eliminating the first, her body weight would have gradually shifted in the

FIGURE 4.4. THERMOSTAT THEORY (AS APPLIED TO SPENDING)

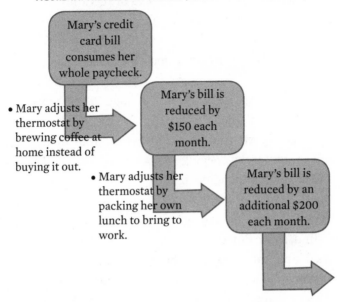

other direction. Behind the scenes and beneath her skin, her body would be undergoing a subtle shift until, after a certain length of time, it would reach a slightly higher setting. The key here is that a random Coke or donut is not what makes the difference. It's when the behavior is repeated the next day, and then the next, and becomes a daily pattern.

Our spending habits and level of financial stability operate in the same way. In Figure 4.4, let's consider a similar example, but one applied to spending. In this case, Mary has difficulty paying her credit card bill each month. If she changes her thermostat setting by making one small change, such as curbing her $5/day Starbucks coffee habit, and if she consistently sticks with it, day after day after day, her new lifestyle will slice $150 off her monthly statement (or provide her an extra $150 to put toward her next bill). If she sticks with this for a whole year, she's looking at about $1,825 in *found money*!

If Mary then changes her thermostat setting again by making a second small change, and does this on a *daily* basis, she will bring her spending setting down another degree. For example, if Mary begins packing a lunch to bring to work instead of spending $10 on lunch, then she will save roughly $200 per month or $2,400 over the course of the year. She will be on her way to liberating her finances and achieving higher and more lasting goals for herself.

Just as diet and exercise work hand in hand for the ultimate effect on your health, your financial situation is affected by income and spending. It is important to first know where your money is going. You may want to start by opening up your credit-card and bank statements and looking at each line item.

Are there services or items for which you are being automatically billed that you no longer use? When you try this exercise, you will probably find, as we did, that we were being automatically billed for things we'd long since forgotten about. It is important to check your statements regularly for these sneaky automatic deductions. Once you find a suspicious or useless automatic charge, *without even stopping to use the bathroom,* go pick up the phone, call the company, and cancel your subscription or service.

The next step is to take a close look at your spending habits. When I did this, I discovered that my statement was riddled with charges from my workplace cafeteria. While I had absolutely no grounds to contest the charges with Sodexho, and arguing about the prices would do little to no good either, I *could* do as Michael Jackson sang and take a good look at the person in the mirror. I could simply change my daily habits. Armed with information on how much money I was literally flushing down the toilet every day at work made it much easier to take the time to pack my lunch each morning.

I invite you to try thinking of small, maybe even ridiculously small, changes in the positive direction that you might be able to make in your own life. Try picking one change and then make it a habit. Do this three days in a row, and you own it. You are on your way to a new pattern, new lifestyle, and, little by little, a new future. What spending habit are you willing to change first?

Your answer: _____

In a seminal book called *The Millionaire Next Door: The Surprising Secrets of America's Wealthy*, authors Thomas J. Stanley and William D. Danko enlightened readers on their counterintuitive finding that, much of the time, people who appear wealthy often have a very low net worth, and those who appear only "average" are often truly very wealthy.[3] This is because truly wealthy people care about retaining their wealth for the long term. On the other hand, people who care more about appearances and immediate gratification often load themselves down with consumer debt and as a result get trapped into a lifestyle that is unsustainable . . . especially when the work stops.

Too many people spend money they haven't earned,
to buy things they don't want,
to impress people they don't like.

WILL ROGERS
American cowboy, actor, and humorist (1879–1935)

When people develop a habit of financing their "wants," one "want" leads to the next, which leads to the next, and so forth. If you are stuck in this pattern, you may have discovered that "having" is not nearly as satisfying as the next "want" is alluring. To make matters worse, you may be suffocating under a mountain of bad debt, surrounded by liabilities that no longer excite you. Consumer debt can be particularly devastating when there is some kind of uncontrollable shift to the income side of the equation. A job loss or divorce could flatten the whole house of cards in a flash. And if it gets bad enough, retirement could become a pipe dream.

Stanley and Danko revealed a surprising fact: Authentic wealth has little to do with income. In fact, those who are authentically wealthy look as "regular" as your next-door neighbor. This authentically wealthy neighbor may drive an old car, buy groceries at discount grocery stores like Aldi, and may even choose to shop for clothes at the local thrift store. The authentically wealthy neighbor will gladly accept a hand-me-down to avoid buying something new, much less putting it on credit. They have daily spending habits that are controlled and based on needs rather than wants the majority of the time. Ultimately, these daily habits serve to keep them on a healthy and sustainable financial plateau.

I learned a valuable lesson from my father when I was about twelve years old. The revolutionary Sony Walkman had hit the American shelves in 1980 and, two years later, was piping hot. This seemingly magical device was a handheld cassette player with radio, and . . . brace yourself . . . it came with earphones! It was a brand-new concept in the early '80s, and as a young teen I desperately wanted one of my own. One day, my dad *finally* took me out to shop for one, even though I had to use my own money that I had been saving up over time. However, we didn't just go out, buy a Walkman, and come home. My dad had another plan for me. As an impulsive pre-teen, I found it to be a thoroughly aggravating plan; but in looking back, I'm now grateful for it.

My dad and I shopped around, test-drove a bunch of devices, both Walkmans and spin-offs, and compared prices across several brands and stores. To make matters worse, he made me come home to think about my options and ponder whether this was really how I wanted to spend my money. His motto was: "*Always go home empty-handed. If you want it bad enough, then you won't mind going back out to buy it.*"

In the end, I decided I really *did* want that Walkman spin-off "bad enough," and we went back out a couple of days later to drop coin for the top (and cheapest) contender on the list. I share this story to pass on the valuable lesson I learned from my dad. The point isn't to avoid spending money on nice things. It's that when you do, make sure you do your research, shop prices (and these days check online reviews), and refrain from impulsive buys. Try to force yourself (and your kids for that matter) to go home empty-handed, as hard as it may be, because . . . if you want it bad enough, you truly won't mind going back out to get it. In fact, I can tell you from experience that you'll quite enjoy the trip!

When it comes to online shopping, you obviously can't drive home empty-handed and then make a second trip back out. However, if you find something online that you really want, try closing the web page and doing something else for the rest of the day. Get outside. Call a friend. Make yourself wait at least a day or two. After a couple days, you might even discover that you'd forgotten all about the item and that it's not all that important to you after all. Give yourself the chance to move on.

How many times have you come to the conclusion that someone you know is wealthy based on their fancy car, large home, or lavish vacations? It's easy to fall for that trick. If we do, then we often fall for the second trick: Measuring our own self-worth or the quality of our lives, or even our happiness, against their stuff. We convince ourselves that we want what they have. But even if we succumb to a new SUV or a fresh set of appliances, do these things truly make us *happy*? Or do they just put us further behind?

The problem is that too much of this kind of spending could jeopardize your retirement prospects in two ways. The first is that you'll have less money to put toward acquiring and maintaining an income-producing asset like a rental property, so you will literally build less potential net-worth energy for yourself. (Refer back to chapter 3, the "Benefits of Rental Property" section, for a refresher on potential and kinetic net-worth energy.)

The second way in which this kind of spending threatens your future finances and retirement prospects is that, if you finance the items, any bad debt you take on comes right out of your net-worth equation. It may not seem so terrible while you are working and able to make payments; however, once you stop working, the monthly payments will continue to take an uncomfortable slice out of your personal monthly cash flow.

My last point, which you probably already know, is that it is essential to pay off any credit card debt that you have. Otherwise, you will be paying interest on the amount borrowed, and then interest on that interest, and then interest on that interest's interest, and so on, putting yourself further and further behind. If the cash-flow numbers work out, you can also refinance an existing rental property to strategically get back to ground zero and start fresh in curbing spending and paying off your credit card every month. Chapter 7 has some other great ideas for cleaning up bad debt.

This chapter was all about "preparing the nest" for good things to come. In other words, this has been about learning new ways of thinking about money, debt, assets, liabilities, and spending. By now, you may be eager to get started in creating a sustainable source of income that will be there for you after you retire. If so, turn the page. . . . You are ready for the first step of taking action: setting your goal! In the next chapter, I've outlined three goals for you to consider taking on as your own, goals that are specifically related to acquiring rental property to aid in a long-term retirement strategy. Then, in chapter 6, I will share five tricks to help you achieve your goal, or any goal, for that matter.

It may be hard for an egg to turn into a bird: It would be a jolly sight harder for it to learn to fly while remaining an egg. We are like eggs at present. And you cannot go on indefinitely being just an ordinary, decent egg. We must be hatched or go bad.

C.S. LEWIS

5

THE PRIMARY AND ULTIMATE GOALS

Setting the Goal That Is Right for You

THE ULTIMATE GOAL

The Ultimate Goal is to pay off your mortgage(s) so that the income from your property or properties can become your monthly living income. Property that is not tethered to a mortgage—that you own free and clear—is all yours. The bank can't take it back, because the bank no longer co-owns it with you. Monthly cash flow is maximized, because you will no longer have to pay the principal and interest, the largest of your property expenses (although, of course, you will need to continue paying taxes and insurance and budgeting for capital expenses). As you will see in Figure 5.1 later in this chapter, once you are liberated from your mortgage payment, the income from your property will shoot up and become an integral part of your retirement plan.

You should always bear in mind the Ultimate Goal. It should be a factor when you are considering a property and evaluating different mortgages. The type of mortgage you attain for your property will be a key factor in your ability to achieve the Ultimate Goal. This is a key theme throughout Part Three of the book, in particular chapter 9, "Hatching Your Plan," and chapter 10, "Do the Chicken Dance!"

DETERMINE YOUR LEVEL I, II, OR III PRIMARY GOAL

It's time to decide your destiny. What do you want your future to look like? In this chapter, I offer three different Primary Goals for diversifying your retirement plan using the tool of real estate. You get to choose your own adventure.

If you simply desire to provide a level of safety for your retirement by diversifying beyond your Social Security and/or mutual fund–based retirement accounts, then you should set and attain the modest and realistic Level I Goal of owning just one rental property.

If you are feeling a bit more ambitious and would like to strive for a higher level of safety, comfort, and peace of mind in your retirement, as afforded by greater cash flow each month, then you should decide to set and attain the Level II Goal.

Finally, if you are seeking complete financial self-sufficiency once all your mortgages are paid off, then the Level III Goal is for you. This is for persons who have the ambition, time, and resources to create enough cash flow to cover all of their living expenses in retirement. With the Level III Goal, Social Security, pensions, and retirement accounts are all considered bonus. If these sources disappear for any reason, the cash flow afforded by your Level III Goal will sustain you and provide the lifestyle of your making for all your living days. These three Goals are outlined in Table 5.1 and described in detail in the pages that follow.

TABLE 5.1. THE LEVEL I, II, AND III GOALS

Level I Goal	One rental property as a retirement backup plan, providing a level of safety through authentic diversification
Level II Goal	Enough rental income to supplement other sources of income in retirement (or once mortgages are paid off), providing a degree of comfort through additional monthly income
Level III Goal	Enough rental income to cover living expenses and property expenses in retirement (or once the mortgages are paid off), providing complete financial self-sufficiency

The Level I Goal: Diversification and Safety Net

The minimal and most modest goal that I hope you will consider setting for yourself upon reading this book is the acquisition of one rental property for the long term. One property, well chosen and well managed, will provide a level of diversification and safety for your later years—beyond the stock market and Social Security—that simply would not otherwise be there. Consider your one rental as an insurance policy against a sudden decline in the stock market—or, worse, a sustained recession, depression, technical failure, identity theft, or even cyberterrorist attack on the stock market, striking just when you need your money most.

As I'll get into in Part Three, there are many ways to acquire your first rental. For example, if you own your own home, one of the easiest and most common ways that people get started is to find a new home for yourself and turn your existing home into a rental. If you don't already own your home, you may want to purchase a two-to four-unit house and move into one of the units. Check out the many stories in Online Appendix B for real-life examples of these commonly employed first moves (look for Venesa, Kevin and Andrea, John, and Deb's stories).

Whether you turn your home into a rental or purchase one from scratch, the rent that you receive every month from your tenants will gradually pay off your mortgage, until you ultimately own it free and clear. You may have only modest cash flow in the beginning, but, whether it takes just a few years or thirty, once you've paid off the mortgage you will have a continuous, sustainable, and healthy amount of income streaming into your bank account every month. As you get older, this income will trend upward. In retirement, this income stream will supplement your Social Security income, and your pension if you are lucky enough to have one, and whatever retirement savings you've accumulated over the course of your life.

Figure 5.1 provides an example of the degree of diversification and safety that you could attain for yourself on a monthly basis with just **one rental property.** This graph shows rents over time with a

FIGURE 5.1. MONTHLY CASH FLOW (AFTER EXPENSES) OVER 30 YEARS (ASSUMING 20% DOWN, NO PROPERTY MANAGER, AND HYPOTHETICAL 2% RENT APPRECIATION PER YEAR)

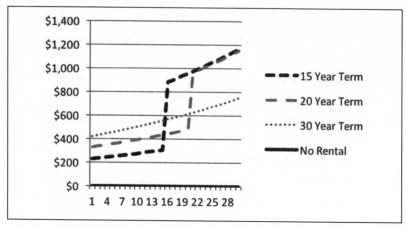

hypothetical 2 percent increase each year to keep up with the rate of inflation, plus a jump in cash flow at the time the mortgage is completely paid off. Note that the 2 percent rent escalation is for example purposes only. It is not possible in all locations at all times, nor is it always in your best interest to implement it.

This graph shows mortgages at terms of fifteen, twenty, and thirty years for comparison. If you are able to sacrifice a little in monthly cash flow in the early years with a fifteen-year mortgage, then you will be able to jump to higher levels of income much sooner. To bring the message home, the graph also shows the impact of not investing at all, as represented by the flat line at the bottom of the chart.

You can see that the small move of acquiring one rental property can add a stream of income to your life, both now and when the property is paid off, that would be otherwise nonexistent. Figure 5.1 is for demonstration purposes only. The actual numbers will vary based on your property and geographic area.

The Level II Goal: Financial Comfort

The Level II Goal brings even more benefits than the Level I Goal just described. Going beyond the realm of modest diversification, the Level II Goal entails creating enough income to supplement whatever it is that you expect to receive in retirement to meet your anticipated monthly expenses at that time. The "Total Extra Needed" formula presented in chapter 3 can help you determine how much cash flow you'll need to create in order to achieve the Level II Goal of financial comfort in retirement.

By acquiring enough rentals, or rental units (in the case of a multi-family home), to supplement your expected income in retirement, you will also create additional flexibility, as described in chapter 8. These rentals will have a lasting effect on your life by providing a modest income before you retire, heightened income once your mortgages are paid off, and ongoing income for your family or favorite charity long after you are gone. In addition, having multiple properties will allow you to sell or refinance one down the road, if you need to, while still enjoying the cash flow of the others.

Keep in mind that owning more than one property should be used in conjunction with your broader retirement plan. In addition, it is important to remember that the Level II Goal should be achieved incrementally. There is work involved in acquiring property, preparing it to be rented, and finding a great tenant. Each rental also demands emergency funds. *Proceed slowly* so that you will be successful in the end.

The Level III Goal: Complete Financial Self-Sufficiency

With the Level III Goal, the cash flow from your rental properties completely pays for your lifestyle once the mortgages are entirely paid off. You are completely self-sufficient, whether or not you have additional income from any other source. If the stock market tanks, you will be fine. If your promised pension vanishes, you will be fine. If your Social Security checks are slashed, you will also be fine.

In fact, if you achieve the Level III Goal, you will be better than fine. In addition to sustainable monthly income, you will have options afforded by greater potential (and eventually kinetic) net worth energy. For example, if you desire early retirement, you may retire as soon as your mortgages are paid off. You also have options in terms of selling and "trading up," as I'll discuss later in the book.

The specifics of this goal are to acquire enough properties that, *once your mortgages are paid off*, your total rental income exceeds your total monthly expenses for those properties *plus* all of your own personal expenses. Depending on the type of properties you purchase and your geographic region, and your expenses, the Level III Goal may be attainable with a handful of single-family properties or one multi-unit building. We attained the Level III Goal of complete financial self-sufficiency with five properties, a couple of which are rented room by room as house-shares. Once our mortgages are paid off, we will be positioned to retire comfortably, with complete financial self-sufficiency.

Another way of looking at this is that the Level III Goal entails completely replacing your current salary with income from your rental properties once the mortgages are paid off. On the "Total Extra Needed" formula of chapter 3, you will want to leave all the income lines blank. The goal here is to create enough rental income that you will be completely self-sufficient, whether or not these other potential sources of income are present. These other items can be the icing on the cake. Sure, they would be nice, but you won't have to rely upon them for your survival or to maintain your current standard of living once you stop working.

Bear in mind that, as with the Level II Goal, the Level III Goal takes dedication, work, time, and adequate emergency funds. If you have the opportunity to purchase a multi-family building, rather than several single-family homes, or if you decide to trade up your Level II Goal properties into one apartment building, that will probably get you to your goal faster with less expense, time, and energy, since everything will be under one roof. Even your CapEx will be lower as a proportion of your total income, as discussed in chapter 3, under "Risk #4, the Risk of Costly Repairs." If an apartment building is your goal, be sure to take time to educate yourself further before taking the plunge!

Beyond the Level III Goal

If the Level III Goal is all about complete financial self-sufficiency after your mortgages are paid off, then going *beyond the Level III Goal* entails amassing enough property that you achieve this outcome even *before your mortgages are paid off.*

If you are looking to get out of the "rat race" in the near future by going beyond the Level III Goal and replacing your job with real estate, keep in mind that this takes time and dedication.

Real estate is a long, slow road, and it is work. If your mind is set on going beyond the Level III Goal, then it is important not to give up on your job (and income!). Think of your job as a means to an end, an opportunity to build some initial investment capital for your real estate investing. Your job will also help you qualify for mortgages, which is an important function in and of itself. Finally, your job will support your daily living expenses, until the day your real estate investments can take over, and the surplus income can help stock your emergency fund to prepare for unexpected real estate–related expenses that come up from time to time.

However, going beyond the Level III Goal is only realistically achievable for those who are truly obsessed with so-called financial freedom. It is reserved for those who have a burning desire, dedication, and drive to become very wealthy in either time or money. These characteristics, plus a willingness to take risks, are essential ingredients of investors who have created significant cash flow and amassed significant wealth through real estate. The methods in this book can certainly put you on the path to catapult you beyond the Level III Goal, if this is your desire.

I should note, however, that *going beyond the Level III Goal is beyond my aim in writing this book.* My mission is simple: It is to help working adults across all walks of life reclaim their retirement dreams and protect their late-life financial security through retirement diversification using the powerful tool of *even just one* income-producing rental property.

Don't be pushed by your problems.
Be led by your dreams.

RALPH WALDO EMERSON
Essayist and Transcendentalist (1803–1882)

Decisions, Decisions

If you are not sure where to start, it is probably best to simply start with the Level I Goal. You can always decide later whether to proceed to Level II or III. If you have already achieved the Level I Goal of owning one rental property, you have conquered your initial fears and gained some experience as a landlord and property owner. If this is your case, and since you are reading this book, you are clearly ready for the Level II or Level III Goal. In fact, I believe that real estate investing might be a little like getting a tattoo. While I am tattooless myself, I've heard that once you have your first tattoo, you are on the lookout for your second, and then your third. . . .

Still others may want to leapfrog right over the Level I Goal by buying a multi-family home or apartment building. This is what Alfredo and Rose (see Online Appendix B) did when they bought an apartment building and moved into one unit. This is not necessarily the easiest or most gradual approach; however, it could get you to the Level II or III Goal in one move if that is your desire.

Setting and achieving a Level I, II, or III Goal could be a pivot point in your life, one away from struggle and stress and toward financial safety, comfort, or even complete self-sufficiency in your later years. And with that, now that you've selected your Goal, it is important to set yourself up to actually achieve it, which is my aim in presenting the next chapter: "Why Did the Chicken Cross the Road?"

Set your mind on a definite goal and observe how
quickly the world stands aside to let you pass.

NAPOLEON HILL

6

WHY DID THE CHICKEN CROSS THE ROAD?

Secrets to Achieving Your Goal (Any Goal!)

Question: Why did the chicken cross the road? *Answer:* Because crossing the road was the chicken's goal. It's that simple. Once the chicken set its eyes on the other side of the road, it didn't turn back. Turning back could have meant getting stuck in limbo-land and eventually getting squashed by the farmer's pickup truck coming around the corner! That chicken just kept going until it reached its goal of getting to the other side.

Like the chicken, you can't arrive anywhere unless you know where you're aiming to go. When you drive to work, you remain focused on where you're going so that you actually get there. Imagine if you whimsically decided to meander off, getting completely sidetracked by the various sites along the way, never making it to your place of work. One or two times of not showing up and you'd probably lose your job!

While this example may seem ridiculous, we so often treat our personal goals this way. And yet, why should we be any less accountable to our own goals than we are to our boss' goals?

The goals we set are vital. They determine where we end up. The goals that we *don't set* are also vital, because they determine where we will *not* end up. If we never set out to own rental property, we never will. If we never set out to diversify our retirement accounts beyond what Wall Street and our 401(k) can offer, we never will. And this could be a decision that we eventually pay the price for . . . severely.

■

Why should you be any less accountable to yourself
than you are to your boss?

K. KAI ANDERSON

BECOMING SELF-SUFFICIENT

At the end of the day, don't we all just want to be taken care of? A good shoulder rub? Free dessert on our birthday at our favorite restaurant? And, most of all, a worry-free, financially secure retirement?

I'm sorry to say that, for this last one, I have bad news for you: Your retirement prospects are completely and totally in your own hands. As I've shown in chapters 1 and 2, if your pension is small or nonexistent, your workplace won't be taking care of you when you walk away from that paycheck. Even if you have an employer-sponsored 401(k), decisions related to how much to contribute and how to allocate funds are entirely in your own hands. The stock market is a gamble in and of itself and may or may not be there for you at the time you need it. Likewise, Social Security may or may not be there for you in the same form it's in today, and it should only be expected to play a minor role after you stop working. Even your financial adviser, if you have one, may not always put your best interests above their own, and they may or may not make perfect decisions along the way. And as for your savings . . . again, there's simply no way to really know how much will be enough and when, or whether, you can ever stop working.

In spite of this, many of us have been conditioned to be passive when it comes to saving for retirement. Whether it's our 401(k), IRA, or financial adviser, we are told to simply sign up, enroll in automatic deductions, put someone else in charge, and never worry about our finances again. The company prospectus is too boring and too confusing to bother reading, something that is probably not an accident. Plus, we are too busy and too overwhelmed with life to bother with the details. We trust that everything will work out fine.

Unfortunately, this hands-off *passive approach* to retirement planning *actively* puts our financial futures at risk. More than ever before, we need to learn an *active approach* to invest for passive income, income that is received on a consistent, regular basis with little effort required to maintain it: for example, monthly rental income.

This book is all about developing self-sufficiency and taking action. One small move now could lock in financial security for years to come. And this one small move is simply buying the right rental property or converting an existing home into a good, cash-flowing rental property.

PREPARE TO ACHIEVE YOUR LEVEL I, II, OR III GOAL

To achieve the Level I, II, or III Goal, it is essential that you first set it as a goal for yourself. Claim it. Thereafter, certain strategies will increase your chances of successfully attaining it. Here are some suggestions to get you started, each of which I'll cover in more depth in this section:

1. Make your goal SMART.
2. Embrace the power of positive thinking.
3. Put your goal in your face.
4. Develop a mantra or a theme song.
5. Persevere.

A goal is a dream with a deadline.

NAPOLEON HILL

Make Your Goal SMART

You may have already heard of the "SMART" acronym for goal setting. It is widely used in goal-setting classes, and for good reason. There is brilliance in its simplicity and on the emphasis on the fact that you'll know when you've achieved it. The letters have taken on slightly different variations over time by different goal-setting gurus. In the context of the Level I, II, and III Goals that I've put forth in this book, my preference is the following:

S—Specific
M—Meaningful
A—Action-oriented
R—Realistic
T—Time-specific

An example of a SMART goal, in the context of this book, might be something like this: "I will purchase one rental property in the next nine months, in order to diversify and protect my retirement, and I will do at least one thing every day that brings me closer to that goal."

You can see that this goal is SPECIFIC to the purchase of one rental property; therefore, you'll certainly know when you've achieved it. It is MEANINGFUL, since there is a *reason* why this goal is important: It is to safeguard and diversify your retirement picture, of course! It is ACTION-ORIENTED, in that you recognize that it is your responsibility and you are promising to do one thing each day to bring yourself closer to achieving your goal. It is REALISTIC, in that this is a feasible goal (whereas one property in the next month, or two properties in nine months, would probably be unrealistic, and even unwise, if you are just starting out). And it is TIME-SPECIFIC, in that you've given yourself a deadline of nine months.

To see the beauty of the SMART goal, it might be helpful to see the absurdity of a related *non*-SMART goal. Consider this non-SMART goal: "I hope to buy a lot of rental properties sometime really soon." It's almost ridiculous! You can see that this non-SMART goal is way too general, not personally meaningful at all, with no action tied to it to make it happen, totally unrealistic, and not at all time-specific. In its complete opposite form, this non-SMART goal is doomed from the start. And yet, this is what people do all the time when they say things like this to themselves:

> "I hope to win the lottery."
> "I'm going to retire one day."
> "I hope my 401(k) account will be enough to retire on."
> "I hope Social Security doesn't go away."
> "I plan to get rich in real estate."
> "I want to buy a rental property, once I have the time."

Harness the Power of the Mind

According to Dr. Srinivasan Pillay, a psychiatrist, brain-imaging researcher affiliated with Harvard University, and author of *The Science Behind the Law of Attraction*, and *Tinker, Dabble, Doodle, Try: Unlock the Power of the Unfocused Mind*, there is scientific merit behind the power of positive thinking. Referencing multiple scientific studies, from monkey studies to neuroimaging studies to obesity studies, he teaches that like attracts like and that thoughts influence reality. These concepts are known as the "Law of Attraction." This law states that we tend to draw things, people, and results into our lives that are directly in line with the thoughts we put out. In other words, positive thoughts attract positive results and negative thoughts attract negative results.

The concepts of the Law of Attraction date back to at least 391 B.C., when the Greek philosopher Plato asserted that "likes tend toward likes" (or "like attracts like"). Fast-forward to the early 1800s, when Phineas Quimby taught similar "New Thought" principles. More recently, these concepts have been popularized by Louise Hay, the "mother of positive thinking" and the author of numerous books on the power of the mind, as well as Esther and Jerry Hicks, authors of *The Law of Attraction: The Basics of the Teachings of Abraham*. Finally, the movie called *The Secret* popularized these concepts and brought them into the mainstream.

We are connected within and without. What we think and feel affects how we will act and how others will act as well. The depth of our feelings and actions is a critical variable in "attracting" what we want to our lives.

SRINIVASAN PILLAY, M.D.

Psychiatrist, brain-imaging researcher, and CEO of NeuroBusiness Group

According to the Law of Attraction, if you state your goal as if you are already on the road to success, then your mind will believe it and make it happen. Consider the difference between the following two messages that we might tell ourselves. On the surface, they seem to mean pretty much the same thing. To the mind, however, they are total opposites. Which one do you think sends a more powerful message to your higher self, and in the right direction? Which one could potentially create a negative result?

> *Admonishing:* "Don't buy clothes that you don't need!"
> *Encouraging:* "Each day I am becoming smarter about purchasing only the clothes that I really need."

Do you see the difference? By the way, this works on others, too! Try this on your child or your partner/spouse. For example, how many times have you told your child, "Don't interrupt," only to have her continue to interrupt? Next time, try this: "You are getting better and better each day about waiting your turn to talk. Keep up the good work!"

I had the opportunity to try out the Law of Attraction with my daughter one day as she was practicing cartwheels in our basement. Just before one attempt, she exclaimed in frustration: "I'm terrible at this. I'm never going to get this!" Then her brain literally guided her body into a "terrible" cartwheel in which she landed squarely on her bottom. Unable to resist this teachable moment, I explained that her brain had literally brought on that outcome itself. I suggested that she declare, before each cartwheel, "I'm getting better and better at this each time!" Lo and behold, her cartwheels did get better and better. That is, until we went outside to the rough ground and she had to start all over again! At that point, being on new terrain, she had to redevelop the confidence that she had just attained inside.

Across many different real estate investing situations, I have discovered the power of staying positive. From navigating the roadblocks in a complicated property purchase to cleaning up our property after our "Tenant from Hell" moved out, and everything in between, the phrase I keep telling myself is this: "I'm getting better and better at this each time!" And it continues to be true.

Similarly, there is something called Ironic Process Theory, a term coined and studied by Daniel Wegner in the 1980s that explains why many of our goals—think New Year's resolutions—fail. According to this theory, our minds tend to see the big picture of what is being conveyed, especially in our world that is overflowing with distractions. We often don't hear, or we mentally overlook, small (albeit important) words like "not," "don't," and "won't." As an example, if we state a goal of "I will not eat junk food!" we will naturally start craving junk food and eat it. This is because we will have created an advertisement or billboard in our own minds that broadcasts "JUNK FOOD" and fails to convey that small, but critical, word "not." You will be much more successful if you state your personal goal (or even your directions to your kids) in the positive. For example, consider this alternative: "I am becoming better and better about choosing healthy foods to nourish my body."

Try to pose for yourself this task:
not to think of a polar bear, and you will see that the
cursed thing will come to mind every minute.

FYODOR DOSTOEVSKY
Russian novelist (1821–1881)

Put Your Goal in Your Face

Napoleon Hill, of the last century, was one of the best-known writers on the power of the mind in achieving our goals. He coined the word "auto-suggestion," defining it as "the agency of control through which an individual may voluntarily feed his [or her] subconscious mind on thoughts of a creative nature, or, by neglect, permit thoughts of a destructive nature to find their way into this rich garden of the mind." In other words, we can control our thoughts, and our thoughts determine our destiny.

He recommended a few key actions. For starters, he urged writing down one's goal and posting it in an obvious place so that you are reminded of it on a daily basis. This could be your bathroom mirror, the dashboard of your car, or even as a reminder on your computer or smartphone. He also recommended saying the goal out loud to yourself at least once or twice daily.

Most importantly, Napoleon Hill spoke of the importance of passion. In his seminal book, he writes: "Your ability to use the principle of auto suggestion will depend, very largely, upon your capacity to concentrate upon a given desire until that desire becomes a burning obsession."[1]

It helps if you can put things in your environment that help you keep your goal in the forefront of your mind. This is because, no matter how important your goal is, there is a natural, albeit self-sabotaging, human tendency to put off important tasks. For example, most of us experience this tendency with seemingly arduous tasks such as creating budgets, consolidating 401(k) accounts, and setting up wills. Getting your first rental is an equally important item on this list.

The thing is, if we put something off long enough, it simply doesn't happen. In fact, and odd as it is, it seems that the larger or more financially significant the goal, the greater the tendency to procrastinate, probably due to our feeling overwhelmed and intimidated. This is why it's good to post reminders, even sticky notes, around your personal world until you've achieved your goal.

As a last word on procrastination, with rental property it really doesn't pay to delay. Consider that the sooner you get your first rental, the sooner the renters begin paying off the mortgage, and the sooner you will achieve the Ultimate Goal of owning a fully cash-flowing asset for your new and truly diversified retirement plan.

Develop a Mantra or a Theme Song

I'm going to share with you my secret for achieving a major goal: Develop a mantra or find a theme song. Say it, sing it, and listen to it as much as humanly possible. Cast it into the background of your brain. In fact, you know how you can sometimes get a song stuck in your head and you can't get it out, no matter how hard you try? Well, this is the opposite. In this case, you want it in there.

You are but the product of your thoughts.
What you think you become.
MAHATMA GANDHI

One of my favorite motivational songs is Rachel Platten's "Fight Song." I very intentionally play that song so much that the words and tune literally run through my mind almost all of the time. Over time, the song has made its way into my subconscious brain and has become an underlying electrical current within my mind. It subliminally fuels me and helps me keep my major goal at the forefront of my mind. (To easily play it on repeat, simply look up "Rachel Platten, Fight Song, one hour loop" on YouTube.)

You might have your own favorite song that you find particularly motivating. Whether it's the *Rocky* theme song from the '80s ("Eye of the Tiger"), or Alicia Keys's "Girl on Fire," find the song that works best for you. If these don't cut it for you, check out my website, www.GetaChicken.com, for a list of other motivational song ideas.

Rachel Platten's "Fight Song" played a major role in my efforts to get back in shape. When I first started jogging again, I began with just two "Fight Songs," jogging out for one song and then back home for the next—which was only 6 minutes and 52 seconds, round trip. Perfect—no excuses. I knew I could do anything for 6 minutes and 52 seconds. I did this for a couple days and then I cranked it up to four "Fight Songs," playing them over and over on my smartphone as I ran. After a while, I bumped it up to six "Fight Songs," and then eventually eight and then nine, and so on.

It's best to start with a goal that you think you can accomplish. With running, I only bump it up little by little. In fact, whenever I get back from a run, my daughter asks me, "How many 'Fight Songs' did you do today, Mama?" (I eventually progressed to running a 5k [roughly ten "Fight Songs"!] and then a half marathon [too many "Fight Songs" to count!].)

When using this method to achieve your real-estate-related Level I, II, or III Goal, it is usually best to break your goal down into pieces. Use your song of choice as motivation to get you through the first action step, and each next action step, until at last you have achieved your goal.

We've actually found this energetic, action-oriented, and positive song to be helpful in raising our daughter. Since she has been exposed to the song (a lot!), she knows it very well. Whether it is learning to ride a bike, passing the deep-water test, or cleaning her room, she enjoys calling whatever goal she's working on, at the time, her "Fight Song" until she's achieved it. Then she finds a new "Fight Song" for her next challenge. Sometimes it takes a bit of encouragement on our part, which is fine. We *all* need encouragement. But the self-confidence and pride she gains from achieving her "Fight Song" *is all hers.*

When your desires are strong enough, you will appear to possess superhuman powers to achieve.

NAPOLEON HILL

Persevere

Another life lesson came during a fierce round of the Dora the Explorer memory game with my daughter. About halfway through the game, she became frustrated because she realized that I had accumulated more matches and therefore I was "winning." In an attempt to teach her another valuable life lesson, I reminded her: "The only way to have a chance at winning the game is to keep on playing the game. Quitting is the same as losing." (When she's older, I'm sure she'll find this kind of advice thoroughly annoying and totally uncool, so I figure now's my big chance to dish it out!)

*If you love life, don't waste time,
for time is what life is made up of.*
BRUCE LEE
Hong Kong martial artist and filmmaker (1940–1973)

Quitting is the same as losing. This is true in all areas of life. Giving up because the task that lies ahead seems too unfamiliar or too hard guarantees only one thing: not achieving that goal. On the other hand, forging ahead with a plan, in spite of the fear, also guarantees one outcome: the chance of success, and possibly great success!

The three main obstacles to success are lack of perseverance, self-doubt, and fear. Gaining some experience will help with these obstacles. However, we need the opposites of each obstacle (perseverance, self-confidence, and courage) to gain that experience. And perseverance—or simply not giving up, no matter what—is the master key. If you can persevere in spite of self-doubt and fear, then you will gain experience, you will begin seeing results, and you will overcome any lingering self-doubt and fear.

As you can see, there is a tension between the mind and the body (or the realm of persevering by taking action). It is one of life's biggest Catch-22s. We lack the confidence to take action (due to inexperience), but we lack the experience to feel confident enough to take action. This is why your mind is your most powerful asset and why it's one of the underlying themes of this book.

It is vitally important to train your subconscious mind to believe this one very important thing: *If you decide that you absolutely* must *achieve your goal, then you know you will not stop until you've achieved it.*

In addition to mastering the domain of the mind, you need to master the domain of action, since any goal needs action of some kind in order for it to come to fruition. I'll spend the rest of this chapter going into this very important concept. The rest of this book is then dedicated to helping you come up with your action plan to achieve your Level I, II, or III Goal. Then you can get to work. Be accountable to your own goal so that one day when you are looking back on your life, you will view this period of time as a crucial pivot point between two radically different outcomes. And on that future day, you'll be grateful that you took action today.

RETHINKING OUR OWN CAPABILITIES

I have a quote taped to my kitchen cabinet that is a modified version of one first penned by Thomas Jefferson. It's a bit tattered because it's been there a long time. It reads: "To get what we've never had, we must do what we've never done." Thomas Jefferson's version (on the next page), actually speaks to the necessity of being *willing* to do something new and unfamiliar. Without a doubt, willingness is the first step. The version taped to my cabinet reaches beyond willingness to the necessity of *doing*. In other words, taking that action by doing what you've never done before . . . in spite of the fear.

If you've never owned a rental property, you may be terrified by the idea. In fact, the very topic is known to generate a lot of fear among those who have no experience in the area. In this book, I attempt to help you move past the fear and show you how rental ownership could eliminate even greater financial worries later in life.

If you want something that you've never had, you must
be willing to do something you've never done.

THOMAS JEFFERSON
Founding Father of the United States (1743–1826)

Overcoming Fear of the Unknown

I live my life by a theory that I've privately (until the publication of this book!) referred to as "corridor theory." My corridor theory has helped me forge ahead with different goals, in spite of not knowing all the answers, or even all the questions, in advance. Can you visualize a long corridor that leads toward your ultimate goal? Along this corridor, there are doors in front of you that you must open along the way to get to each next section of the corridor. There is no way to anticipate each new challenge that you might find behind each new door. In spite of the not-knowing, little by little you work your way down the corridor, opening doors as they present themselves. Eventually, you reach the end. You reach your goal!

If you let your fears stop you from opening the doors along the way, you never get to the end, where your prize is waiting. You must trust that you will be able to handle whatever challenge lies behind *only* the very next door in front of you. Don't worry about all the doors that may or may not be in your path later on down the corridor. Only focus on the door that is directly in front of you, and have faith that as you go, and as you overcome each new challenge, the more equipped you will be to open the doors that follow.

If ye have faith nothing shall be impossible unto you.

MATTHEW 17:20

I offer the corridor theory as a visual reminder to remain calm and steadfast when working on a goal that is new to you. Calling upon this corridor theory has helped me countless times throughout my real estate investing, and in life.

Overcoming Other Mental Roadblocks

Another roadblock to action is the belief that we must first get out of debt. Nothing could be further from the truth. Don't wait until you are out of bad debt to start creating good debt: this might never happen. Instead, create good debt to help you pay off your bad debt by creating a lifelong, potentially appreciating asset, one that you eventually own free and clear.

Also, don't let yourself be a victim to perceived lack of start-up capital. There is no reason to let this stand in your way. Check out chapter 7, "Borrowing a Chicken," on generating cash without ownership. These income-generating moves are a terrific way to meet two goals at the same time: getting out of debt (or saving money), and developing some familiarity with making money through real estate. Furthermore, as you will see in chapter 8, you may find that you have more resources than you first thought.

Another barrier to taking action is a belief that you are not educated enough to get started. Granted, a certain degree of education is important, as discussed in the next section in this chapter, but there comes a point at which you must just get out and do it. You don't want to fall into the trap of being a simple observer, or "tire kicker," forever. This won't get you any further ahead in life. In fact, the more tire kicking you do without making offers and going through with purchases, the worse off you will be in the future. This is because, later on, in addition to simply not having the financial options made possible by a rental property, you also will know deep down that it didn't have to be this way. You may regret having not pushed through your fears.

There are a number of natural fears that scare people off from securing their first rental. If you are not careful, these fears could be paralyzing. Here are some of the top fears that you should expect to bubble up:

1. I won't find a tenant.
2. The tenant might not pay their rent.
3. The tenant will destroy my property.
4. I will get phone calls in the middle of the night.
5. I'll be too busy to manage the property.

If you think your fears might be significant enough to prevent you from taking necessary action, remember that a good property management company can eliminate many of the fears. (See the *R.O.R.E. Blueprint for Success: A Step-by-Step Companion Guide* at www.GetaChicken.com for tips on selecting an excellent and trustworthy property manager.) On the other hand, some fears might be legitimate red flags that should be taken seriously. Do your homework as you look at properties, and walk away from any properties with legitimate issues (financial, legal/title, zoning, structural, major cosmetic, etc.). Again, see the *R.O.R.E. Blueprint for Success: A Step-by-Step Companion Guide* on evaluating and inspecting properties.

Do not wait; the time will never be "just right."
Start where you stand, and work with whatever tools
you may have at your command, and better tools
will be found as you go along.
NAPOLEON HILL

I can't claim that I was without fear when I bought my first rental. You will probably have some fear as well. Keep in mind that you should simply expect a certain degree of fear along every step of the way. With this expectation in mind, you won't be surprised by it when it hits you in the face. Nor will you feel the need to back out of a deal that could have been your saving grace in retirement had you gone through with it. Again, just be smart about it. Go over the numbers; bounce them off of professionals or experienced real estate investors whom you trust; expect some fear; and if the property continues to make sense, keep moving forward in a positive, results-oriented direction.

BUILDING YOUR KNOWLEDGE

The number one person with the greatest vested interest in your financial future is . . . (drumroll) . . . you! This means that *you* must be the one to take the reins. This will entail educating yourself, educating yourself some more, and then taking action.

I recommend starting with free resources. If you want to start online, check out the highly reputable website on landlording and property management called www.biggerpockets.com. In terms of books, I've shared my favorites in Online Appendix C, *Recommended Reading and Other Resources*, at www.GetaChicken.com. You can also explore your local library offerings and go to a local real estate–investor club meeting. Club meetings are a great way to learn from the experiences of others and to meet people with similar goals and aspirations. (As a side note to all the ladies in the house, many cities also have female-specific real estate investing clubs.) You can find experienced investors within these clubs who can help you analyze deals before you purchase. To find these clubs, simply google "real estate investment clubs" or look them up on a networking site like www.meetup.org.

Live as if you were to die tomorrow.
Learn as if you were to live forever.
MAHATMA GANDHI
Leader of the Indian independence movement and the inspiration for
nonviolent civil rights movements worldwide (1869–1948)

FINDING SUPPORT

Children need to know that you believe in them. As adults, we need that, too. And since you are the grown-up in this situation, you are the one who must take control of believing in yourself. To do this, it's essential that you funnel positive messages to your own mind constantly. If you have positive, supportive adults within your own personal sphere, all the better.

If you feel that you are lacking in this area, find people who understand your various life goals and can support you along the way. As I mentioned in the previous section, attending local real estate–investor club meetings is an excellent and quite natural place to start. And yet positive, proactive people can be found just about anywhere. You could decide to meet regularly with a friend or a small group of friends who are working toward their own personal goals, whatever they may be. You can each be a support or accountability partner to one another.

Better yet, find a buddy or put together a small group of friends who are also interested in protecting or even thriving in their golden years. You can work together through the *R.O.R.E. Blueprint for Success: A Step-by-Step Companion Guide* available at www.GetaChicken. com. You can help each other stay motivated. You can evaluate potential deals together. You might even end up partnering on a property. After all, owning half a rental is certainly a fine place to start. It's still infinitely more than owning nothing. Plus, the experience that this affords is incredibly valuable. If you decide to buy a second property, it will be that much easier for you.

Becoming self-sufficient doesn't mean doing it all on your own. It simply means being the conductor of your own orchestra. From time to time, you will most likely need to employ various experts across a range of different areas, such as:

- A real estate agent
- A mortgage broker (one who can get you the best rates)
- A title company or real estate attorney
- A tax accountant (CPA) who is familiar with real estate investing
- A good home inspector (one who will be thorough and take his or her time walking you through the house)

- An insurance company (for both homeowner's insurance policy and a landlord "umbrella" general liability policy)
- A handyman who is honest and can tackle most issues and can be available on short notice
- A property manager (optional)

It is best to find these people through word of mouth. Other landlords and investors are probably the best resource. Take the time to interview these professionals and ask for references so you can lower your chances of discovering the hard way that they're no good. You may want to steer clear of hiring friends or relatives, because if things don't go as they should, it could be difficult or awkward to confront them and potentially destructive to your goals, the relationship, or both.

Sources of Bad Advice

You certainly wouldn't look for legal advice from your plumber. And you wouldn't seek plumbing advice from your lawyer. (Even though each might feel inclined to dish out such advice in casual conversation!) When it comes to buying and managing rental properties, it is amazing how many people love to share their opinions, even when they have no experience at all on the subject. Here are three reasons you should be careful when you receive such advice.

First, anyone who is not investing in real estate for the long term themselves simply has no business providing guidance on the subject. Advice is most relevant from those who can speak from personal experience. Rather than accepting advice based on your friend's friend's experience (or your friend's friend's friend!), get that individual's phone number and talk to him or her yourself. There is probably a good amount of wisdom you can gain—both negative and positive—by having an actual conversation with that person.

The second reason not to take advice from those who are not long-term real estate investors is because there is a ton of unwarranted fear circulating on this subject. Yes, there are challenges, and yes, it involves work at times; however, we learn from the challenges and we benefit from the work in the long run. The future payoff, in terms of owning an income-producing asset, is unbeatable. Again, instead of indulging the fears of those who are inexperienced, seek out wisdom from those who are.

Even though misery loves company, there is nothing more miserable than settling for misery just because everyone else has done the same.

K. KAI ANDERSON

The third reason is simple. How *dare* they squash your dreams and goals!?! Don't allow them to do this to you. Nothing is more depressing than seeing someone's ambition or passion in any area of life squelched by a naysayer. And when it comes to securing your future economic needs by converting an existing home into a rental, or purchasing a new rental, the long-term consequences of *not taking action* could be dire. If this person is your spouse, encourage them to read this book with you from the beginning. (My wife was very skeptical of real estate until she began seeing that it meant we will *actually* retire one day.)

As you begin opening up the conversation beyond your inner circle of close family and friends, you will discover many individuals across every walk of life who own rental property. You'll also find people who used to own rental property. You'll notice that some of these former owners wish they'd stayed in the game. Others may be glad to be out; however, I'm not sure they will maintain this opinion in their older years when they are still working, or as they chip away at a visibly shrinking nest egg. The takeaway here is that everyone will have their own recommendations, based on their own unique set of experiences. The truth is, you can learn from them all.

Beware of Scams!

There are many real estate–investing classes, programs, seminars, coaching lessons, and even "boot camps" out there. Many are legitimate, but just as many may be either total scams or simply hyper-expensive for what they are worth. This section aims to help you sort out the lemons from the sweet oranges. I, and many people I know, have benefited from a little hand-holding when getting started in real estate. However, you want to stay away from courses that smell like fish. They could burn you financially and destroy your faith in real estate investing.

First, let's look at one way in which a common training scam works. Using radio, television, postcards, Google Ads, or even the Goodyear Blimp, an instructor or company offers a free introductory class to the public. Their hope is that you will later enroll in their follow-up course, at cost, sometimes substantial cost. Note that this is not a red flag in and of itself. This is simply a form of marketing. On the other hand, if you are taking a free (or even paid) introductory course and the instructor starts trying to "empower you" by having you contact your credit card company to raise your credit limit, then you are most likely sitting in front of a scam artist. At this point, I would get out of there as quickly as possible. You can be sure that, toward the end of the session, the instructor will start dropping hints that you should pay for an expensive follow-up course with your credit card, while attempting to reassure you that the results of the course will far outweigh its cost.

When I was getting started in real estate, I would never pass up a free training session. This means that I've been witness to many courses, and spiels for courses, some seemingly legitimate and others downright fishy, with price tags ranging from a couple of hundred bucks to more than $30,000! Regrettably, I did end up purchasing a couple of products that were grossly overpriced for what I received. However, and thankfully, I did not fall prey to the most egregious of all scam attempts that I witnessed. I had enrolled in a free two-day seminar sponsored by the "Enlightened Wealth Institute." It sounded pretty awesome at the time. It also seemed legit, given that a best-selling author's name was attached to it. Indeed, the first day was packed with information! Our homework that evening consisted of a few items, including contacting our credit card companies to request that our credit limits be raised. The second day involved a hard sell for a course priced at over $30,000! They claimed we would make our money back within the first couple of months. You can now find countless reviews and personal stories on sites like Bigger Pockets and the Ripoff Report of how this company cheated people out of thousands of dollars and sometimes even people's entire life savings.[2,3,4,5]

In her e-book *The Guru Manifesto*, Vena Jones-Cox, a seasoned investor and past president of the Cincinnati Real Estate Investors' Association (REIA), the Ohio REIA, and the National REIA, provides additional tips for sorting out the legitimate courses from the worthless ones.[6] For instance, if the refund policy is the mere three-day minimum that is required by most states, then do not purchase the product. Legitimate courses will have refund policies that are at least thirty days or, in some cases, even unlimited. Legitimate instructors stand by their product. Scam artists, however, bet on your not opening up, or otherwise initiating, the course within the first three days, leaving you stuck with a rotten apple and an expired refund policy.

Another red flag is a training program—and its table of contents— that are impossible to check out before you purchase. In Vena Jones-Cox's own words, "If you can't view the contents of the course because they're online, or because it's shrink-wrapped, be especially careful that the return policy is generous, and that you understand any 'gotchas' in that policy."

Diligence is the mother of good fortune.
BENJAMIN DISRAELI
Two-time British Prime Minister (1804–1881)

Use common sense. If something seems too good to be true, it probably is, *even* if it is connected to a celebrity or well-known author. Also, if it seems too expensive for your personal budget, it probably is. It is best to avoid purchasing a seminar on the spot. The speakers do a phenomenal job of hyping you up. They usually suggest that their "low price" is only available for a limited time. If you are really tempted, and not wanting to lose a great deal, do some quick online research on your phone. Google the name of the presenter and the name of the course with the word "scam" or "complaints" to see if anything pops up. However, keep in mind that this method is not foolproof. Some legitimate courses have had their reputations tarnished by a couple of disgruntled individuals, while other dishonest courses have continued conning people out of their hard-earned money by simply changing their business name.

To summarize, you can often identify fraudulent real estate courses from the following three questions:

1. Did the instructor suggest raising your credit limit and/or paying with a credit card?
2. Did the course fail to offer a money-back guarantee of at least thirty days?
3. Are the course and its table of contents impossible to view prior to purchase?

If you are considering a training program, *and* if the answer is "no" to each of the above three questions, *and* if you can afford it within your current budget, then you just might have a legitimate course *for you*. Legitimate courses can be well worth their money. For example, I was very happy with the in-person approach of the bricks-and-mortar Investors United™ School of Real Estate Investing in Baltimore, Maryland. You can also find courses through your local real estate–investor association meetings and through the online discussion forums at www.BiggerPockets.com. Investor clubs can be good sources for finding high-quality training programs, since most clubs vet the courses before sharing them with their members. Finally, investor clubs and Bigger Pockets can be valuable resources, in and of themselves, because of human interaction (both in-person and online) with other individuals who genuinely want to share knowledge with no strings attached.

PART THREE

THE CHICKEN

How to Protect Your
Retirement Dreams with
Real Estate

7

BORROW A CHICKEN

How to Make Money in Real Estate Without Actually Owning Property

orrow a chicken? I know this sounds weird, but you can make money legitimately in real estate without actually owning property in your own name. Borrowing a chicken has to do with leveraging resources you already have and leveraging other resources.

Start by doing what's necessary; then do what's possible; and suddenly you are doing the impossible.
SAINT FRANCIS OF ASSISI
"Patron Saint" of All Living Things (1182–1226)

Regardless of your age, if you have very little in retirement savings or other savings, you probably want to start by earning some extra money with real estate. This money can be used to pay off any existing consumer debt you may have, build an emergency fund, and/or start a launch pad for your first real estate purchase. Of course, extra cash can also be used to expedite the payoff of your existing mortgages as well.

The two main ways you can earn some extra dough, especially as you are preparing the rest of your game plan, are to:

1. Generate quick, steady income (and hopefully some pleasant company) by renting space in your own home.
2. Create cash flow by setting up a "lease/sublet" in someone else's home.

RENT OUT SPACE IN YOUR HOME

Whether you own your own home or rent someone else's, one of the easiest ways to come up with a little extra cash is to rent out extra space in your home. House-sharing is an excellent and very commonly used strategy to generate a little extra money in exchange for the work of finding roommates with whom to share a home. While it is most common among young people, house-sharing is also becoming more and more common among persons of all income levels and age groups, thanks in part to the recent rise of a number of online resources that have made the concept attractive, safe, and easy to implement.

Your first step is to decide whether you prefer more frequent, shorter-term stays with multiple individuals, and little to no ongoing personal relationship; or an ongoing commitment and an in-house relationship with a housemate. This decision will affect how you market your space and screen your tenants.

If you decide to go with *multiple, shorter-term arrangements*, you can use Airbnb (www.Airbnb.com) or other similar websites to rent out your extra space on a nightly or weekly basis, much like a bed-and-breakfast. With Airbnb, you have a couple of choices. You can rent out an extra room, with shared bathroom and kitchen privileges, for someone to use while you are also in the home. Alternatively, you can rent out your entire home for use while you are out of town. If your goal is to earn a little extra cash, then you can even make arrangements to stay somewhere else, temporarily, and hand over the keys to your whole house or apartment on an as-needed basis. This can be a very lucrative strategy if you live in an area where there are times of high demand, such as college graduations or when large events or conventions take place in your town.

*Regard it as just as desirable to build a chicken house
as to build a cathedral.*

FRANK LLOYD WRIGHT
American architect (1867–1959)

To rent space in your home on a temporary basis, you will want to take some nice photos and list your home or your extra room on www.Airbnb.com or a similar website. Airbnb has a screening process that includes a requirement that users upload their driver's license. You can also require additional levels of verification such as providing references, connecting to social media accounts like Facebook, and so forth.

In spite of the recent popularity of Airbnb, there are many reasons why you might prefer to go with a *longer-term housemate or housemates (as a house-share)*. For one thing, whether you are young, old, single, coupled, divorced, widowed, parenting, or empty-nesting, you might discover that having a friendly person in your home can brighten your days and make your mealtimes more interesting. We know this from firsthand experience after having rented out our finished basement on a couple of occasions to different (mature) college and graduate-school students.

If you are in need of extra cash and have some space in your home that you're willing to sacrifice, your first step is to decide that it is not beneath you. There is no shame in sharing your space. Think of it as generosity! You are helping someone else out just as much as they are helping you. (Before deciding to do this, however, be sure to research local laws regarding renting space in your home.)

You may want to start out with a short-term agreement, for example one or two months, in order to see how it goes with a given individual. You can mention this in your ad and discuss, up front, that the agreement can be extended if the situation seems to be working for both parties. Take some nice photos and list your space for rent on www.Craigslist.org, another website, or with a real estate agent who lists rental properties. You can also use Facebook or word of mouth within your network of friends and family to find someone compatible to share your space.

Screen your new housemate just as stringently as you would screen a tenant for a rental property. This includes a background check, credit screening, references (including current and past housemates), and the like. For detailed information on how to screen and select quality housemates (and tenants) for your property, be sure to review the *R.O.R.E. Blueprint for Success: A Step-by-Step Companion Guide* available at www.GetaChicken.com!

As a part of your screening, get to know the person before they move in. Have them to dinner. Also be sure to visit them in their current home. Doing so will provide valuable information to you about their state of cleanliness and orderliness and whether they might be a good fit. If they currently have housemates, it will also help to see how they get along with those people as well as how they talk about them when they are not there.

Last but not least, don't be a rescuer! As you get to know your prospective housemate, if there seems to be something wrong with the person, there probably is. If you sense that they will not be able to pay their rent on time (as evidenced by whether they can pay their security deposit and first month's rent at one time), don't let them move in. If there seems to be a lot of drama surrounding this person and their social relationships, stay away. Otherwise you will soon become part of the drama. If they have a negative personality, or even some random personality trait that you think might drive you insane, a polite "I don't think this will work out" will do. If they appear to use alcohol, cigarettes, pot, oregano, or anything else beyond your comfort level, then your answer again should be "no." You will be sharing your personal living space with them, and you have every right to pass and wait for a better fit.

If everything checks out and they seem to be someone who you might enjoy, or at least get along with, then there is no harm in giving it a try for a month or two, with the option to extend. To be on the safe side, be sure to first lock away your valuables and all paperwork that contains account numbers and personal information. Also, be sure to check your local laws about the nuances related to renting space in your home.

Most people are taught to live within their means. . . .
Try pursuing the means to live your dreams.
GARY KELLER

LEASE/SUBLET: RENT OUT SPACE IN SOMEONE ELSE'S HOME

The lease/sublet is a win-win-win arrangement. Under the lease/sublet strategy, you rent a property from one person and then rent it out to one or more other people for a higher amount. You are the middle-person. You are simply a tenant signing on with an owner, *with the owner giving you permission* in your signed lease to sublet the property to another tenant or to multiple individuals in the form of a house-share. This is a win-win-win arrangement because it can be incredibly helpful to owners who are out of state or otherwise too busy to find tenants for their property. You also provide some of the property management duties, such as arranging for maintenance and repair-service people, without being liable for the cost.

The second win is for your tenants. House-shares are a terrific way to provide affordable housing to the community. You create a group of a few individuals (sometimes coming as friend-pairs or groups) to rent by the room with shared access to all common areas. Your tenants will pay significantly less in a house-share than they would in a studio or one-bedroom apartment in the same area. Plus, many people love being a part of an instant community. This can be an awesome social benefit if they are new to town or otherwise "starting over" in life.

The third win is for you. The lease/sublet will boost your monthly cash flow and help you get some landlording experience at the same time. You can use the additional income to accelerate the payoff of any debt that you may have, to build up your reserves, and to save up for the purchase of a long-term real estate investment. The best part about an arrangement like this is that you are not responsible for the cost of any of the repairs or maintenance. Meanwhile, if you don't own any other rental properties yet, the lease/sublet will boost your comfort level with many aspects related to "managing" a property.

I put "managing" in quotes because you are not technically assuming the role of property manager. In this strategy, you rent a home from an independent landlord, and then, with the owner's permission, you rent it out to others. It is critical that you do *not* sign a property management agreement with the owner. Property management agreements should be saved for the professionals. I learned this lesson the hard way, which I will share with you shortly! However, as a side note, you should know that as you gain comfort with landlording, you will find friends and acquaintances coming to you with requests to manage their properties. Sometimes they may even find themselves pleading with you to help them manage their space! If there is enough margin, you could propose the lease/sublet as described in this section. Otherwise, the answer should always be a firm "No, thank you. I recommend you call a professional property management company."

We learned this distinction the hard way when we agreed to help an acquaintance find roommates for her and her husband's house-share. To keep a long and painful story short, we foolishly agreed to sign a short property management agreement that they had pulled from the internet rather than doing a lease/sublet agreement. I secured roommates for their home, and a couple months later the owners suddenly decided to sell their property. Without giving the required two-month notice, they told the tenants they had to move out. Understandably, one of the tenants felt that his rights were being violated and he reacted by suing the owners.

The owners, who had been so friendly up to that point, then threw me in front of the oncoming bus. They filed a lawsuit with us, deflecting all responsibility that was rightfully theirs onto me as the "property manager." At this point, fearing thousands of dollars in court fees, with the very likely outcome of being held personally liable in the end, I kept it friendly with both sides and negotiated a deal where both the owners and I would each pay the displaced tenant a sum of money to cancel the lawsuit. This was an expensive lesson, which I hope will benefit you as well. The lesson is this: never, *ever* sign a property management agreement with your name listed as the property manager (even if it is with a friend or family member!) unless you are an actual professional property manager. In the end, it's what's on paper that matters, and it can bite you on the bottom if you're not careful!

While the lease/sublet move may sound a lot like being a property manager, the risk is much lower. The difference is that under the lease/sublet you are simply another tenant who happens to be subletting the home; the owner is still ultimately responsible. However, if you've signed something saying that you are the property manager, then all legal responsibility falls on you: property registration, inspections, maintenance, safety, and virtually everything else.

If you choose to take on a lease/sublet, then you should know that it takes a fair bit of time and energy to establish. Therefore, it is best suited for those who have the time (especially in the beginning) and who live fairly close to the property. Check local laws on subletting a property and putting together a house-share before proceeding. As always, keep track of your income and expenses and report both to the IRS at tax time.

A number of factors are essential for a lease/sublet strategy to work. You need a good property, a good property owner, and good tenants. First, you need a nice-looking, well-maintained property with multiple rooms (ideally, four or more) in a desirable area. To find your property, simply look for "for rent" postings on Craigslist, in newspapers, and on bulletin boards at local cafés.

To make it worth your time, the income minus total expenses must be well into the positive. The rent you pay to the property owner should be for an amount that is at market value or slightly below. On the other side of the equation, I've found that it works out best, from a financial point of view, when there are four or more bedrooms, rented separately in the form of a house-share, rather than renting as a whole house or apartment. Be sure to check city- and county-level laws before you do this, because in some cities or counties no more than four unrelated persons are allowed to occupy a property. However, in other areas this number might be as low as two. This lease/sublet strategy might not be realistic if there are fewer than four rooms because the sum of the rooms may not be higher than the going rate for the entire home.

Equally important is the property owner. The owner of the property must be fully on board. He or she must know exactly what you plan to do and must agree to it. Out-of-town landlords are the best candidates, because you will be simplifying their lives. You need an owner who is willing to make any necessary repairs or minor cosmetic upgrades that are or become necessary, in order to attract and keep quality tenants. Also, the property must not be managed by a property management company. You will be serving as the middle-person, and it is unlikely to make sense if there is a property manager also in the middle.

Finally, you need great tenants. If you are in a popular area, it will be easier to find excellent tenants. If you are in a university area, then your work will be that much easier, because younger people are more inclined to join a house-share. When renting by the room, it is most challenging to find your very first tenant. By definition, the first person to sign on will be someone who is willing to take that initial risk of committing without knowing their future housemates. You need to hold out for someone you believe will be *well liked by others*. When it comes to house-shares, personalities matter. Many prospective house-share tenants care more about the personalities of their prospective housemates than they do about the home itself. Plus, the personalities of the people you find will determine the personalities of the others who agree to sign on.

The first step in putting together a lease/sublet is to enter into a long-term lease with the property owner, for example for three years or more. Getting everything set up for just one or two years may not be worth your time, especially if you need to furnish the common areas. For your protection, negotiate with the owner to add a clause to the lease stipulating that you don't begin to pay rent until you have secured tenants. Also, be sure the lease with the property owner specifies that you plan to sublet the property to other individuals on separate or joint leases. Finally, be sure to specify in writing that the owner is responsible for all costs related to maintenance, repairs and necessary cosmetic improvements over the course of the lease.

Second, you will enter into separate room-share leases (assuming you are renting by the room). This time, you will be the sublettor and they will be the tenant. As always, you should require that the tenants get renters' insurance and list you (and the owner) as additional insured.

Few people realize that luck is created.
ROBERT KIYOSAKI

Here is how this worked for us: I contacted a landlord with a non-local phone number who had a four-bedroom property listed for rent in a very trendy neighborhood and within walking distance of a university. This neighborhood has a main street on which artsy boutiques, trendy restaurants, salons, and spas are popping up all the time. The property owner was worried about finding a tenant quickly enough to cover his mortgage, as he lived in another state. I explained on my initial call that I would be interested in renting it from him for his asking price of $1,600. I also mentioned that I would like a long-term lease of five years (which was music to his ears!) and that I would like permission to sublet it out, by the room. He said he had never heard of anything like this, but he was open to giving it a try.

We then entered into a typical lease agreement, using his standard rental lease, with him as the landlord and myself as the tenant. On this agreement, we crossed out the section of the lease that indicated "no subletting" and replaced it with a clause to indicate our mutual agreement of my intention to sublet the property out to other tenants either as a whole or on a "room-by-room" basis.

At this point, the owner completed some repairs and provided a whole housecleaning and painting of some key areas. I had lobbied for this in order to make the home more appealing to potential tenants. I then posted the rooms for rent on Craigslist and furnished the common areas, for little to no cost, using resources such as www. freecycle.org and www.craigslist.org (always going to the free section first, and settling for a low-cost purchase if absolutely necessary). I've been happily surprised with the quality of some of the items that we've been able to get for absolutely no cost at all.

We furnished the home and provided a security system, utilities, and Wi-Fi for the tenants in an amount totaling about $350 per month. At the writing of this book, the amount we receive in rent from these "all-inclusive" rooms is $2,525 ($575, $650, $675, and $625 for the four rooms). This means that our monthly cash flow from this property is $575.

Incoming rent:	$2,525
Outgoing rent:	–$1,600
Outgoing expenses:	–$350
Total monthly cash flow:	$575

The monthly cash flow from this real-life example is not too shabby for a few hours of initial setup. If you were so inclined, you could put a few of these lease/sublet deals together and even call it a part- or full-time job.

While there are great benefits to the lease/sublet strategy, remember that this move will not increase your ultimate net worth. At the end of the day, you will not enjoy any of the other benefits of the property besides the immediate cash flow it provides. The potential appreciation, the tax benefits, and the ultimate ownership of a property without a mortgage will never be yours in an arrangement like this. In addition, it comes with the same risk of vacancy (see chapter 3, Risk #3) as when you own rental property in your own name, which is why you need a property in a hot area, multiple rooms, and an owner who is willing to keep it in a nice state of repair over your long-term lease. With all these considerations in mind, however, the lease/sublet is a powerful strategy that could get you closer to your goal of owning rental property by simultaneously creating income and property managment experience.

There's only a small difference between living a great life in your head and living a great life in reality, but that small difference makes all the difference. People who lead great lives allow their big thinking to direct them to action.

GARY KELLER

8

OWN A CHICKEN

How to Get Your First (or Next) Rental Property

This chapter is all about getting your chicken: that is, your own egg-laying rental property. As you'll see in this chapter, whether you are seeking your first rental, your second, or your fifth, there are many different ways to acquire it. You can:

1. Find the golden chickens in your life
2. Do a traditional purchase
3. Think outside the box (or chicken yard!)
4. Put your nest egg to work
5. Put your chicken to work

If this sounds mysterious, don't worry. I'll explain each of these five general ways in this chapter. Keep reading! Buying or acquiring your first (or next) rental may not be as hard as you think.

*Our only limitations are those we set up
in our own minds.*
NAPOLEON HILL

FIND THE GOLDEN CHICKENS IN YOUR LIFE

There are many ways to acquire rental property without actually spending money of your own. You just need to find the golden chickens that are already in your life. As you will see, these moves are not rocket science, nor are they the privilege of the elite class. These are quite basic moves. They are the building blocks behind many investors' success, both in getting started and in continuing to build financial safety, comfort, and even self-sustainability for the long term.

Move (and Keep Your Old House as a Rental)

If you own your own home, the easiest way to acquire your first investment property is simply to move and convert your existing house to a rental. In fact, as you will see from reading the stories of real-life people I call "not-chickens" in Online Appendix B, this is without question the most common way most of the people whom I interviewed for this book acquired their first rental. (It's also how we got started ourselves.) Converting your existing home into a rental is an excellent, fairly simple, and relatively affordable way to acquire a rental property without actually purchasing one from scratch.

Many people assume they need to sell their house when they buy their next one. This isn't necessarily true, especially if you are able to take advantage of a low-down-payment mortgage (see the "Think Outside the Chicken Yard" section of this chapter) or another low- or no-down-payment strategic move as described in this chapter. Many people also fear that tenants will destroy their beloved home. The cure to this fear is a matter of shifting one's mindset from viewing it as a home to thinking of the property as a long-term investment. The house is still the same house—it's just that its function has shifted.

Converting your existing home into a rental makes sense in many life stages. Perhaps you are midlife and eager to move up from that starter home that you purchased when you were younger. Maybe you've finished raising your children and are ready to downsize. Or perhaps you've been relocated or you've accepted a job in another state. Whatever the case may be, and whether you are planning to move near or far, consider hanging on to your home and renting it out rather than letting go of it.

The main deciding factor should be whether the expected rent will cover your anticipated expenses. Since you know your home intimately, you probably already have a pretty good idea of the expenses. The next step is to do your research to get a feel for what your home may be worth in terms of the market rent. If you have reason to believe—after checking with a realtor or doing your own research on Craigslist, Zillow, or another rental platform—that the rent will be greater than your mortgage payment and other expenses, then the decision is easy. Keep it. In fact, it is a brilliant way to get around the fear hump in terms of going out and purchasing an investment property from scratch. Simply converting an existing home into a rental can significantly ease that transition and speed up your achievement of the Level I Goal.

If you wish to move and keep your existing home as a rental, it is essential that you contact your mortgage holder. Explain why you would like to move. If you have a Federal Housing Administration (FHA) loan, you are probably fine as long as you've occupied the house for at least a year. Other types of loans can vary. However, it is important that you talk to your bank in advance, because with some loans, if the lender discovers that you've moved, they have the right to call the loan due in full. It's always safest to call and get permission, in advance, before you move and rent out your home.

I should mention here that there is a powerful piece of the U.S. tax code called the "Primary Residence Exclusion" (PRE), which allows you to sell your home without paying capital gains taxes, as long as you meet certain criteria.[1] To qualify, you need to have lived in your home for at least two of the past five years. In addition, the profit from the sale of your home must be less than $250,000 if you are single, or less than $500,000 if you are married and file jointly.

Many people assume that they need to buy a more expensive new home for themselves in order to take advantage of the PRE. Others just assume it's something they *should* do. The truth is that, if you decide to do a PRE, you can do whatever you like with the proceeds. If you are considering a move, I encourage you to consider all your options.

The first option is probably the most common use of the PRE: Sell your first home, tax-free, and use the proceeds from the sale to afford the down payment on a next home, usually (though not necessarily) of a higher price tag. Depending on your stage of life and if, for example, you are aiming to move to an area with better schools, this might be a very real priority. However, keep in mind that if you do this, you may be trading one liability for a greater liability (with a potentially more expensive mortgage, tax bill, utility bill, etc.). That said, since there is no limit to the number of times you can benefit from the PRE, you can always sell your new home down the road (after at least two years), tax-free, and then downsize and/or buy an investment property with the proceeds.

This brings us to the second option. If the numbers work out, you can keep your existing home and turn it into a rental property. If you choose this option, you will have converted a liability (since your house costs you money each month) into an asset (by generating monthly income). Plus, depending on your income, this could lower your income taxes each year or increase your refund, due to your being able to write off the depreciation and other deductions. (See the "Taxable Income" section of the *R.O.R.E. Blueprint for Success: A Step-by-Step Companion Guide* available at www.GetaChicken.com.) If you convert your home to a rental, again, there is flexibility. You can still sell your property using the PRE if you do so within three years of operating the home as a rental (as long as you lived in it for at least two years prior to that). If you are past the three-year mark of renting it out (assuming, again, that you lived in it for the two years prior to that), then you have the option of trading into another investment property using the 1031 Exchange, another tax-free method for selling property, which is discussed later in this chapter at length. You can also keep the property as a rental, indefinitely, and continue to pay off the mortgage so that it may provide extra income and additional options further down the road.

As a third option, you can sell your home and purchase another investment property, tax-free, using proceeds from the PRE. Simply use the profit from the sale of your home to buy a single-family home, multi-family house, or apartment building. If you go with a multi-unit option, you can live in one of the units, if you want to, although you don't have to, of course.

Table 8.1 shows the comparison between the three options just discussed. If you like the idea of the second or third option, don't forget to run your numbers! (Again, check out my free Cash Flow Analysis [CFA] Tool at www.GetaChicken.com.) Remember, it's only an asset if the rental income is equal to or greater than all of the monthly expenses, combined.

TABLE 8.1. COMPARISON OF THE TYPICAL "PRIMARY RESIDENCE EXCLUSION" (PRE) MOVE VERSUS TWO OTHER OPTIONS (ASSUMING RENTAL INCOME SURPASSES RENTAL EXPENSES)

	SCENARIO 1: PURCHASE ANOTHER HOME (USING THE "PRE")	SCENARIO 2: CONVERT YOUR 1ST HOME INTO A RENTAL PROPERTY AND BUY A 2ND HOME	SCENARIO 3: PURCHASE AN INVESTMENT PROPERTY (USING THE "PRE")
YOUR FIRST HOME:	Sell your liability	Convert your liability into an asset	Sell your liability
YOUR NEXT HOME:	Purchase a new liability	Purchase a liability	Purchase a Level II or III Goal asset
NET RESULT:	1 liability (with potentially higher expenses)	1 asset + 1 liability + Lower income taxes (or greater tax refund)	1 major asset + Lower income taxes (or greater tax refund)

When Two Hearts Become One

It is often the case that when two formerly single, divorced, and/or widowed individuals fall in love, they each have their own home. Rather than seeing this as a problem, see it as an opportunity! Instead of selling one house and moving into the other, consider keeping one as a rental. Even better, start fresh in a new home together and keep both properties as rentals. Just because two hearts become one doesn't mean that two houses must also become one. Instead, let them become three!

Save the Family Home

Have you, or you and your siblings, recently inherited the family home? If so, I recognize that this inheritance comes with the loss of someone who may have been very dear to you. It may be hard to let go of the home that is filled with memories. In fact, I believe you should seriously consider keeping it, especially if it is completely paid off. Even if it's not, if the potential rent is equal to or greater than the monthly expenses and/or if it will be paid off within the next couple of years, then you should seriously consider keeping it as an asset. You may want to hire a property management company if you are worried about the work involved in managing it or unfairly burdening one sibling. A property manager will take on the job of finding a tenant, collecting rent, attending to repair needs, and depositing money directly into your and your siblings' bank accounts each month.

Save Your House from Foreclosure

If you are at risk of losing your home to foreclosure, time is of the essence. For whatever reason, if you can no longer afford your payments, then you may have a couple of options. The first option is to create extra income by renting out a room or part of the house and informing your lender about this plan to become current on your payments.

Another option is to rent out your entire home. The simple fact that you can't afford your payment doesn't mean there isn't someone else out there who can. If you are at risk of losing your home and if you can rent it out for at least your monthly mortgage payment, I urge you to not passively let the bank take your home. Instead, consider *quickly* renting another (more affordable) place for yourself, cleaning up your home, and renting it to someone else. Note that if it feels too tight, financially, it may work out better to rent out the rooms in your home separately as a house-share to generate substantially more income (see chapter 7). Again, notify your lender of your plan to become current and check with your local property registration office to be sure you are in compliance with local laws and filing requirements.

Saving your home and renting it out will benefit many people. Your new tenant will benefit from the housing that you are able to provide. You will benefit by not destroying your credit, by keeping your home for the long term, and by converting your home into an asset. Your neighbors, and their property values, will also benefit by your avoiding foreclosure. Eventually, you will find yourself actually making money off the house that you once came so close to losing.

Save Your House from a Custody Battle or Loss in Divorce

If your marriage or significant relationship is on the rocks, you may want to try to do something to save it. Whether it's getting healthy, getting counseling, enrolling in an Imago workshop, or checking out "hot yoga," you just never know. It just might be possible to resuscitate your relationship. But . . . if "over" means over, then, if you own a home with your ex, you will need to decide what to do with that home. Assuming you are still capable of making decisions together, then you might want to consider keeping it as a rental and hiring a property manager. The property manager can issue two separate checks (or direct deposits) and two separate sets of monthly reports. Depending on your relationship with your ex, this may or may not sound like a realistic idea. If your ex wants nothing to do with you *or* the house, then by all means take the house (as long as the cash flow works out positively)! You can turn it into a rental or house-share yourself if there is positive cash flow and make lemonade from this lemon-like situation.

Use a Home Equity Line of Credit (HELOC)

Whether you're buying your first investment property, or a next one, a common and powerful strategy is to use the equity in a property that you already own as funds for the down payment on the next. You'll see from reading the stories of other "Not-Chickens" (Online

Appendix B) that many of the people I interviewed have used this strategy to advance to the Level I, II, or III Goal and enjoy a consistent stream of income in their retirement years.

There are generally three ways to leverage your existing property to purchase rental property, without having to come up with money out of your own pocket, for the down payment:

1. Refinance your existing property (personal residence or rental property) at a higher amount and use the additional funds for a down payment and closing costs.
2. Obtain a tax-deductible home equity line of credit (HELOC) on your primary residence.
3. Open a tax-deductible home equity loan on your primary residence.

Your choice will depend on a number of factors. If you have a low interest rate on your first mortgage, or if you are several years into your loan, refinancing may not be the best route. In this case, a second mortgage in the form of a HELOC or home equity loan may be best. The downside to a HELOC, however, is that the rate is variable and as interest rates go up, so does your payment. If it's possible to refinance at a lower term length—for example, jumping from a thirty-year term to a fifteen- or twenty-year term—while also pulling money out at a low interest rate, then this would be an ideal scenario for refinancing.

Your options will depend on what interest rates are doing at any given time, a factor that is out of our control. Get a range of numbers from your mortgage broker or banker (such as the interest rates and associated payments at different term lengths and total values) and spend some time doing the math. Remember, too, that doing a refinance will cost you some money, including the cost of a new appraisal. Ask your mortgage broker or banker if any of the closing costs and fees can be wrapped into your new mortgage and what that associated payment would be. In the end, it may very well be worth it; however, these costs should be factored into the equation.

It is essential that you do some additional math before initiating this move. Your cash-flow calculations must always include the total amount financed from all sources. In this strategy, the total amount financed should include your new property's primary mortgage payment plus the extra amount that you will be paying each month on your existing property. Add both together and complete the Cash Flow Analysis (CFA) Tool on my website at www.GetaChicken.com to determine your monthly cash flow and return on investment *before* moving ahead with this move.

The housing crash that began in 2007 taught us all an invaluable lesson about converting property equity into cash to pay for fun stuff that doesn't pay you back. However, recall from chapter 4 that debt used to purchase an income-producing asset is actually good, productive debt. When you take action, in this way, to purchase a good, cash-flowing rental property, then you are joining a select—but not altogether uncommon—club of individuals who have created lasting wealth by leveraging resources they already own . . . in other words, by using the golden chickens already in their lives.

TRADITIONAL PURCHASE

Using a Real Estate Agent or Broker

The most common way to purchase rental property is with the assistance of a licensed real estate agent or broker. Working with a good real estate agent can be very advantageous. For one thing, real estate agents are professionally trained in all aspects of the home-buying process, so you can rely on them to be your advocate through the entire process, from the offer to the inspection to the closing table. They also have access to those little black lock boxes that are on every house listed on the retail market. Your agent has access to literally all homes that are listed on the market, even bank-owned foreclosures. This means that you and your agent can go and view a ton of properties and get a feel for the market, even in just one afternoon.

Here are some tips for using a real estate agent or broker to buy a rental property:

1. You are not required to sign an exclusivity agreement with a buyer's agent to work together. However, as a matter of integrity, if you want to submit an offer on a given property, it is important that you go through the agent who originally showed it to you.

2. Know what you are looking for, share your criteria with your agent, and be stringent about adhering to your criteria. (Use the *R.O.R.E. Blueprint for Success: A Step-by-Step Companion Guide* at www.GetaChicken.com to design your criteria for your ideal rental property.)

3. View as many properties as possible in your key geographic areas. Get to know your key areas inside out and get to know the types of properties, and their property values, that are typical in those areas. If you start feeling pressure from your agent to hurry up and "just buy something," or if he or she hints that you are wasting their time with low offers or multiple viewings, then you should simply quit and find another agent.

4. Make offers on many properties. Ultimately, one will be accepted.

5. Keep your offers low. Aim for 20 percent lower than market value. Only make offers or accept counteroffers that fall within your cash-flow parameters.

6. Say no to creep! What this means is that if your upper bound is $200,000, don't go a dollar over $200,000. You need to stay in control. Otherwise, in negotiations you will find yourself agreeing to a higher and higher price tag. If this property doesn't work out within your financial parameters, don't worry. Another one will.

7. Never get attached to investment property. If it doesn't make sense financially or isn't practical for some other reason, just move on.

Mortgages

The mortgage is what separates real estate investing from other means of investing. The power of real estate is that you are able to borrow money from a bank, or another lender, to purchase an income-producing asset, that would otherwise be completely unattainable, but that you eventually own in full. Not only *can* you use a mortgage, almost everyone *does*. In fact, nobody expects you to buy a property with "all cash," though that certainly is an option if you happen to have the means and want to hit the ground running in terms of strong cash flow.

This means that rather than footing the entire cost of the property, we only need to come up with money for the down payment. The down payment is the portion of the purchase price that you typically must pay from your own funds to demonstrate to your lender that you will not walk away from your obligations to pay your mortgage. The bank likes you to have a little skin in the game. Whether it's for our personal residence or our Level I, II, or III Goal, it is the mortgage that makes our dreams possible. It is the paying off the mortgage(s) that makes our dreams come true (The Ultimate Goal).

When it comes to purchasing a property that you plan to use for rental purposes, if you go with a conventional bank you have very few options in terms of the amount you will be required to provide as a down payment. Usually you will be required to provide 25 percent of the purchase price. That said, there are a number of options for a no- or low-down-payment mortgage on an investment property, which I cover, later in this chapter, under the section "Think Outside the Box (or Chicken Yard!)."

Remember that the short-term goal of your investment property is to generate cash flow. The lower your down payment is, the higher your mortgage and the lower your cash flow will be. This means that if you use a lower-down-payment program, be sure the cash flow works out. As long as your interest rate is fixed and you are in an area with strong rental demand, you should have no issues meeting your monthly mortgage obligation and paying down your mortgage with the Ultimate Goal of paying it off.

Understanding Your Monthly Payment

Each monthly payment is typically composed of four elements: principal, interest, taxes, and insurance. These four elements are often referred to by the acronym PITI.

- *Principal:* The P in PITI is your principal. This is the portion of your payment that goes toward the total amount remaining on your loan (also referred to as the principal) with each payment. The principal component of your PITI directly lowers the amount that you owe on your total balance each following month. Over time, as the overall amount owed becomes smaller, your equity increases (assuming your property does not go down in value).

- *Interest:* The first I in PITI refers to the "interest," or the amount you pay to your lender, with every payment, for the privilege of having a mortgage with them. It's basically your (non-optional) way of saying "thank you." After all, it's your lender who has made it possible for you to purchase this property in the first place. It's an expensive thank-you, but ultimately this thank-you will be paid by your tenants, on your behalf, with their monthly rent, as I've explained in chapter 3, "Why You Need a 'Chicken.'"

    You can shop around for the best interest rate to a certain degree, or pay "points" at the time of closing for a lower rate. A point simply refers to an amount of money equal to 1 percent of the total loan amount. Two points correspond to 2 percent of the mortgage amount, and so on. Each point typically reduces the interest rate by one-eighth to one-quarter of a percentage point.

- *Taxes:* The T in PITI refers to the real estate property taxes that are owed to your jurisdiction. They are usually held in escrow by the bank and folded into your mortgage payment. Bear in mind that as your property value increases over time, it is not uncommon for your property taxes to creep up as well. If you believe your assessed value (for taxes) is higher than the actual or appraised value, then you usually have the right to appeal.

- *Insurance:* The last I in PITI refers to insurance, specifically property or homeowner's insurance. All conventional lenders require borrowers to insure their property, in the event the asset experiences some kind of trauma that affects its value. You can shop around for different insurance quotes to find one that works best for you.

Be sure to enter all these factors into your Cash Flow Analysis (CFA) Tool at www.GetaChicken.com. You can plug in the various terms of the loan (term length, interest rate, and total loan amount) and it will calculate your actual monthly payment (principal and interest portions only).

Selecting Your Mortgage Term

Whether you are purchasing a new property or refinancing one that you already own, you generally have four options regarding the length of your mortgage: ten, fifteen, twenty, and thirty years. These terms equate to the number of years until your asset will be completely paid off. Shorter terms get you to your goal faster, but have higher payments, which lessen your monthly cash flow and increase your overall risk.

Make sure to compare the payments associated with different mortgage options carefully before selecting a product. If you are concerned about safety, you will want to select a more conservative term like a thirty-year mortgage. This keeps your monthly payment lower than the alternatives and increases your cash flow. You always have the option of paying it down faster, if you like, for example at the payment amounts associated with the ten-, fifteen-, or twenty-year mortgages. However, when cash flow is tighter or if times get tough, you can always simply resort to your actual thirty-year payment amount.

If you have sufficient potential cash flow, you may want to select a lower-term mortgage so that you can be ambitious in paying down your principal and building equity. This will help you achieve your

Ultimate Goal of having one income-producing property owned free and clear. If you are a Level II or III Goal investor, you can eventually use the equity to purchase additional property.

Note, however that it is often the case that a ten-year mortgage has the same interest rate as a fifteen-year mortgage. This means that there would be no clear advantage to locking yourself into a ten-year rate with a higher payment. Rather, it would be better to secure the same rate on a fifteen-year product and then, if your cash flow allows, pay the principal down using the payment amount associated with the ten-year mortgage. The fifteen-year mortgage will be safer and provide more flexibility than the ten-year mortgage, at no cost in the interest rate.

Creative Mortgages—A Cautionary Word

I love creativity! From the arts to ideas to inventions to personalities, creativity is what makes each of us interesting. It's what makes our whole world interesting. However, when it comes to mortgages, you are better sticking to the plain vanilla "fixed-rate mortgage" of whatever length best meets your needs.

There are several different types of so-called "creative" mortgages that had a heyday during the housing bubble of 2005–2007. In large part, they (and the unscrupulous mortgage brokers issuing them) are responsible for the bursting of that housing bubble.

The three most common creative mortgages are balloon, interest-only, and adjustable-rate. At best, unlike fixed-rate mortgages, these products offer no protection against the forces of inflation over time. At worst, they can be downright lethal.

Balloon mortgages are mortgages in which, after a set period of time making payments, the entire balance of the mortgage becomes due in full, also known as "ballooning." Some people get balloon mortgages intending to sell or refinance before the remainder of the loan is due. However, if the market changes and the value of the property drops, you may not be able to go through with this plan and could be at risk of losing the house. No matter what your intentions are, it is risky to get a balloon mortgage.

Interest-only mortgages are mortgages in which the principal is *never* paid down (unless you proactively make extra payments). Also, similar to a balloon mortgage, interest-only mortgages become due in full at some specified point in the future. In other words, you could be stuck with the original balance of your mortgage forever, like a mouse running on a treadmill, until it is suddenly due in full. As I shared in chapter 3, in the "Equity" section, an interest-only mortgage comes with the risk of forcing your property to achieve equity only through appreciation, rather than by paying down the principal. In the event your property doesn't appreciate in value, and assuming you don't make extra payments toward the principal over time, the interest-only aspect of the mortgage makes it impossible to gain equity, reduces your options for selling or refinancing, and elevates your risk.

Finally, an adjustable-rate mortgage, also called an ARM, is a mortgage that boasts a low "introductory" interest rate and monthly payment. However, after a given period of time—usually two to five years—the rate and payment can jump up, sometimes dramatically. From there, the rate can continue to increase gradually. There is a "lifetime cap," or maximum amount to which it can increase, but this cap can be significantly higher than the introductory amount. Sadly, some lenders allow borrowers to qualify for these mortgages based on a seemingly affordable initial payment, rather than the lifetime cap, resulting in an unaffordable mortgage a few years down the road.

To wrap up, I cannot emphasize enough that you want a fixed-rate mortgage for your personal and investment properties. Don't gamble on these other dangerous types of mortgages that I just described. If you currently have one of these mortgages, it would very likely be in your best interest to refinance as soon as possible into a fixed-rate mortgage. If necessary, you can mix and match a bit—for example, by refinancing two properties and using equity in one to pay the other down to a level that allows it to be refinanced. (See chapter 10 for more refinancing ideas.) Get as creative as you like, but do get out of your creative mortgage.

Whether you think you can or you can't, you're right.

HENRY FORD

THINK OUTSIDE THE BOX (CHICKEN YARD!)

Become the Queen Bee of Your Own Hive

If you don't mind living next to your tenants, you can massively jump-start your Level I, II, or III Goal by buying a multi-family investment property. The property could be as small as a duplex or as large as an apartment building.

What makes this move particularly doable is that you can buy your multi-family personal residence using a low-down-payment program (3 percent) from the Federal Housing Administration (FHA). If you purchase a property that is in the Fannie Mae HomePath program or the Freddie Mac HomeSteps program, investors are allowed to purchase with only 10 percent down. See www.homepath.com and www.homesteps.com for more information and a list of available properties across the United States.

If you are a veteran, a Veteran's Administration (VA) loan can provide 100 percent financing (in other words, no down payment) if you purchase a duplex, triplex, or four-unit apartment building, as long as you plan to live in one of the units yourself for at least a period of time.[2] This can be an excellent way to get started in real estate investing, while paying virtually nothing out of your own pocket as en entry fee and having your rental income pay for your own living expenses. Note also that while VA loans cannot be used to purchase single- and multi-family properties that you do not plan to reside in, they can be used to refinance a rental property that you formerly occupied as your personal residence. VA loans are available even to those who have been affected by bankruptcy or foreclosure.

The immediate appeal of this strategy of buying a multi-family home and living in one of the units is that the rent from the other

unit(s) either partially or totally covers your mortgage, thereby reducing your own personal living expenses dramatically! The mid-
range appeal is that, after some time, you can either stay or move out.
Either way, you've got your chicken. The longer-term appeal is that
once your mortgage is fully paid off, you will have a fully cash-flowing
multi-unit property and you will have achieved the Ultimate Goal.

This strategy of buying a multi-family house and living in one of
the units is an extremely common way that people get started in owning rental property. This method can work well for so many types,
whether you are younger or older, newly married or freshly divorced,
nonparents, parents, or empty-nesters. In Online Appendix B, I share
the stories of many individuals and couples who got started in this
way. John started as a young single guy looking to save a little money.
Deb was newly divorced with two young children looking to start
over in a more strategic way. Also check out Alfredo and Rose's story
in which, as newlyweds, they literally leapfrogged over the Level I
and II Goals and settled right in with the Level III Goal in one almost
breathtaking move. Finally, this is an awesome plan for those who are
a little older in years to downsize their living space while acquiring
an income-producing asset at the same time. See Enid and Marisha's
stories at www.GetaChicken.com, both of whom are forward-thinking
later-life Queen Bees who have created a way to live humbly in their
own "all expenses paid" self-built communities.

Similar to the house-share concept, a main benefit of a multi-unit
property is that if one tenant leaves, the vacant unit only accounts for
a portion of the total income rather than the entire income, as it
would in a single-family house. Plus, the CapEx costs will be less than
they would be across multiple homes since the components are all
under one roof. See chapter 3, Risk #4, the Risk of Costly Repairs, for
a review of CapEx. This move comes with two potential headaches.
Tax time could be difficult, since personal and investment expenses
will need to be separated. Also, you might regret living right next
door to your tenants! On the other hand, like Marisha, you may actually enjoy the convenience and potential sense of community that
it provides.

People who have used this strategy have literally catapulted their investment goals. After a period of time, usually after a year or two or whenever their lender gives approval, some people move and find a tenant to take their unit. Those with aggressive goals, like John, Deb, Enid, Marisha, and Jake and Mary, have repeated the process with additional multi-family homes. See Online Appendix B for their amazing stories and additional warnings and suggestions.

Buy Your Home with an Investor's Eye

Another strategy for cleverly acquiring a rental property is to purchase—with an investor's eye—a single-family home for yourself. The idea here is to use the three critical rental-property criteria (see the *R.O.R.E. Blueprint for Success: A Step-by-Step Companion Guide* available at www. GetaChicken.com) to select a property. Then, after a certain length of time, you find a quality tenant, move out, and turn the property into a rental. Before you implement this strategy, it is important to talk with your lender about the length of time that you'll be required to live in the property before being allowed to convert it into a rental.

The reason this is a powerful strategy is because it costs less to buy a property that you plan to live in (single family, duplex, or multi-unit) than it does to buy one that you plan to rent out from the beginning without residing in it at all. You can get a better interest rate, and you are allowed to use a smaller down payment. Traditionally, the down payment is 20 percent, as compared to the 25 percent that is required for an investment property. However, there are plenty of programs that allow you to purchase a property for your own residence with much lower down payments than the traditional 20 percent.

For starters, many cities and jurisdictions have special programs for first-time home buyers. You can find these online by searching "First-time home buyer program" with your city or town name. Many areas also have special low-down-payment programs for teachers, police officers, or veterans. In addition, some areas offer "live-near-your-work" home-buying programs and some universities, hospitals, and companies offer similar programs as well. In addition, Table 8.2

shows a number of different loan options that are available to home-buyers as of the writing of this book.

TABLE 8.2. NO- AND LOW-DOWN-PAYMENT LOAN OPTIONS

DOWN PAYMENT BY TYPE OF MORTGAGE		SOURCE OF MORTGAGE	NAME OF MORTGAGE PROGRAM[3]
INVESTMENT PROPERTY	PERSONAL RESIDENCE (OR LIVE-IN INVESTMENT)		
N/A	0%	Veteran's Administration	VA Loan
N/A	0%	USDA	USDA Loan
10%	3%	Freddie Mac	HomeSteps
10%	3%	Fannie Mae	HomePath
N/A	3%	Fannie Mae	HomeReady
N/A	3%	Fannie Mae	Standard 97% LTV
N/A	3%	Federal Housing Administration	FHA Mortgage

The point of this section is to encourage you to be forward-thinking when you buy your primary residence. Rather than simply thinking of your immediate needs, or even thinking of it as your forever-home, if you buy a primary residence with an investor's eye, then you give your-self options that will last your whole life. Think of what other people, specifically your future potential tenants, will be looking for in a home and what rents they might be willing to pay. When permitted by your lender, and when it makes sense in your life, you will have the oppor-tunity to move out and keep the property as a long-term investment.

Check out the "Determine Your Criteria" section in the *R.O.R.E. Blueprint for Success: A Step-by-Step Companion Guide* available at www.GetaChicken.com to help identify the best financials and other qualities for this purchase. Table 8.2 shows a number or no- and low-down-payment options available for the purchase of a property in-tended as a primary residence (or, in the case of multi-unit properties, for combined investment and personal residence purposes). Compare these down payment options to the 25 percent that is typically needed for property that is purchased for investment purposes from the get-go and it is clear why this such a powerful strategy.

It is worth noting here that—unlike the loans issued in the housing crisis of the 2000s—Fannie Mae and Freddie Mac are now run by the government. These programs are primarily designed to help individuals, whose income supports a mortgage, but who have difficulty saving for a down payment. In the case of a duplex or multi-unit property, the income from the rented units is allowed to count toward your qualifying income. If you are using one of these no- or low-down-payment options to purchase a new primary residence, be sure that the interest rate is fixed and that your job is stable, to ensure that you can continue making the payments for as long as you keep it as a residence.

Purchase with Seller Financing

With seller financing, the seller plays the role of the bank. Also called owner financing or a "purchase-money mortgage," this move entails making payments directly to the person who is selling you their property, at a given interest rate, over a certain period of time, just as you would make payments to a bank. The main benefit to the buyer is that the terms are more negotiable than what you typically find with bank financing. Seller financing can be used for either a portion of the total purchase price of a property or the whole amount. In fact, everything is negotiable with seller financing. This is because the agreement is only between you and the seller. As long as both parties agree, the sky is the limit in terms of how creative you can get. Be careful, however, not to get into a creative mortgage, like one of the three types I described earlier in this chapter, where your payment jumps up after a period in time or where your entire loan is due after a specified time period. Be sure to run everything by an accountant before you proceed, and have a lawyer draft or review your seller-financing document.

Seller financing can come in handy if you have trouble qualifying for a standard mortgage or if you've maxed out the number of mortgages that you are allowed. Note that while most banks have a five-mortgage limit per borrower, some small banks (shared within the Online Appendix C, *Recommended Reading and Other Resources*) are less restrictive. There are also fewer closing costs at settlement since many of the loan origination fees are eliminated for the buyer, accounting for nearly 2 to 5 percent of the total loan price.

Seller financing has benefits for the seller, too, of course. These are good to understand as you pitch the idea to potential sellers and in the event you want to provide seller financing to someone else one day. First, if an owner is eager to sell, this expands the available options for the owner and allows him or her to avoid having to list the property. It also provides payments with interest and has the tax advantage of spreading out the seller's capital gains over multiple years, rather than taking them all in one lump sum the year of the property sale. Another tax benefit to spreading out the gains is that it may prevent the owner from getting bumped into a higher tax bracket. Finally, if the seller is older in age, seller financing can be a way to provide for one's loved ones by ensuring a continuous stream of income after death without them having to deal with property management.

While seller financing might sound like a gimmick reserved for late-night "no money down" infomercials, it is more common than you may realize. It is estimated that about 10 percent of homes sold in the United States involve some sort of seller financing.[4] And yet, keep in mind that in spite of the benefits, if you are able to strike a seller-financing deal, it is important not to sacrifice your criteria in terms of the quality of the home and your cash-flow requirements. You do not want to end up with the headache of "one person's trash" if they were unable to sell the property to anyone else. As an example, we once landed a seller-financing deal with the owner of a large rental property portfolio. This good-humored, older gentleman agreed to sell us his two-unit property, with financing of 80 percent of the purchase price. We put the property under contract with a $1,000 earnest-money deposit, fully refundable if we were not completely satisfied with the results of the property inspection. (See the *R.O.R.E. Blueprint for Success: A Step-by-Step Companion Guide* at www.GetaChicken.com for other essential escape clauses to include in your contract.) Indeed, the inspection revealed an excessive amount of deferred maintenance and old systems, basically a looming CapEx nightmare (see chapter 3), so we backed out and our deposit was returned.

Purchase Your Landlord's Rental

Are you currently renting either a single-family home or an apartment in a multi-family home that you wouldn't mind owning? Or do you have older kids or a college student who is renting a place that you would consider owning or even jointly purchasing with your daughter or son? If so, then a very smooth move for acquiring real estate is to approach the landlord about purchasing the property.

This is not such an unusual strategy. After all, in many areas, your landlord is actually required by law to give you the "first right of refusal" if he or she plans to sell their single family home. With yourself, or your grown children, as the "owner occupants," you will be able to get better terms than purchasing as an investment. For example, the down payment will usually be smaller and the interest rate will usually be a bit lower. Refer back to the "Buy Your Home with an Investor's Eye" section of this chapter.

Whether you approach the landlord or whether the landlord approaches you (or your daughter or son), you might want to ask the landlord about the possibility of seller financing. Since you are a known entity to the landlord and have ideally been making the rent payments faithfully and on time, the landlord/owner may be willing to provide a loan in place of a traditional lender's mortgage. This "seller financing" option, just discussed, means that you could potentially buy the property with a smaller down payment than you would need with a regular bank. Depending on the willingness and helpfulness of the landlord and if the property is owned free and clear of a mortgage (and your negotiation skills!), you may not need to come up with a down payment at all.

Remember, everything is negotiable. If your landlord trusts you and has no urgent need for the entire proceeds from the sale, he or she may be interested in providing some financing. Remind the landlord that if you default on your loan, the property would simply revert back to him or her. Make sure to have everything drawn up in writing and be sure that the property fits in with your ideal purchase criteria. (Again see the *R.O.R.E. Blueprint for Success: A Step-by-Step Companion Guide* at www.GetaChicken.com.)

After you are the proud owner of your landlord's property, you may want to use the house-share strategy of renting out extra rooms in your home, as discussed in chapter 7. Eventually, when it comes time for you (or your kids, if you are the parent) to move out of this home, you can keep it and rent it out or you can trade up into another property, tax-free, using the PRE discussed earlier. Whether or not you buy or rent your next home after you ultimately move out, you will likely be further ahead than if you had not purchased the property. Even if you become a tenant again, you will benefit from the tax advantages of owning investment real estate and you will benefit in the long term by having a cash-flowing asset with a mortgage that your tenants are gradually paying off on your behalf.

If there is something to gain and nothing to lose
by asking, by all means ask!
W. CLEMENT STONE
Entrepreneur and "New Thought" author (1902–2002)

Lease/Sublet with Option to Buy

The "lease/sublet with option to buy" is similar to the lease/sublet discussed in chapter 7, except you have the added benefit of being allowed to purchase the property within a certain window of time, if you wish. The lease/sublet with option to buy is a way of acquiring a property for a long-term investment rather than using it only as a time-limited source of monthly income.

The lease/sublet with option to buy is similar to—yet also different from—other real estate arrangements that you may have heard of, such as "rent to own," "rent with option to buy," and "lease option." Rent-to-own and renting with option to buy are most commonly used in reference to a tenant renting a home and having the option to buy it within a specific period of time, if they so choose. "Lease option" can also mean this; however, the term has been given new meaning by Wendy Patton, author of *Investing in Real Estate with Lease Options and "Subject-To" Deals*. Using her method, an investor can use a lease option to make money as a matchmaker between a buyer and seller in a rent-to-own arrangement.

However, our goal is to create sustainable income for the long term, and the lease/sublet with option to buy can be an excellent entry point for this goal. Before taking ownership, you have the opportunity to gain property management experience (if you don't already have it), test out the property (and discover any potential chronic issues), and test out the rental market, all while boosting your own personal monthly income or saving up for the down payment. It is critical that your agreement with the owner specifies that, as in a lease/sublet, he or she is responsible for all maintenance and repair costs during the period of time before you own the property. Then, if and when you decide that you want to move forward with the purchase, and assuming you are able to line up financing to purchase the property, you go to settlement with the seller, and the property officially becomes an important part of your long-term retirement portfolio. However, if, for any reason, you don't want to purchase the property, you do not have to exercise your option to purchase. At this point, depending on the structure of your agreement and your desires, you could either continue operating it as a lease/sublet or you could part ways with the seller.

You have a number of options for financing the purchase, should you decide to move forward. You can use conventional financing from a bank or mortgage broker. Or you can ask the owner of the property if he or she would be willing to provide financing. Your chances of a "Yes" are greatly enhanced if you are consistent and flawless in your rent payments (using automatic monthly withdrawal from your bank to ensure this!) *and* if you consistently maintain an attitude of respect and helpfulness with the owner. Some sellers may agree to provide financing, while others will be eager to sell their property, collect their money, and move on with their lives.

Share the Wealth (Partnering)

Partnering is a common financial strategy, especially among more seasoned investors. Equity partnerships mean that all partners are co-owners and are entitled to a share of the distribution of the profits (rather than working for a fee or a salary). Roles in an equity partnership can be shared and/or divided in any number of different ways. In one version, sometimes called an "elephant and mouse" partnership, one person ("the elephant") finances the property, while the other ("the mouse") invests his or her time in all aspects related to managing the property. They typically split the profits 50/50. This can work out equally well for those with more money but less time, as well as those with more time but less money.

There are many potential pitfalls to partnering, so it is best to sit down together and write down all the details of your agreement. Discuss all potential situations and worst-case scenarios that you can think of, and decide in advance how you would handle each. Meet with your own accountant and lawyer to further understand how things could unravel and how to best protect yourself and your personal assets if they do. Finally, an independent lawyer should draw up the understanding into a legal operating agreement, which should also be reviewed by your personal accountant and lawyer before you sign on the dotted line.

Surprise your doubts with action.
DANIELLE LAPORTE

PUT YOUR NEST EGG TO WORK

There are many ways you can purchase investment property using resources that you might not realize you have. When it comes to leveraging (and diversifying) your retirement accounts, you have a few options, though your choice will be guided by where your money currently resides. If you have a 401(k) or another type of employer-sponsored retirement plan, you can loan yourself money. If you have an IRA or self-employed 401(k), you can convert a portion of your account into a self-directed retirement account that allows you to invest in real estate. Finally, if you are over age 59½, you can use your retirement funds—wherever they reside—to buy a rental property. The following section goes into each of these options.

Loan Yourself Money from Your 401(k)

If you have a retirement plan through your employer, or former employer, then you are in possession of a valuable resource. The same is true if you have a self-employed "solo" 401(k). And yet, if you are like the vast majority of people, you will let that resource sit there on autopilot for decades, almost forgetting about it, while it builds slowly over time.

There is another option. And I'm not talking about early withdrawal. After all, pulling money out of these retirement accounts before age 59½ comes with a 10 percent penalty, a loss of money that is rightfully yours. Rather than withdrawing money early, I'm talking about a *very* different thing: loaning yourself money to purchase an investment property.

In this strategy, under current regulations, you can access up to $50,000 or half of your account value, whichever amount is smaller. You have the ability to use this loan any way you wish; however, I'm only recommending that you use it to purchase cash-flowing rental property. The interest rate is typically very low and—believe it or not—the interest payments go right back into your own account. You are literally a bank unto yourself in this move. You typically have up to five years to pay yourself back, which means that even though the interest rate is low, the payments are relatively high. Needless to say, the monthly loan repayment amount must be factored into the cash-flow analysis equation when you are deciding whether to undertake this strategy.

If you use this method to purchase a rental property, you will create two asset streams, from where there had formerly been just one. When you take a loan from your 401(k) or similar type of retirement account, you are literally giving yourself "seed money" for the down payment on an income-producing property. Then you are obligated to pay yourself back, on a monthly basis, over the course of five years or less. However, again, since you are both the lender and the borrower in this case, the small interest payment actually goes back into your retirement account.

If you opt for the relatively slow train of paying yourself back over the entire five years, then you use the cash flow from your rental to make the minimum payments. Then, if you were so inclined, you could systematically use this strategy to acquire a new rental every five years.

However, you don't need to take the whole five years to pay back your 401(k) loan. There are a few other options. For example, if you buy below market value, or if you improve your property in a way that increases its value, then you may be able to refinance the entire amount (your primary mortgage plus your 401[k] loan) into a new mortgage and pay your account back that way. You typically need to wait until the property has "seasoned" for at least 365 days before refinancing. This is because if you get an appraisal within one year after purchasing it, the appraisal will usually include the price that you paid for the property as one of the comparable properties.

Another option, if you have equity in another property, is to refinance that other property at a higher amount and use those extra funds to pay off your 401(k) loan. Again, be sure that the refinanced amount fits into your cash-flow calculations for your property or your overall portfolio.

Once you've paid back your 401(k) loan, you'll then have a 401(k) plus a rental property, rather than just a 401(k). See Figure 8.1. As you'll read in Online Appendix B, Jen and Rachel have used this strategy a couple times, as have we. It is an excellent way to put your retirement funds to work in achieving the Level I, II, or III Goal. Loan to self, purchase, improve, rent out, refinance . . . and—for the Level II and III Goals—repeat!

FIGURE 8.1. USING ONE RETIREMENT ACCOUNT TO CREATE TWO ASSET STREAMS

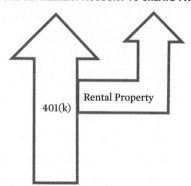

There are two main considerations when thinking about a 401(k) loan. The first is whether your numbers will work well enough to keep you afloat for the five-year period in which you are paying yourself back. If there is any uncertainty in your numbers—particularly in terms of the rent you will be able to charge—then you may not want to embark on this kind of move. Don't be overly optimistic when running your numbers. For example, always run your numbers with the rent at the lowest end of the realistic range. If they still work, then this could be an excellent way for you to acquire a property.

The second consideration is that the amount that you loan yourself will be taken out of the stock market until you have paid yourself back in full. This means that if there is particularly strong growth in the stock market, you will miss out on that period of escalation. On the other hand, stepping out of the stock market is not always a drawback. For example, if the stock market is in a period of either flat growth, volatility, or outright decline, then this move could be an excellent way to pull out temporarily by essentially moving your money to "cash" (out of stocks) while making it productive at the same time. The challenge is—of course—predicting whether stocks will go up or down, a task that befuddles even the most expert financial analysts! That said, the goal here is not to attempt to time or predict the market: The goal is to leverage your existing resources to acquire a tangible asset for a truly diversified long-term retirement plan.

As a last note of caution, please recall—from chapter 4—the difference between assets and liabilities. Loaning yourself your precious retirement money, to purchase items or experiences that do not generate income, will only put you further behind and jeopardize your long-time financial safety. This strategy described here is reserved only for the acquisition of cash-flowing rental property.

Self-directed IRA (Roth and non-Roth)

If you have a sizable IRA (either Roth or non-Roth), you might want to consider rolling a portion of it into a *self-directed Roth or non-Roth IRA*. Rather than leaving all your eggs in one basket, you can diversify by buying a cash-flowing rental property with your IRA funds, just as we did.

The self-directed IRA is a well-kept secret, known only to the most savvy real estate investors but available to all. The self-directed IRA allows you to control your own retirement funds, rather than simply parking your money with a mutual-fund company. Once you've transferred a portion of your IRA funds into a new self-directed IRA account, you are allowed to invest this money however you like. In addition to purchasing real estate, some self-directed IRA companies allow you to invest in other things such as stocks, precious metals (silver, gold, platinum), oil, restaurants, your best friend's start-up company, and the like. You can even play banker by lending money and collecting payments with interest.

In addition to the freedom to invest in creative ways under your own direction, there are other reasons that people like to invest with a self-directed IRA. The first is simply that this happens to be where they have the bulk of their savings. They may not have a lot saved up anywhere else, but they may have an IRA. These IRA funds can serve as an easy source of down-payment funds to broaden their retirement portfolio with the purchase of a rental property.

The second reason people like to invest with a self-directed IRA is that investments are protected from capital-gains taxes. This means that you can sell a property owned within your self-directed IRA without any tax consequences, and then reinvest your money in a next property or in another way. Even better, if your self-directed IRA is a *Roth-type*, then your investments are not subject to income tax when you withdraw them after age 59½. It is for this reason that a Roth IRA is typically far more advantageous than a non-Roth IRA.

If you are young and just starting out, it is a good idea to open up a Roth IRA or a self-directed Roth IRA and start socking money away every year. You can always convert a standard Roth IRA, managed by a mutual fund company, to a self-directed Roth IRA, later on, so don't waste precious time by worrying about the details. Get that Roth IRA open, start making contributions, and let them grow with the market.

It is important to note that you are strictly prohibited from combining your self-directed IRA funds with your own personal funds. For example, all expenses related to a property owned by that account must be paid by that account, and all income received from that property must go directly back into that account.

In spite of the tax benefits of the self-directed Roth IRA, there are some potential downsides to consider. First, because investments in an IRA are already tax-deferred, depreciation expenses within an IRA do not offset your personal taxable income as they do with other investment property. Also, expenses must be handled by the self-directed IRA management company or a property manager, which come with a fee and can make administrative functions somewhat complicated.

Additionally, there are two types of taxes that may adversely affect some investments in a self-directed IRA: Unrelated Debt-Financed

Income (UDFI) and Unrelated Business Income Tax (UBIT). UDFI is a tax that you pay for carrying a mortgage on a rental property rather than purchasing it solely with your retirement funds. The good news is that the tax is proportionate to the amount financed and can be lessened by deducting the property-related expenses. In years where there is no taxable income within the IRA, this tax does not apply.

The second type of tax, UBIT, affects those who use their self-directed IRA for active businesses, including fix-and-flip–type real estate ventures. It is essentially a tax assessed when an IRA invests in active income, instead of passive investment income such as rental real estate. This tax does not apply if, after renovating, you rent the home out for a period of time before selling.

With a property owned by your self-directed IRA, the rental income goes right back into the IRA account. It is not taxed annually, and if it is a Roth-type account, it will not be taxed upon withdrawal either (assuming withdrawal after age 59½). There is also no tax if you sell the property and reinvest the proceeds into another investment property.

I converted my Roth IRA into a self-directed Roth IRA in order to use the pool of money that I'd been growing over about fifteen years to invest in real estate. With this goal in mind, I purchased a property with "all cash" (i.e., no mortgage) for $75,000 in a neighborhood where purchase prices were typically between $120,000 and $140,000 at the time. The house was in desperate need of some renovation, bringing the total cost much higher than I'd originally planned. I hired a property management company, who rented it out for $1,300/month to start earning money back on the investment. I plan to eventually sell the property and redirect the funds from the sale into a multi-unit property, using a non-recourse loan and the UDFI tax that comes with it.

The *R.O.R.E. Blueprint for Success: A Step-by-Step Companion Guide* at www.GetaChicken.com has all the details on how to make this strategy work best for you. For more information on the self-directed IRA and whether it makes sense for your individual situation, consult with an accountant who has knowledge of and experience with self-directed IRA products.

Self-directed Solo Roth 401(k)

The Solo 401(k), also known as the Self-Employed 401(k) or the Individual 401(k), is a retirement plan for self-employed individuals. There are two types of Solo 401(k)s. The first type is the more common variety that is operated by a broker and involves investing in the stock market and mutual funds. The second type of Solo 401(k) is self-directed. Like the self-directed IRA, the self-directed Solo 401(k) allows you the freedom to invest in a variety of types of investments, including real estate.

The self-directed Solo 401(k) is actually more advantageous than the self-directed IRA for many reasons. For starters, the self-directed Solo 401(k) is not subject to UDFI or UBIT taxes, thus allowing more flexibility. Also, unlike the self-directed IRA, but similar to a typical 401(k), you are allowed to borrow up to $50,000 or 50 percent of your account value (whichever is smaller) from your account, without any taxes or penalties. In addition, the self-directed Solo 401(k) allows for higher annual contributions than the self-directed IRA.

Even better, in 2006 Congress created the Roth version of the self-directed Solo 401(k). This means that, like other Roth-type investment products, you can pay a small amount of tax up front, grow your account over time, and eventually withdraw your funds (after age 59½) tax-free. To repeat, you can legally buy and sell homes, rent homes, or conduct other investments, all without paying any tax on the earnings using the Roth version of the self-directed Solo 401(k).

With all these advantages in mind, you may be wondering, "Why would anyone choose a self-directed IRA over a self-directed 401(k)?" The answer is relatively simple. Where is your money? If you already have an IRA, then the self-directed Roth IRA is for you. If you are self-employed, then the self-directed Solo 401(k) is for you. If this is your case, you can simply roll over a portion of your existing 401(k) accounts (from previous employers) and/or your Solo 401(k) into your new self-directed Roth Solo 401(k) account and get started investing in real estate. As always, it is best to discuss your own particulars with an experienced accountant before you begin.

Tap Your Retirement Account After Age 59½

If you are over age 59½, then you have earned the freedom to access your retirement accounts without penalty whenever you like and for any reason. So, instead of leaving all your eggs in that one basket, you may want to use this opportunity to move some of your funds into rental property. Any time you withdraw money from your retirement account after age 59½, it is called a normal distribution, because there is no penalty. If it is a Roth product, then you may withdraw your funds in as few or as many different normal distributions as you like without paying any tax. If you don't have a Roth product, then you will need to pay income tax on your normal distributions.

As we discussed back in chapter 1, we are required to take regular withdrawals after age 70½ in what is called the RMD (required minimum distribution). This means that you have an eleven-year window (between ages 59½ and 70½) in which you are allowed to take out as much or as little money as you would like. Some people who have high account values on a non-Roth retirement account use the strategy of taking enough distributions during this eleven-year window so that both their balance and their tax bracket are lower once they are forced to begin withdrawing it regularly after age 70½. You will definitely want to consult a tax adviser to further understand how you will be affected by various IRS rules and how to best strategize your spending during these critical years.

The other factor to consider is that if your adjusted gross income from your RMD is over a certain amount, then you won't receive the Social Security benefits that you may be expecting. In this scenario, up to 85 percent of your Social Security income could be lost to taxes. This is something many people with higher retirement account balances may not take into account when they are planning for retirement, something that is also definitely worthy of a conversation with your CPA at least a few years before turning 70½.

For both of these reasons, this eleven-year window of time, from age 59½ to age 70½, is an excellent time to withdraw some funds to purchase rental property, without a mortgage, if possible, so that it can provide solid monthly income for you right away. An experienced property manager will lessen the work entailed and allow you to relax and enjoy your well-earned retirement.

PUT YOUR CHICKEN TO WORK

Trade Up with a 1031 Exchange

Once you are the proud owner of one or more rental properties, you are allowed to sell your investment property and buy another one, tax-free. Perhaps you want to trade your property for one that has more income potential. Maybe you have your eye on a part of town that is becoming "hot" where you feel there may be greater appreciation potential. Perhaps you have had a difficult time finding quality tenants for your existing property. Or maybe you want to sell your single-family investment property and purchase a multi-unit building to generate greater cash flow and achieve the Level II or III Goal. Whatever the reason, trading up using 1031 Exchange is an excellent strategy to sell one investment property, and buy another investment property, without paying taxes on the sale of the first.

This advanced move is called the "1031 Exchange." The 1031 Exchange gets its name from the piece of tax code to which it refers, and this code has a number of rules. I'll go over the most important ones here, though you should consult with an experienced accountant and title agent before embarking on the 1031 Exchange:

1. You must have owned the original rental property for at least one year plus one day.
2. The purchase price for the new property must be equal to or greater than the sales price of the original property, and all the proceeds from the sale of the original property must be directed to the purchase of the second rental property. Any of the proceeds that you don't direct into the new property is called "boot" and is taxable.

3. Both properties must be "like-kind" investments, which include virtually any kind of real estate held for investment purposes. It excludes personal residences, fix-and-flip properties, as well as other capital gains–type investments like stocks, bonds, oil, and precious metals.

4. Vacation properties qualify as replacement properties as long as there is an investment intent and as long as they meet both of the following two conditions for at least two years following the purchase: a) You rent it out at fair market rental rates to other people (not family members) for at least fourteen days each year; and b) You limit your personal use and enjoyment of the property to less than fourteen days each year or 10 percent of the number of days that it was actually rented out to other people.

5. If you are trading out of or into a multi-family home, in which you have been or will be residing, the 1031 Exchange only applies to the portion that can be considered investment.

6. You must enlist the services of a third party, called a "qualified intermediary," to aid in the transaction. (Often your title company or closing agent can either serve as a qualified intermediary or recommend someone.)

7. Within forty-five days after the sale of your first property, you must identify to your qualified intermediary up to three potential properties that you would like to purchase. The property you end up purchasing must be on this short list.

8. Finally, you have exactly 180 days (or one half of a year) to purchase one of the properties that is on your list.

With the 1031 Exchange, you direct the proceeds from the sale of one or more investment properties into the purchase of a higher-priced investment property. For the balance, you can either obtain a mortgage or negotiate seller financing. As long as your equity (the difference between the amount you owe and the ultimate sales price) on the property that you are selling meets the down-payment requirements of your lender, you will not need to come up with additional down-payment funds.

For example, imagine that you own a couple of properties and, after a significant period of time, you sell them both under a 1031 Exchange. The amount remaining after paying off the existing mortgages is $600,000. Whether your aim is to buy an apartment building or a vacation property (to be rented for at least two years), if the purchase price is $1,000,000, then since the amount of funds is greater than 25 percent of the purchase price, you will not need to come up with additional money for the purchase. You can apply the $600,000 toward the purchase and use a mortgage for the remaining 40 percent of the balance. Needless to say, you would only act on this advanced strategy after having an experienced real estate accountant verify that the income will cover the mortgage and all expenses.

Reinvest and Build Net Worth

In chapter 3, I explained net worth in terms of potential and kinetic net-worth energy. You put work into creating your potential, and then you manifest that potential, in the form of kinetic net-worth energy, the moment you finish paying off your mortgage. If you go for the Level II or III Goal, you will not only boost your cash flow, but you will also boost your overall net worth once the mortgages are paid off. In other words, achieving the Level I Goal of owning one rental property is an excellent measure of safety, but owning more rentals can be even more powerful because the total mass is greater.

One way to build mass is to accumulate more value, through more property. If you are younger, you will have more time in which to do this. If you have set a Level II or III Goal of owning more than one property, you may want to do what many successful people do: They reinvest their equity in one property by refinancing it, pulling cash out, and using that money to purchase an additional rental property. I did this, as did a great number of people I interviewed. See the stories, online, of Deb, John, Jake and Mary, and Catherine, to name a few.

For easy math, as an example, say you invest $20,000 into a $100,000 rental property in a middle-class neighborhood. See the Cash Flow Analysis (CFA) Tool, Form #5 at www.GetaChicken.com. In this example, the return on investment is 23 percent. Over time, if the property appreciates to $120,000, you will have made back your initial investment of $20,000 in the form of equity. At this point, you can refinance 80 percent of the new property value, by obtaining a new $96,000 mortgage on the property and pulling out the remaining 20 percent ($24,000) to reinvest in another property.

In theory, when you have periods of appreciating values, and assuming positive cash-flow analyses, you could do this exponentially, with one property becoming two, two becoming four, four becoming eight, and so on. In fact, in the words of Robert Kiyosaki, "Professional investors invest their money in an asset, get their money back without selling the asset, and move their money on to buy more assets."[5] Using this formula can have a significant impact on your net worth down the road and can catapult your achievement of the Level II or III Goal.

This chapter provided an almost dizzying array of options, from acquiring your first rental to buying your next rental(s) and leveraging what you have to ensure that your long-term financial plan—your nest egg—is shatterproof. The next chapter, "Hatching Your Plan," breaks these down and provides guidance based on your unique set of personal circumstances. Turn the page, and craft a plan that best meets your needs and circumstances and is *best for you.*

9

HATCHING YOUR PLAN

Strategies for Every Age and Level of Resource

N
ow that you have a mission—should you choose to accept it—
and now that you are armed with almost countless strategies
to acquire rental property (chapter 8), or even make money off
property you don't own (chapter 7), it is time to hatch a plan. In this
chapter, I break down these various moves by age and level of resource so that you can construct a strategy that is best for you.

This strategy chapter is divided into six sections, by the three age
groups and two levels of resource categories ("little in savings" and
"healthy amount of savings"). I've intentionally left the level-of-
resource definitions open to your own interpretation. The reason is
that it's all subjective. The meaning of any given figure depends on
your lifestyle, the spending habits of your spouse or partner, your
earning potential, and where you live, among other factors. For example, while $300,000 could be a grand sum for one person, it might
only buy a year or two for someone else.

I've broken down the strategies by three general age brackets: 20–
40, 40–60, and 60+. Those who are 20–40 include individuals who are
just starting out on their own, as well as young singletons, couples and
families. Those in the 40–60-year-old bracket are those, like me, who
are "midlife" and starting to think seriously about saving for retirement and saving for their kids' future college tuitions. Those in the

60+ age bracket may literally be looking retirement in the face, perhaps feeling an urgent need to develop a plan for the remainder of their lives.

Due to the urgency of the highest age bracket, I've actually presented the age categories in reverse order in this chapter. Keep in mind that these age brackets are meant to be approximate. Depending on what's going on in *your* life, the information in one bracket may be more fitting than the information in your actual age bracket; and therefore, you may want to read this chapter in full.

See Table 9.1 for a breakdown of optimal mortgage terms by age. As always, discuss the strategy that is best for you and your own circumstances with your accountant or other trusted adviser, preferably one with personal real estate investing experience.

To achieve your Ultimate Goal of owning rental property with no mortgage, you must first achieve your Level I, II, or III Primary Goal of actually *acquiring* one or more rental properties. That said, a *major factor in your ability to attain the Ultimate Goal* depends on the type of financing you use to purchase your property or properties.

In general, the older you are, the shorter the term you are going to want for your mortgage. For example, for those who are younger and have more time, the thirty-year mortgage often makes the most sense. However, if you are midlife, you may want a shorter mortgage to accelerate your Ultimate Goal of owning rental property debt-free. The same goes if you are over 60, of course. In fact, if you are over 60 and are able to purchase or otherwise acquire a rental property with no mortgage, this will probably be your best option. At this stage in your life, you probably want to enjoy the unencumbered cash flow made possible by rental property with no mortgage strings attached.

TABLE 9.1. OPTIMAL MORTGAGE TERMS BY AGE

	AGE BRACKET		
	20–40	**40–60**	**60+**
Ideal Length of Mortgage*	20–30 year mortgage	15–20 year mortgage	10–15 year mortgage, or no mortgage at all

*Assuming the cash-flow analysis reveals that the payment plus all other expenses are less than the rental income.

No matter which strategy you choose, be sure not to put *all* your savings in real estate. The goal is to *diversify* and create a monthly income stream. If you put all your funds into real estate, you are not diversified. It is also important to have funds set aside as an emergency fund, as discussed in chapter 3. The proportion of your savings that you want to invest in real estate should be a decision you make with your CPA and/or your "fiduciary"-type financial adviser. (Revisit chapter 2 for the important distinction between types of financial planners.) With that, we will jump into the first of our six overarching groups: those who are over the age of 60 and have little in savings.

According to the effort is the reward.
RABBI BEN HEI
Author of *Ethics of the Fathers*, 5:26

STRATEGIES FOR AGES 60+

Ages 60+ with Little in Savings

According to a 2015 U.S. Government Accountability Office (GAO) study, more than half of U.S. households age 55 and older have no retirement savings at all. And one quarter have less than $148,000 saved up.[1]

If you have little to no savings and are over age 60, it is understandable that you may feel particularly worried right about now, especially if you do not have a pension. However, feeling anxious, feeling bad about yourself, or feeling angry at the system (no matter how justified!) will not help your situation at this point. Worry, blame, and anger only tend to lead to rumination, which can lead to escalating levels of worry, blame, and anger. In the end, the one who will suffer will be you (and, by extension, your loved ones). What you need now is action. You need to take the reins of the rest of your life.

If you are over age 60 and have no pension and have very little in savings, your first order of business is to start building income. Whether you rent or own, the easiest way to do this without taking on another job is to rent out space in your home or make money from your other stuff. (Revisit the section on how to turn a liability into an asset, chapter 4.) You can use those funds to pay off your existing mortgage or other debt, to build up your emergency fund, or to save up for the purchase of a rental property.

Being over the age of 60, you also have a number of the options I shared in the last chapter. For example, if you own your own home you can tap the equity to purchase a rental, as discussed in Chapter 8. Being over the age of 59½, you can also withdraw some of your retirement funds, without penalty, for the purchase of an income-producing property. Another option is to downsize, even becoming a tenant in a more affordable place if necessary, and convert your existing home into a rental. Another way of downsizing is to do what Marisha does (see her story in Online Appendix B). If you own your own home, you can sell it using the Primary Residence Exclusion (discussed in chapter 8) to avoid paying taxes on the sale, and then purchase a two-unit or multi-family property, taking up residence in one unit while renting out the other(s). This strategy provides cash flow as well as community. The best part is that you can purchase a multi-family home using a low-down-payment program for residential purchasers if necessary (see chapter 8). If you have trouble qualifying based on your age, consider buying jointly with your adult children or another younger friend or family member. Joint ownership will also facilitate the transfer of assets once you eventually pass on. Needless to say, you should discuss the details of your particular situation with your attorney.

Once you purchase a property, you'll probably want to pay off the mortgage as quickly as possible so that you can get to the point of unencumbered cash flow, especially in the event that you want to, or need to, stop working. When it is fully paid off, you will have a solidly income-producing asset to provide a level of safety that would otherwise be nonexistent.

Ages 60+ with a Healthy Amount of Savings

If you are in retirement, or near to it, and you have a substantial amount of retirement savings, you are in the minority. In fact, did you know that, among households ages 55+ with any retirement savings, only 15 percent have over $500,000?[2]

If you are over 60 with a fair bit of a nest egg, your biggest decisions will be how many properties to buy and whether to purchase with a mortgage. Your Level I, II, or III Goal will determine how many properties to buy. Other factors will include the amount you want to spend and the type of property you want to purchase. If you have the resources, you may want to skip over the "four green houses" stage (as in Monopoly) and jump right to the "red hotel" ... or apartment building. If you feel inclined to do this, be sure to educate yourself further on investing in apartment buildings and find a buyer's agent who specializes in these types of properties.

Since you have a fair bit in savings and since your retirement-account funds became available to you at the age of 59½, purchasing property without a mortgage is particularly feasible for you. Furthermore, as discussed in chapter 8 in the "Put Your Nest Egg to Work" section, doing something major and practical with your money in the eleven-year span of time before you are obligated to start taking your required minimum distribution (RMD), at age 70½, is a great way to reduce the amount of money that you will be required to withdraw and therefore be taxed on (if your investments are non-Roth). If you purchase without a mortgage, then you will enjoy strong cash flow right from day one. This is the best option if you have the funds and don't want to wait or don't feel like you have the time to wait ten to fifteen years for a mortgage to be paid off. For example, if you have concerns about your health or possible disability, then this could be the path for you. Just be sure to enlist the help of a good attorney, accountant, and property manager—all of whom are tax-deductible—to help you get your ducks in a row.

Your attorney will help with all aspects of your estate planning, ensuring that you purchase the right way, right from the start, with a plan for your properties after you die. Your accountant will help you make decisions to lessen any tax consequences for yourself and your heirs. Your property manager will liberate you from all of the work involved in operating the property and keeping it rented. With these three professionals working for you, you can simply sit back and enjoy a steady stream of income generated by an asset owned with no mortgage right from the start. Furthermore, you can enjoy peace of mind in knowing that, rather than spending down your savings, you can live off your income-producing property and leave it to your surviving spouse or heirs so that they may ultimately benefit as well.

No matter how you decide to purchase your rental, be it with or without a mortgage, at this stage of your life you may want to consider hiring a property manager. Activities like unclogging toilets and showing properties to prospective tenants may not be how you want to spend your free time in retirement. The best decision you could make (second to your decision to purchase one or more rental properties in the first place!) is to hire a competent property management company. Your property and your property manager will allow you to earn sustainable income with minimal oversight on your part, even as you travel to far-off lands or lounge on a beach in Florida!

STRATEGIES FOR AGES 40–60

Ages 40–60 with Little in Savings

If you are between the ages of 40 and 60, and if you have little to no savings, you are not alone. However, at this point the odds are severely stacked against you in terms of your ability to quickly save enough money to live off of for the last third of your life. If you are in this group, I hope you hear the call loud and clear. As I see it, real estate may be your best option for a financially safe retirement and later-life financial security. If you have little to no savings and if you don't take action on at least the Level I Goal, right now, you could be setting yourself up for serious financial troubles later on. But if you do take action right now, you could set yourself up for a safe, comfortable, or even financially self-sufficient life once your mortgages are paid off.

Shatter the legacy that's holding you back.
DANIELLE LAPORTE

If you are starting out with very little, your first order of business is to begin making some money beyond whatever income you are already earning. Renting out space in your own home or someone else's, as discussed in chapter 7, is an excellent way to do this. You can use this cash to pay off existing consumer debt and build your emergency fund, a critical component to the next phase of your investing plan.

Once you've built your emergency cushion, your next order of business is to acquire or buy a rental property. There are two main methods for acquiring or buying a property with few resources beyond your emergency fund, both of which are described in detail in chapter 8. Virtually all the individuals I interviewed used one of these two methods to get started.

If you own your own home, the easiest method is to move and convert your existing home to a rental. You can move in with someone else, or better yet, buy a new home with one of the low-down-payment programs described in chapter 8. If you have equity, you can also refinance, pull money out, and apply it toward the purchase of a rental property.

Whether or not you own your own home currently, a second popular way to get started is to buy a multi-family home, using a low-down-payment program or seller financing, and occupy one of the units. If you want to purchase a rental from scratch, you still have some time to use leverage to your advantage and turn around your situation using the powerful tool of real estate. *In fact, leverage is the golden ticket at this stage in your life, especially if you are starting out with very little.* It is the ability to *build something big* with the assistance of a mortgage (eventually to be paid off) that makes real estate powerful and far more advantageous than other investments, like mutual funds and stocks, where you must personally contribute the full amount of the money invested.

It does not matter how slowly you go
as long as you do not stop.
CONFUCIUS
Teacher and philosopher, known as "The Great Sage" (551–479 B.C.)

Ages 40–60 with a Healthy Amount of Savings

If you are in the 40-to-60-year bracket and if you have managed to accumulate some retirement savings, then congrats are in order! You've been working hard to get where you are now. Or maybe your money is the result of an inheritance. In either case, at this stage in your life your spend/save/invest decisions are critical. As a side note, if your savings *are* the result of an inheritance, you may be a little less practiced in scrimping, saving, and/or investing, which means that setting and attaining at least the Level I Goal will be all the more important for you. If you hold your money in real estate, it will be less likely to evaporate.

When analyzing a potential property to purchase, you'll want to find the right balance between cash flow and the length of mortgage. On my website, www.GetaChicken.com, you can download a free Cash Flow Analysis (CFA) Tool. If your cash flow analysis reveals that you will have sufficient cash flow, then you may want to go with a lower-term mortgage. A property that is paid off in fifteen years is better aligned with the Ultimate Goal than one that won't be paid off for thirty years. And yet, if cash flow will be tight, or if you want to be more conservative, it is safer to go with a longer-term mortgage with a lower monthly payment. Remember that you can always put additional money toward the principal and pay your mortgage off sooner.

If you have money invested in an IRA or self-employed (Solo) 401(k), then you have access to another powerful move that you can put to work. You can roll some of your money into a self-directed IRA or self-directed Solo 401(k) in order to invest tax-free in real estate. This is a powerful strategy, but there are some catches, so be sure to read the relevant section of chapter 8 carefully and discuss the subject with your CPA before taking the plunge. If you have an employer-sponsored retirement plan, you can also loan yourself money to cover the down payment toward the purchase of a rental property and pay your account back over the next five years. Finally, you can tap your equity in an existing property to finance the down payment for a next rental. So many options! Lucky for you, all of these advanced moves were described in detail in chapter 8.

STRATEGIES FOR AGES 20-40

Ages 20–40 with Little in Savings

If you are under 40, then you have time on your side! And yet, as with any kind of investing, sooner is always better for getting started. For example, the thirty-year mortgage was designed with young people in mind. Using this standard mortgage product, if you purchase a property at age 30, it will be paid off by the time you're 60. Furthermore, if real estate appreciates at at an average of 4 percent per year, then by the time you reach age 70, its value will have more than doubled.

The will to win, the desire to succeed, the urge to reach your full potential . . . these are the keys that will unlock the door to personal excellence.
CONFUCIUS

Being on the younger end, you have plenty of options. One way to get started is to begin making money in real estate without actually owning property, as described in chapter 7. If you are unattached, the easiest way to do this is to simply find a home to rent for yourself and then sublet the other rooms. If you already have a home that you rent or own, you can do the same thing by renting out a spare room. Once you've gotten the feel for screening potential roommates and executing a lease, a next logical move could be the lease/sublet, either with or without the option to buy. As explained in chapter 7, the lease/sublet involves finding a landlord from whom you can rent a house or apartment without actually living there yourself, and then subletting the rooms to individuals in the form of a "house-share."

When you are ready, you should move steadily forward with your Level I, II, or III Goal, the essential ingredient for increasing cash flow and boosting your net worth over the remainder of your life. One powerful strategy is to purchase a duplex or multi-family building and live in one unit while allowing the rent from the others to cover most or all of the mortgage. There are low-down-payment options for purchasing such a property, as long as you plan to live in one of the units (see chapter 8). Another option is to purchase a starter home for yourself using one of the low-down payment programs shared in chapter 8, but to select one with an investor's eye.

For those of you in this group who already own a home but want to upsize or move to a neighborhood or school system that is better suited for kids, you may want to hold on to your starter home when you move. This is, by far, the most common way people get started in owning residential rental property. Again, see chapter 8 for tips on how to best implement this move.

Ages 20–40 with a Healthy Amount of Savings

If you are young and have a substantial amount of savings, you are in the best position of all our six groups. After all, and as magazine covers so vividly portray, who doesn't want to be young and rich (and beautiful!)? Plus, you have time . . . time to grow your money, time to try new ways of investing, and time even to make mistakes and recover.

If you are in this group, you basically have access to many of the options discussed for the other five groups. Your best opportunities will depend, in part, on where your money is. If your savings are tied up in a retirement account, your options will be different than if they are sitting in a checking account. The section "Put Your Nest Egg to Work," in chapter 8, goes into the several different ways you can leverage your retirement account funds to diversify your portfolio to include real estate. Otherwise, you'll probably want to go with a traditional purchase.

Remember that when you buy a rental property or a multi-family home—rather than a single-family home or condo for yourself—you are buying an asset instead of a liability. When you purchase real estate as an investment, the government gives you the gift of a break on your *existing* income taxes that you already pay, right now (see chapter 3). This is on top of monthly income from an asset that typically appreciates in value over a long stretch of time.

Alternatively, you may wish to buy a home for yourself before buying a rental. If so, I encourage you at least to buy your residence with an investor's eye, so that you have more options down the road in terms of moving and keeping it as a rental. Be sure to review the financial and other criteria for selecting your ideal investment property in the *R.O.R.E. Blueprint for Success: A Step-by-Step Companion Guide,* which is available on my website (www.GetaChicken.com).

Finally, if you want to get started with an investment property *and* a personal residence at the same time, a home with a separate apartment unit, or a multi-family home, is the way to go. The method of living in one unit and renting out the other(s) is a strategy used by many of the people, whom I interviewed, to get started. This move can be very advantageous in both the short and long term. Your tenants' rent will help out with the mortgage, often drastically reducing your own personal living expenses. You can use the income to expedite your achievement of the Ultimate Goal, becoming the proud owner of a mortgage-free, multi-unit house or building that provides multiple streams of income. Needless to say, as your priorities in life shift, you can eventually move into a new home for yourself or even start the process again in a second multi-unit.

Whether you buy a property as a personal residence, as an investment, or as a simultaneous residence/investment, the time to get started is now. In fact, if there is one consistent message that rang through all my interviews, it was this: Those who bought their first property at a young age were glad they did. And those who didn't, wished they had. Your time is now.

10

DO THE CHICKEN DANCE!

Achieving the Ultimate Goal

Once you've successfully converted your home into a rental, bought a new rental property from scratch, or purchased a multi-family property (in which you may plan to also reside), congratulations are in order! At this point, you will have diversified your nest egg through the ownership of at least one rental property. You will have achieved the Level I Goal. (Remember that all tools for identifying, purchasing, and managing your perfect rental property are presented in painstaking detail in the *R.O.R.E. Blueprint for Success: A Step-by-Step Companion Guide,* available at www.GetaChicken.com!)

Once you've achieved the Level I Goal, you need to decide whether you are satisfied with this modest degree of diversification, or if you want to advance to the Level II Goal of building a little extra comfort into your retirement picture. If you do, simply circle back through the many techniques of chapter 8 and the age/resource-related strategies of chapter 9. The anticipated comfort of the Level II Goal does come with work and time, however, plus additional emergency fund requirements, so it is best to move slowly toward this next goal. I recommend you give yourself *at least* a year as a new landlord and investment-property owner before you acquire additional property.

If you are interested in the Level II Goal of increased comfort, or the Level III Goal of self-sufficiency once your mortgages are paid off, you may notice a tension between your desire to pay down your existing mortgages and your desire to acquire more property. You can actually work on both simultaneously, with some give-and-take between both goals at various times. For instance, you may decide to strategically increase the mortgage balance on one property by refinancing, in order to purchase a next property and then resuming your efforts to pay them both down.

Achieving the Ultimate Goal of paying off your mortgage, or mortgages, takes significant time and patience. Your success also depends, in part, on the type of mortgage(s) you select in the first place. See chapter 8 sections "Selecting Your Mortgage Term" and "Creative Mortgages—A Cautionary Word." Also refer back to chapter 9 on how to select the best fixed-rate mortgage given your circumstances.

When it comes to paying down your regular fixed-rate mortgage, you can do so aggressively, or you can take the slow road. Some people prefer to put as much as possible toward their principal, to gain equity quickly and pay off the mortgage faster. Others are content with the slower road. In part, this decision depends on your cash flow, as well as how much surplus money you have through other sources like your regular job or the techniques shared in chapter 7. Age is also a factor. If you are older and closer to retirement (or even *in* retirement), you'll want to pay off your mortgage as quickly as you are able, so that the income potential is maximized and you can get the most benefit out of the property.

There are three general ways to speed up your attainment of the Ultimate Goal of paying off your mortgage or mortgages. The first way is fairly obvious, but nonetheless quite powerful: Put extra money toward the principal each month. For example, consider a $100,000 mortgage with a 5 percent interest rate and a thirty-year term. Putting an extra $50 toward the mortgage each month would shave five years and two months off the total length of the mortgage. (This also comes with a savings of $18,534 in interest, though this matters less since the mortgage interest is covered by the rent from your tenants, as discussed in chapter 3.) In this example, pushing even harder by paying $200 over your minimum payment each month would skyrocket your payoff goal by sixteen years and nine months! Check out www.mortgagecalculator.org/calculators/what-if-i-pay-more-calculator.php to see how seemingly small extra amounts paid each month can profoundly impact your attainment of the Ultimate Goal.

A second simple but powerful strategy to shorten the time you have on a mortgage and more quickly achieve the Ultimate Goal is to refinance from a thirty-year mortgage to a fifteen- or twenty-year mortgage, *assuming you have the opportunity to drop your interest rate.* However, if your new rate is not a fair bit lower than your original rate, don't refinance. If it is the same or greater, you are better off keeping your original rate and going with the extra-payment method just described. Another consideration before moving forward with a refi is that you need to verify that the monthly rent will be greater than the new mortgage amount, plus all other expenses and your cash-flow needs. If it is too tight, it is again better to go with the extra payment method so that you don't get locked into an obligation to make a higher payment. You can consult the Cash Flow Analysis (CFA) Tool on my website at www.GetaChicken.com to verify your numbers.

If you have more than one property, a third powerful strategy is to consider the properties as players on your own personal team, and you are the head coach. There are a couple of ways this can be done. The first is to use the above two strategies to focus all efforts on paying off the mortgage on just one of your properties. It is usually best to focus on the one with the lowest principal, or amount owed, assuming all your interest rates are roughly the same. Once you pay off that property, it will be liberated from the mortgage payment and you can direct all those funds into the aggressive payoff of your next property. This is similar to the popular snowball approach that many budgeting experts advise when it comes to paying off credit card bills.

The second "properties-as-team" approach is to refinance one property in order to pull money out and pay off another (assuming it can be completely paid off with those funds). This strategy really only works when one property has sufficient equity to refinance and completely pay off the mortgage of another. If these two factors are in alignment, then this strategy will increase your first monthly payment by a small amount, but you can use the extra income from that mortgage-free property to pay off your next property, and then your next, and so on.

It is important to note that you can, and should, use all these strategies on your personal residence as well. In fact, all your properties are on your same team. As a profound example, imagine that you have a $300,000 mortgage on your home with a thirty-year term and a 4.5 percent interest rate. If you aggressively put an extra $800 toward your mortgage each month (for example, by taking in a housemate) then the mortgage will be completely paid off after just fourteen years and ten months, roughly half its original thirty-year term!

The sooner you pay off all your mortgages in full, including your own home, the sooner you will achieve the rewards of financial safety, comfort, and/or complete financial self-sufficiency to last the rest of your life. At this point, you will have achieved your Ultimate Goal.

FINAL WORDS

There are three main reasons why rental property is an essential ingredient to an authentically diverse retirement plan. As a refresher, to be diverse means to be different in *as many ways as possible*, not merely diverse across different risk-tolerance levels within the same vehicle.

First and foremost, rental property operates on a different time scale from typical retirement accounts. Instead of building up a fixed—and exhaustible—pool of funds over your lifetime (the "nest egg"), rental property operates on a monthly income scale, similar to a paycheck or a pension . . . or even a chicken. By definition, it is unending. It makes unnecessary the ever-vexing question with which we all grapple: "How will I know when I've saved up enough to retire?"

Second, rental property offers diversification because it operates on a different earnings premise than the stock market. Most stocks and mutual funds operate on the premise of buying at one price, waiting for appreciation, and selling at a higher price. While you *can*, and often do, make money in real estate from capital-gains, as long as appreciation works in your favor, the strategic approach of buy-and-hold rental property is based on building a safe and secure financial future through rental income.

Finally, rental property offers actual, practical diversification in this modern, computer-oriented world of virtually—and even internationally—accessible bank accounts and retirement accounts. The tangible, physical quality of real estate offers solid protection in a world of increasingly common risks related to identity theft, cyberwarfare, technology glitches, and other computer-related errors. With real estate, your account balance can't simply vanish into thin air in an instant.

By now, I bet you've identified your Level I, II, or III Primary Goal and you're ready to get started. You know whether one property will be enough for your situation or whether you feel more ambitious, preferring the additional financial comfort or even complete financial self-sufficiency of the Level II or III Goal. However, if you are like most, you will simply start out with the Level I Goal of acquiring and managing just one rental property. You'll test-drive the experience for at least a year, and then, if the experience is positive, you will consider taking it to the next level.

In addition to your Goal, you probably now have a feeling for which moves are best suited to your circumstances and interests. You've found a strategy for achieving *your goal* that is appropriate to where you are in life in terms of your age and your resources of time, money, and energy.

It's now time to take action. At this point, I enthusiastically urge you to turn to the *R.O.R.E. Blueprint for Success: A Step-by-Step Companion Guide,* available on my website at www.GetaChicken.com. Like a real-world workbook, this guide will walk you, step by step, through every technique shared in this book and more. It reveals how to find, inspect, and evaluate potential rental property, including the critical aspect of calculating and understanding property financials, with the goal of landing the *perfect* income-producing rental property for your retirement portfolio. It shows you how to conduct your own high-quality tenant screenings and also how to find a trustworthy and competent property manager, if that is your preference. I also offer Online Appendix C, "Recommended Reading and Other Resources," for further information on some of the subjects covered in this book and resources that I have found to be particularly useful.

It is up to you to decide what to do with the information presented in this book. It is my hope that you will at least go for and—with the goal-attainment strategies presented in chapter 6—*accomplish* the very attainable Level I Goal of acquiring just one cash-flowing rental property. This one move alone will diversify your retirement portfolio by creating one everlasting stream of income to support you in your post-working days. Taking action in this one way will be a significant step toward both protecting your financial future, as well as having an appreciable asset to pass on to the next generation.

People often avoid making decisions out of fear of making a mistake. Actually the failure to make decisions is one of life's biggest mistakes.
RABBI NOAH WEINBERG

The Ultimate Goal is to pay off your mortgage(s) in full so that you can fully realize the earning potential and other opportunities made possible by your asset(s). Once you've achieved the Ultimate Goal, you will have greater income pouring into your bank account month after month for life. One rental property will provide a level of diversification that simply would not otherwise be there. Additional properties will get you to the place of additional financial comfort or complete self-sufficiency in retirement. And now, as we peer into that crystal ball, looking ten, twenty, or thirty or more years into the future, I am confident that you will feel both grateful and relieved that you took the bold and brilliant move of acquiring your first rental property back in the day. And yes, the future's "back in the day" is actually today. It is right now.

Our deepest fear is not that we are inadequate. Our deepest fear is that we are powerful beyond measure. It is our light, not our darkness that most frightens us. We ask ourselves, Who am I to be brilliant, gorgeous, talented, fabulous? Actually who are you not to be? You are a child of God. Your playing small does not serve the world. There is nothing enlightened about shrinking so that other people won't feel insecure around you. We are all meant to shine, as children do. We were born to make manifest the glory of God that is within us. It's not just in some of us; it's in everyone. And as we let our own light shine, we unconsciously give other people permission to do the same. As we are liberated from our own fear, our presence automatically liberates others.

MARIANNE WILLIAMSON
American spiritual teacher, peace advocate,
and author of *A Return to Love*

Our Story

The course of my life changed permanently the day I read *Rich Dad Poor Dad* by Robert Kiyosaki. From this master I learned the revolutionary concept of "Your house is not an asset," among many other lessons related to the benefits of creating passive income through rental property.

My launch into real estate investing entailed the simplest kind of all rental property acquisitions: moving and converting my home into a rental. My girlfriend (now wife) and I were at the point in our relationship where we were ready to take that next step. However, my one-bedroom condo felt too small for the two of us, and her house-share was also not ideal for obvious reasons. As luck would have it, we noticed one day that the tenant of the two-bedroom unit across the hall from my condo was moving out. We jumped on the opportunity and called the owner. Within a matter of only a couple of weeks, I had gone from being the owner of a small condo to being the landlady of that condo and a tenant of another.

This is how I first learned about the power of cash flow. As landlady, I received $1,100 each month for the smaller, but nicer, unit that I owned. As tenants, we dished out only $1,000 per month for a larger unit that was rougher around the edges. The net result of this move was an extra $100 each month (plus a lot of extra space!).

Having considered real estate investing for much of my life, this first taste of being a landlady was thrilling! Plus, I discovered that it really wasn't that hard. A few months later, I enrolled in an on-site real estate–investing program at the Investors United™ School of

Real Estate Investing. Over the course of a full year, I purchased my first two investment properties, which I found by sending letters to landlords of properties along busier streets in popular areas of town.

I ended up selling that small condo just as the housing meltdown was beginning, a move that I was happy about since the condo fees seemed to be steadily increasing. The two rentals were breakeven with respect to expenses and income, with much of the maintenance and repair costs coming out of my regular salaried income. We eventually made a change that had a powerful impact on our cash flow. We switched both properties into "house-shares." In this way, instead of renting each house as a whole, we rented to separate individuals on a room-by-room basis. Given that the homes were both within walking distance of a major university, and that the rents were considerably lower than they would have been for a one-bedroom apartment, it has always been easy to rent by the room. Most of all, our tenants have enjoyed the sense of community that our house-shares offer.

In the aftermath of the housing crash, we bought our next three homes to aid our retirement goals. For two of the three, we temporarily leveraged my retirement funds using a 401(k) loan for the down payment, coupled with fifteen-year mortgages. For the third property, we converted my Roth IRA to a self-directed Roth IRA and used those funds to purchase a fixer-upper, which came with many life lessons! All the techniques we used, and many more, are described in detail in this book, as are our various successes and setbacks!

At this point, we have achieved the Level III Goal. And once the mortgages are completely paid off, in ten to fifteen years, we will have achieved our Ultimate Goal. At that point, the income from our handful of properties, after expenses, will be equal to our current income from our jobs. Our plan is to pay down the mortgages on our existing properties as quickly as possible. Before retiring, however, we plan to use the monthly income from the rentals to pay our daughter's future college tuition. We will then use the income to fund our safe, comfortable, and financially self-sufficient retirement.

We feel a certain sense of calm knowing that we will *never* have to worry about whether we will run out of money in retirement or have to work for the rest of our days. Sure, we have other retirement funds doing their thing in their traditional mutual fund–based retirement accounts. If we're lucky, we may also have Social Security benefits in some form or another. But, because we have used rentals—like chickens—to create an infinite flow of eggs, rather than just building up one risk-laden, finite "nest egg," we know that we will have created a safe and secure retirement not only to last the rest of our days, but also to provide income security for the next generation. And that feeling is priceless.

Acknowledgments

I would first like to acknowledge my lovely, loving, and wonderfully awesome wife, Kara, for supporting my passion for real estate investing and for supporting me through the entire process of writing this book. I couldn't have done this without you, Kara, nor would I have wanted to. Thank you for your incredible support and for making each day of the journey a delight!

I would also like to acknowledge our now eight-year-old daughter. Even as young as you are, your enthusiasm for the book (especially its chicken-and-egg theme!) has been awesome to witness. When she was just five years old, she commented, "Do you remember in *Frosty the Snowman*, there were eggs in a magician's hat and he said 'Ta Da!' and the eggs came down and cracked on the floor. Splat! Then he wiped the floor and said [in a funny voice] 'Messy! Messy! Messy!'" Little did she know that she was spot-on. You see, if we put all our nest eggs in one magician's hat, and then wait, simply hoping for the best, then our financial futures and retirement prospects could indeed be "Messy! Messy! Messy!"

I am grateful to Amanda Han, CPA, not only for her expert accounting guidance over the years, but also for writing the foreword to this book. Her early involvement reminds me of the famous story of the Velveteen Rabbit. In that story, the Velveteen Rabbit became real only after it was blessed by the nursery fairy. Similarly, my manuscript became "real" the moment Amanda blessed it by writing the foreword. Again, thank you, Amanda!

Robert and Kim Kiyosaki, I am deeply indebted to you both! Robert, you introduced me to a new way of thinking about income, debt, assets, and liabilities that changed my life forever and served as a catalyst to my own real-estate-investing side-gig. Kim, you furthered my thinking by teaching concepts related to the advantages of monthly passive income over savings accounts. It is no exaggeration to say that your many *Rich Dad Poor Dad* and *Rich Woman* teachings have literally changed the course of my life as well as countless others (including many people I interviewed for this book!) for the better. On behalf of all of us . . . Thank you!

Similarly, Charles and Ian Parrish, father/son co-founders of the Investors United™ School of Real Estate Investing, I am indebted to you both. Thank you for teaching me much of what I know about the technical aspects of investing in real estate. I wouldn't be where I am in life now had I not stumbled upon and had the courage to enroll in your Investors United™ training program.

There are not enough words to express my gratitude to Kevin Harrington, the original "Shark" on ABC's *Shark Tank* and inventor of the infomercial. Kevin, thank you for your enthusiasm for my book! Your endorsement has meant the world to me. Similarly, I am humbled and deeply grateful to Dr. Todd Sinai, Professor of Real Estate and Business Economics and Public Policy at the University of Pennsylvania, Wharton School of Business, for his expert technical review and improvement of this book and his endorsement. Likewise, I would like to thank Vena Jones-Cox, host of the *Real Life Real Estate Investing* radio show, for her critical input and improvements. I am equally grateful to Brandon Turner, senior editor of BiggerPockets.com and co-host of the BiggerPockets Podcast, for his review of portions of this book.

A heartfelt thank-you also goes to my volunteer readers. Thank you, friends, for taking time out of your own busy lives to read and improve various draft versions of my manuscript: Amy Foell, Leila Hanna-Kohen, Justin DeCleene, Louise Suggs, Michael Anderson, Elisha Hawk, Renee Guengrich, and Rebecca Walden. I would also like to thank my friend, Connie Rankin, commercial real estate pro and author of *God Gave Us Wings*, for her support and encouragement.

ACKNOWLEDGMENTS

I am much indebted to my developmental editor, Maria Gagliano. Maria's efforts have truly raised the quality of the manuscript. Working with her has also been a true delight. Maria, I'm grateful for your positive attitude, your dedicated and efficient work ethic, and your candor in helping me improve my writing so that I can effectively share my message. I feel incredibly lucky to have been referred to you by Niki Papadopoulos, to whom I am also grateful for having made this referral!

I would also like to express my heartfelt appreciation for my initial copyeditor, Kristina Stewart. Kris, thank you not only for your technical expertise in reviewing my early manuscript, but also for your enduring enthusiasm, encouragement, and positivity, every step along the way.

I would like to thank Timothy Burgard, and others at AMACOM Publishing, for their professionalism and outstanding quality in all aspects related to publishing, distributing, and marketing my book. It has truly been a pleasure! Equally so, I am thankful to Pauline Neuwirth, and her team at Neuwirth and Associates, Inc., including managing editor Mary Daniello, as well as copyeditor Phil Gaskill, among others, for working their magic to transform my manuscript into an actual book. Again, the professionalism and high standards of excellence far exceeded my already high expectations!

I am deeply indebted to Steve Harrison for his expert guidance on matters of publicity. Amy Scott, of National Public Radio's *Marketplace,* and Julekha Dash, formerly of the *Baltimore Business Journal,* thank you both for providing invaluable feedback in the early stages of this book's development. Danette Kubana, former producer for *Oprah,* thank you for sharing your wisdom and insight on aspects related to marketing my book. I am thankful to literary agent Barbara Collins Rosenberg, as well as author Justine Blau and publishing expert Judith Briles, for their generous gifts of time during the early stages of this book. I am grateful to Ed Tyll of the *Ed Tyll Show* (Starcom Radio Network), Frankie Boyer of the *Frankie Boyer Show* (on BizTalk Radio), and Jennifer Hammond of the *Jennifer Hammond Show* (SiriusXM Radio), for having me on the air long before my book was officially out to help me get the word out about the importance of diversifying our retirement planning beyond mutual funds and Social Security.

I am much indebted to the many persons who shared their personal stories with me to help put faces on the many strategies shared within this book: Amanda Han, Catherine Campinos, Lynne Yansen, Enid Wright, Beth, David, Kevin, Andrea, Venesa, Heather, John, Marisha, Svetlana, Jake, Mary, Deb, Jen, Rachel, Lauren, Eric, Alfredo, and Rose. Even though I changed some of your names to protect your privacy, you know who you are, and thank you!

I am grateful for my dear friend Amy Foell for believing in me and supporting my dreams and for being the very first reader of my manuscript in its original, terribly rough, rendition and for helping me keep my eyes on the prize. I am also grateful for my dear friends Cintra Harbold, Maryam Keramaty, and Annette Dratch, as well as my siblings, Sandy Storer, Scott Anderson, and Brett Anderson, and their families, for being with me through thick and thin.

I would also like to acknowledge my mother-in-law, Lora Ker, and my (now late and terribly missed) father-in-law, Bruce Ker, for their tremendous love, enthusiasm and support throughout this journey. Thank you, also, for allowing me to use your story in chapter 1.

Finally, I would like to acknowledge my parents, who always supported my various endeavors, and who taught me, through example, about being brave and taking chances. Mom, as a two-time author, you have been my role model for completing such a major project as writing a book. And as a mother, you have been a tremendous source of love, encouragement, and support throughout this entire project and throughout my life in general. Dad, you worked hard your whole life, only to be robbed of it shortly after stepping into retirement. You are the inspiration behind this book. You were an incredible, outspoken, creative, and loving role model. I know that you have been with me in spirit, lifting me up to share what I've learned about the retirement industry and the use of rental property as a way to protect one's retirement dreams and late-life financial security. Thank you.

Notes

All website references were last accessed January 7, 2017.

PREFACE

1   News conference in which Bill Gates announced plans for full-time
    philanthropy work and part-time Microsoft work, June 15, 2006,
    Redmond, Washington. http://abcnews.go.com/Technology/PCWorld/
    story?id=5214635&page=4.

CHAPTER ONE

1   "The Retirement Gamble" (episode of PBS *Frontline*, produced by
    Marcela Gaviria and Martin Smith) April 23, 2013. www.pbs.org/
    wgbh/pages/frontline/retirement-gamble/.

2   Burkins, Glenn. "Johnson Cos. Bought By British Company."
    Philly.com. June 14, 1990. http://articles.philly.com/1990-06-14/
    business/25914534_1_employee-benefits-retirement-plans-johnson-
    cos.

3   Gandel, Stephen. "Why It's Time to Retire the 401(k)." *Time*. Oct. 9,
    2009.

4   Ibid.

5   Kujawa, Patty. "A 'Father's' Wisdom: An Interview with Ted Benna."
    Workforce Management. January 20, 2012. www.workforce.com.

6   "Fact Sheet." Social Security Administration, SSA Press Office 440
    Altmeyer Bldg 6401 Security Blvd. Baltimore, MD 21235 410-965-8904.
    https://www.ssa.gov/news/press/basicfact.html.

7   Van de Water, Paul N., Arloc Sherman, and Kathy A. Ruffing. "Social Security Keeps 22 Million Americans Out Of Poverty: A State-By-State Analysis." Center on Budget and Policy Priorities. Oct. 25, 2013. http://www.cbpp.org/sites/default/files/atoms/files/10-25-13ss.pdf.

8   "Policy Basics: Top Ten Facts about Social Security." Center on Budget and Policy Priorities. August 12, 2016. http://www.cbpp.org/research/social-security/policy-basics-top-ten-facts-about-social-security?fa=view&id=3261.

9   "Income of the Population 55 or Older, 2012." Social Security Administration. SSA Publication No. 13-11871. April 2014. http://www.ssa.gov/policy/docs/statcomps/income_pop55/2012/sect09.html#table9.a1.

10   Salisbury, Dallas. "The Future of Retirement Plans." *Wall Street Journal*. 2008. http://online.wsj.com/ad/article/employeebenefits-future.

11   Powell, Robert. "Social Security is Crucial to the Middle Class." MarketWatch. August 22, 2013. http://www.marketwatch.com/story/social-security-is-crucial-to-the-middle-class-2013-08-22.

12   "How Do Benefits Compare to Earnings?" National Academy of Social Insurance. https://www.nasi.org/learn/socialsecurity/benefits-compare-earnings.

13   "What is the average monthly benefit for a retired worker?" Social Security Administration. March 11, 2016. https://faq.ssa.gov/link/portal/34011/34019/Article/3736/What-is-the-average-monthly-benefit-for-a-retired-worker.

14   "Benefit Calculators." Social Security Administration. http://www.ssa.gov/OACT/quickcalc/index.html.

15   Goss, Stephen C. (Chief Actuary for the Social Security Administration). "The Future Financial Status of the Social Security Program." Social Security Administration. 2010. http://www.ssa.gov/policy/docs/ssb/v70n3/v70n3p111.html.

16   "How Do Benefits Compare to Earnings?" National Academy of Social Insurance. https://www.nasi.org/learn/socialsecurity/benefits-compare-earnings.

17   "Normal Retirement Age." Social Security Administration. http://www.ssa.gov/OACT/ProgData/nra.html.

18   Martin, Michel. "Can Extending Retirement Age Help Social
     Security?" National Public Radio. June 6, 2012. http://www.npr.
     org/2012/06/06/154432626/can-extending-retirement-age-help-
     social-security#.

19   "Social Security Fact Sheet: Increase in Retirement Age." Social
     Security Administration. https://www.ssa.gov/pressoffice/IncRetAge.
     html.

20   "EBRI Databook on Employee Benefits: 401(k) Plans." Employee
     Benefit Research Institute. July 2014. http://ebri.org/pdf/
     publications/books/databook/DB.Chapter%2007.pdf.

21   Ibid.

22   "FAQs About Benefits—Retirement Issues: What are the trends in U.S.
     retirement plans?" Employee Benefit Research Institute. 2015. http://
     www.ebri.org/publications/benfaq/index.cfm?fa=retfaq14.

23   Christoff, Chris. "Detroit Pension Cuts From Bankruptcy Prompt
     Cries of Betrayal." Bloomberg News. Feb. 5, 2015. http://www.
     bloomberg.com/news/articles/2015-02-05/detroit-pension-cuts-from-
     bankruptcy-prompt-cries-of-betrayal.

24   Butrica, Barbara A., Howard M. Iams, Karen E. Smith, and Eric J.
     Toder. "The Disappearing Defined Benefit Pension and Its Potential
     Impact on the Retirement Incomes of Baby Boomers." Social Security
     Administration. 2009. http://www.ssa.gov/policy/docs/ssb/v69n3/
     v69n3p1.html.

25   Ibid.

26   Zuckerman, Mortimer B. "The Great Jobs Recession Goes On." *U.S.
     News and World Reports*. Feb. 11, 2011. http://www.usnews.com/
     opinion/mzuckerman/articles/2011/02/11/the-great-jobs-recession-
     goes-on.

27   "20% Of American Workers Have Lost Their Job During Last 5 Years."
     RT-TV. Sept. 30, 2014. http://rt.com/usa/192008-rutgers-heldrich-
     employment-report/.

28   Meckler, Laura, and Rebecca Ballhaus. "More than 800,000 Federal
     Workers are Furloughed." *Wall Street Journal*. Oct. 1, 2013. http://www.
     wsj.com/articles/SB10001424052702304373104579107480729687014.

29   Ortiz, Jon. "Schwarzenegger Orders More Furloughs for State Workers."
     Sacramento Bee. July 28, 2010. http://blogs.sacbee.com/the_state_
     worker/2010/07/schwarzenegger-orders-more-fur.html.

30 "Oklahoma: Workers Hit with Furloughs, Loss of Pension, More Pay Cuts." Communications Workers of America News. March 7, 2011. http://www.cwa-union.org/news/article/oklahoma_workers_hit_with_furloughs_loss_of_pension_more_pay_cuts/.

31 Johnson, Alan. "Unions for state workers get ready to discuss contracts." *Columbus Dispatch*. Oct. 16, 2016. http://www.dispatch.com/content/stories/local/2015/01/06/unions-get-ready-to-discuss-contracts.html.

32 Hakim, Danny. "Cuomo Secures Big Givebacks in Union Deal." *New York Times*. June 22, 2011. http://www.nytimes.com/2011/06/23/nyregion/new-york-reaches-deal-with-largest-public-employee-union.html?_r=0.

33 Gandel, Stephen. "Why It's Time to Retire the 401(k)." *Time*. Oct. 9, 2009.

CHAPTER TWO

1 "Older Americans Fear Outliving Money, Retirement Savings, Assets: Running Out of Money Worse than Death." AARP. June 2010. http://www.aarp.org/work/retirement-planning/info-06-2010/running_out_of_money_worse_than_death.html.

2 "15th Annual Transamerica Retirement Survey: Influences of Gender on Retirement Preparedness." Transamerica Center for Retirement Studies. Aug. 2014. http://www.transamericacenter.org/docs/default-source/resources/center-research/tcrs2014_sr_compendium_gender.pdf.

3 "2014 Retirement Confidence Survey Fact Sheet #5: Gender and Marital Status Comparisons Among Workers." Employee Benefit Research Institute. http://www.ebri.org/pdf/surveys/rcs/2014/RCS14.FS-5.Gender.Final.pdf.

4 Whitby, Jason. "What's the Minimum I Need to Retire?" Investopedia. http://www.investopedia.com/articles/retirement/09/1-million-retire.asp.

5 Updegrave, Walter. "How much retirement income will $1 million generate?" CNN Money. July 22, 2015. http://money.cnn.com/2015/07/22/retirement/retirement-income/.

6 Sommer, Jeff. "The $1 Million Nest Egg." *New York Times*. June 10, 2013. http://bucks.blogs.nytimes.com/2013/06/10/the-1-million-nest-egg/?_r=2.

7   Jeszeck, Charles A. "Most Households Approaching Retirement Have Little Savings." The United States Government Accountability Office. May 2015. http://www.gao.gov/assets/680/670153.pdf.

8   Eisenbrey, Ross. "Why we need Retirement USA." Economic Policy Institute. March 10, 2009. http://www.epi.org/publication/why_we_need_retirement_usa/.

9   Gandel, Stephen. "Why It's Time to Retire the 401(k)." *Time.* Oct. 9, 2009.

10   Gaviria, Marcela, and Martin Smith. "The Retirement Gamble." *Frontline.* April 23, 2013. www.pbs.org/wgbh/pages/frontline/retirement-gamble/.

11   Cited from the book, *Unfair Advantage*, by Robert Kiyosaki.

12   "Voices: Mitch Tuchman, on Why Advisers Can't Beat the Market." *Wall Street Journal.* July 21, 2014. http://www.wsj.com/articles/voices-mitch-tuchman-on-why-financial-advisers-cant-beat-the-market-1405978258.

13   White, Doug, and Polly White. "Are Investment Advisers Worth the Investment?" *Entrepreneur.* May 12, 2015. http://www.entrepreneur.com/article/244997.

14   "Madoff's Victims." *Wall Street Journal.* March 6, 2009. http://s.wsj.net/public/resources/documents/st_madoff_victims_20081215.html.

15   Woodruff, Judy, and Diana Henriques. "How are Bernie Madoff's fraud victims coping five years later?" *PBS News Hour.* Dec. 11, 2013. http://www.pbs.org/newshour/bb/nation-july-dec13-madoff2_12-11/.

16   Seal, Mark. "Madoff's World." *Vanity Fair.* March 4, 2009. http://www.vanityfair.com/news/2009/04/bernard-madoff-friends-family-profile.

17   Maglich, Jordan. Ponzitracker: The Ponzi Scheme Authority. 2015. http://www.ponzitracker.com/2015-ponzi-schemes/.

18   "Fast Answers: Ponzi Schemes." U.S. Securities and Exchange Commission. Oct. 9, 2013. http://www.sec.gov/answers/ponzi.htm.

19   Vernon, Steve. "How to Protect Your Retirement Savings from Identify Theft and Internet Fraud." CBS Money Watch. Jan. 21, 2011. http://www.cbsnews.com/news/how-to-protect-your-retirement-savings-from-identity-theft-and-internet-fraud/.

20 Lachance, Naomi. "Malware Attacks on Hospitals Put Patients at Risk." National Public Radio. April 1, 2016. http://www.npr.org/sections/alltechconsidered/2016/04/01/472693703/malware-attacks-on-hospitals-put-patients-at-risk.

21 Ibid.

22 Gorman, Siobhan. "Electricity Grid in U.S. Penetrated By Spies." *Wall Street Journal*. April 8, 2009. http://www.wsj.com/articles/SB123914805204099085.

23 Sanger, David E., and Martin Fackler. "N.S.A. Breached North Korean Networks Before Sony Attack, Officials Say." *New York Times*. Jan. 18, 2015. http://www.nytimes.com/2015/01/19/world/asia/nsa-tapped-into-north-korean-networks-before-sony-attack-officials-say.html?_r=0.

24 Davidson, Joe. "Months after government hack, 21.5 million people are finally being told, and given help." *Washington Post*. Oct. 1, 2015. www.washingtonpost.com/amphtml/news/federal-eye/wp/2015/10/01/21-5-million-feds-others-being-officially-notified-of-personal-information-cybertheft-and-id-theft-services/.

25 Ellyatt, Holly. "Cyberterrorists to target critical infrastructure." CNBC. Jan. 27, 2015. http://www.cnbc.com/2015/01/27/cyberterrorists-to-target-critical-infrastructure.html.

26 Wikipedia, definition of "Cyberwarfare." https://en.wikipedia.org/wiki/Cyberwar.

27 McCrank, John. "NYSE shut down for nearly four hours by technical glitch." Reuters. July 9, 2015. http://www.reuters.com/article/us-nyse-trading-idUSKCN0PI25A20150709.

28 Forelle, Charles. "In Greece, ATM Lines, Bank Transfer Limits Enter Second Week." *Wall Street Journal*. July 6, 2015. http://www.wsj.com/articles/in-greece-atm-lines-bank-transfer-limits-enter-second-week-1436209482.

29 Robbins-Early, Nick. "Here's How Ordinary Greeks are Living with Closed Banks And ATM Limits." Huffington Post. July 7, 2015. http://www.huffingtonpost.com/2015/07/07/greece-capital-controls_n_7743624.html.

30 Chrysopoulos, Philip. "Capital Controls Likely to Stay Indefinitely, Says Greek Bank Official" *Greek Reporter*. Sept. 19, 2016. http://

greece.greekreporter.com/2016/09/19/capital-controls-likely-to-stay-indefinitely-says-greek-bank-official/.

31   "Thrift Savings Plan Highlights." U.S. Office of Personnel Management. July 2010. https://www.tsp.gov/PDF/formspubs/high10c.pdf.

32   "A Look at 401(k) Plan Fees." U.S. Department of Labor, Employee Benefits Security Administration. Aug. 2013. http://www.dol.gov/ebsa/publications/401k_employee.html.

33   Gaviria, Marcela, and Martin Smith. "The Retirement Gamble." *Frontline*. April 23, 2013. www.pbs.org/wgbh/pages/frontline/retirement-gamble/.

34   Ridgeway, James. "Who Shredded Our Safety Net?" *Mother Jones*, May/June 2009. http://www.motherjones.com/politics/2009/05/who-shredded-our-safety-net.

35   "The Effects of Conflicted Investment Advice on Retirement Savings." Executive Office of the President of the United States. Feb. 2015. https://www.whitehouse.gov/sites/default/files/docs/cea_coi_report_final.pdf was lost. To preserve the incredible value of this work, I have made this document available on my website at: www.GetaChicken.com.

36   Salisbury, Ian. "The Big Business of 401(k) Plans." *Market Watch*. March 20, 2012. http://www.marketwatch.com/story/the-big-business-of-401k-plans-1331829641132.

37   "Recommendation of the Investor Advisory Committee: Broker-Dealer Fiduciary Duty." U.S. Securities and Exchange Commission. http://www.sec.gov/spotlight/investor-advisory-committee-2012/fiduciary-duty-recommendation-2013.pdf.

38   Ibid.

39   "The Retirement Gamble" (episode of PBS *Frontline*, produced by Marcela Gaviria and Martin Smith). April 23, 2013. www.pbs.org/wgbh/pages/frontline/retirement-gamble/.

40   Sanford, James. "Confessions of a Financial Adviser." June 19, 2014. www.cnbc.com/2014/06/19/confessions-of-a-financial-adviserpersonal-financecommentary.html.

41   "FACT SHEET: Middle Class Economics: Strengthening Retirement Security by Cracking Down on Backdoor Payments and Hidden Fees."

The White House Office of the Press Secretary. Feb. 23, 2015. https://
www.whitehouse.gov/the-press-office/2015/02/23/fact-sheet-middle-
class-economics-strengthening-retirement-security-crac.

42   Carson, Brett. "Is Your Financial Adviser a Fiduciary?" U.S. News and
World Report. March 19, 2015. http://money.usnews.com/money/
blogs/the-smarter-mutual-fund-investor/2015/03/19/is-your-
financial-adviser-a-fiduciary.

43   "The Effects of Conflicted Investment Advice on Retirement Savings."
Executive Office of the President of the United States. Feb. 2015.
Note that with the Administration change from Obama to Trump,
the functionality of the website (https://www.whitehouse.gov/sites/
default/files/docs/cea_coi_report_final.pdf) was lost. To preserve the
incredible value of this work, I have made this document available on
my website at: www.GetaChicken.com.

44   Ibid.

45   Miller, Kevin. "The Simple Truth about the Gender-Pay Gap (Fall
2016)." American Association of University Women. Fall, 2016. http://
www.aauw.org/research/the-simple-truth-about-the-gender-pay-gap/.

46   "15th Annual Transamerica Retirement Survey: Influences of Gender on
Retirement Preparedness." Transamerica Center for Retirement Studies.
Aug. 2014. http://www.transamericacenter.org/docs/default-source/
resources/center-research/tcrs2014_sr_compendium_gender.pdf.

47   Ibid.

48   Copeland, Craig. "Individual Retirement Account Balances,
Contributions, and Rollovers, 2012; With Longitudinal Results 2010-
2012: The EBRI IRA Database." Employee Benefit Research Institute.
May 2014. http://www.ebri.org/pdf/EBRI_IB_399_May14.IRAs.pdf.

49   "15th Annual Transamerica Retirement Survey: Influences of Gender on
Retirement Preparedness." Transamerica Center for Retirement Studies.
Aug. 2014. http://www.transamericacenter.org/docs/default-source/
resources/center-research/tcrs2014_sr_compendium_gender.pdf.

CHAPTER THREE

1   Foldvary, Fred E. *The Depression of 2008*. Gutenberg Press. http://
www.foldvary.net/works/dep08.pdf.

2   Hanke, Steve H. "The Great 18-Year Real Estate Cycle." CATO
Institute. http://www.cato.org/publications/commentary/great-
18year-real-estate-cycle.

3   Blackman, Matt. "Market Cycles: The Key To Maximum Returns." Investopedia. http://www.investopedia.com/articles/technical/04/050504.asp.

4   "U.S. Historical Study of its Real Estate Cycles." Economic Indicator Services. http://www.businesscycles.biz/realestateresearch1.htm.

5   Blackman, Matt. "Market Cycles: The Key To Maximum Returns." Investopedia. http://www.investopedia.com/articles/technical/04/050504.asp.

6   "List of recessions in the United States." Wikipedia. https://en.wikipedia.org/wiki/List_of_recessions_in_the_United_States.

7   Vermeulen, Chris. "Investors Who Don't Understand the Power of 7 will Lose Money in 2015." The Street. Nov 30, 2014. http://www.thestreet.com/story/12969173/1/investors-who-dont-understand-the-power-of-7-will-lose-money-in-2015.html.

8   Blackman, Matt. "Market Cycles: The Key To Maximum Returns." Investopedia. http://www.investopedia.com/articles/technical/04/050504.asp.

9   "Residential Rental Property." Publication No. 527. U.S. Department of the Treasury, Internal Revenue Service. https://www.irs.gov/pub/irs-pdf/p527.pdf.

10   "Taking the Mystery out of Retirement Planning." U.S. Department of Labor. Dec. 2014. www.dol.gov/ebsa/publications/nearretirement.html.

11   McMahon, Tim. "What is the Current Inflation Rate?" InflationData.com. Dec. 15, 2016. www.Inflationdata.com/inflation/inflation_rate/currentinflation.asp.

12   "Fund Category Performance: Total Returns." Morningstar. http://news.morningstar.com/fund-category-returns/.

13   Hodges, David. "Why 3% Inflation?" SMA Reserves. 2015. http://www.smareserves.com/why-3-inflation/.

14   http://www.jchs.harvard.edu/sites/jchs.harvard.edu/files/sonhr14-color-ch5.pdf.

15   Turner, Brandon. "How to Estimate Future CapEx Expenses on a Rental Property." Bigger Pockets. April 26, 2016. www.biggerpockets.com/renewsblog/2015/10/13/real-estate-capex-estimate-capital-expenditures/.

16 Keller, Gary. *The Millionaire Real Estate Investor*. McGraw Hill, 2005.

17 Turner, Brandon. "How to Estimate Future CapEx Expenses on a Rental Property." Bigger Pockets. April 26, 2016. www.biggerpockets. com/renewsblog/2015/10/13/real-estate-capex-estimate-capital-expenditures/.

CHAPTER FOUR

1 There are 12-Step programs for almost any addictive behavior. These free, self-help groups include Alcoholics Anonymous, Cocaine Anonymous, Narcotics Anonymous, Overeaters Anonymous, Gamblers Anonymous, etc.

2 "Tax Information for Homeowners." Publication No. 530, U.S. Department of the Treasury, Internal Revenue Service. https://www. irs.gov/pub/irs-pdf/p530.pdf.

3 Stanley, Thomas J., and William D. Danko. *The Millionaire Next Door*. Longstreet Press: Atlanta, GA, 1996.

CHAPTER SIX

1 Hill, Napoleon. *Think and Grow Rich*. Fawcett Crest Books, 1960.

2 "Book and Course Reviews and Discussions." Bigger Pockets. https:// www.biggerpockets.com/forums/79/topics/31955-rober-allens-enlightened-wealth-institute.

3 "Complaint Review: Enlightened Wealth Institute, Robert Allen, Ultimate Wealth Building Success Team." Ripoff Report. April 6, 2008. http://www.ripoffreport.com/r/Enlightened-Wealth-Institute-Robert-Allen-Ultimate-Wealth-Building-Success-Team/Sandy-Utah-84070/ Enlightened-Wealth-Institute-EWI-Robert-G-Allen-Ultimate-Wealth-Building-Success-Team-324144.

4 "Complaint Review: Robert Allen - Enlightened Millionaire Institute— EMI - Enlightened Wealth Institute - EWI." Ripoff Report. April 8, 2008. http://www.ripoffreport.com/r/Robert-Allen-Enlightened-Millionaire-Institute-EMI-Enlightened-Wealth-Institute-EWI/Provo-Utah-84604/Robert-Allen-Enlightened-Millionaire-Institute-EMI-Enlightened-Wealth-Institute-EW-229644.

5 "Complaint Review: Robert Allen Institute—RAI - Enlightened Wealth Institute—EWI - Dynatech." Ripoff Report. Sept. 27, 2011. http://www. ripoffreport.com/r/Robert-Allen-Institute-RAI-Enlightened-Wealth-

Institute-EWI-Dynatech/RichmondVancouver-British-Columbia/
Robert-Allen-Institute-RAI-Enlightened-Wealth-Institute-EWI-
Dynatech-SCAM-SCAM-S-287225.

6   Jones-Cox, Vena. "The Guru Manifesto: How to Avoid Real Estate
     Education Ripoffs and Learn What You Need to Know to Make
     Millions in the Most Profit Driven Investment in America Today."
     2014. http://gurumanifesto.com/_download/guru-manifesto.pdf.

CHAPTER EIGHT

1   "IRS Publication 523." U.S. Internal Revenue Service. https://www.irs.
     gov/publications/p523/ar02.html.

2   Moon, Grant. "Using Your VA Loan as an Investment." Military.com.
     2013. http://www.military.com/money/va-loans/using-va-loan-as-
     investment.html.

3   Table data sources: Reeves, Samantha. "Why VA Loans Don't
     Require a Down Payment." Veterans United. Feb. 1, 2016. http://
     www.veteransunited.com/realestate/why-va-loans-dont-require-a-
     down-payment/; Mortgage Application information through the U.S.
     Department of Agriculture. http://www.usdaloans.com/; Freddie
     Mac home-buying program. www.homesteps.com; Fannie Mae home-
     buying program. www.homepath.com; "Expanded 97% LTV Options."
     Fannie Mae. Sept. 2016. https://www.fanniemae.com/content/fact_
     sheet/97-ltv-options.pdf; "Expanded 97% LTV Options." Fannie Mae.
     Sept. 2016. https://www.fanniemae.com/content/fact_sheet/97-ltv-
     options.pdf; "Let FHA Loans Help You." U.S. Department of Housing
     and Urban Development. http://portal.hud.gov/hudportal/HUD?src=/
     buying/loans.

4   Perkins, Broderick. "Seller Financing: How it works in home sales."
     Nolo. http://www.nolo.com/legal-encyclopedia/seller-financing-
     home-sales-30164.html.

5   Kiyosaki, Robert, and Sharon L. Lechter. *Rich Dad's Cashflow
     Quadrant*. Warner Books, 2000.

CHAPTER NINE

1   U.S. Government Accountability Office. "Retirement Security: Most
     Households Approaching Retirement Have Low Savings." May 2015.
     http://www.gao.gov/assets/680/670153.pdf.

2   Ibid.

Index